"*Since we cannot know what knowledge will be most useful in the future, it is senseless to try to teach it in advance. Instead we should try to turn out people who love learning so well that they will be able learn whatever needs to be learned*".

John Holt (1964)

FOREWORD

This is an extraordinary book, written by an extraordinary man. I feel very honoured to have been asked to write this foreword by Derek Betts.

I cannot imagine that there is anyone else in the world who feels such an emotional attachment to Balfour Primary School as does Derek Betts. His quite unique lifetime bond with the school began as a child on his first day at the school, in 1945, when his Mum brought him in for the very first time.

Since that very first day, Derek has remained incredibly loyal to the school and to the community that the school serves- as a pupil, as the Chair of Governors and currently as the Chair of the Teaching and Learning Committee of the Governing Body. The publication of this book is the best present the school community could have had as it celebrates its 110th Anniversary on 1st May 2015.

Derek's passion in researching the history of the school from its opening day on 1st May 1905 to 1955 to when he first joined the school as a pupil has been truly admirable and his infectious enthusiasm has touched us all at school.

It is a wonderful coincidence for me that Derek was at the final stages of this book as I took on the post of Headteacher of Balfour Primary School in January 2014. I say wonderful because there is nothing I have enjoyed more in my relatively short time at the school than sharing in Derek's passion and enthusiasm whilst sharing with me so many of the anecdotes that go to make up this book. The determination and enjoyment with which Derek looked for, researched and interpreted the vast quantity of material he came across is truly unique and will serve as a truly invaluable record for all that have known or will know the school.

The book offers a fascinating insight into how the school evolved since it was first founded in 1905 and I think it will be a very enjoyable and meaningful read with tremendous value to anyone that comes across it, because I think that the book has been written in a way that reflects how Derek is as a person. By that I mean that rather than the book being merely a historical recount, I found it full of human warmth and with fascinating insights into educational pedagogy.

Derek introduces us to all the historical figures in a way that makes the reader feel very fond of them. It comes across very clearly that everyone was trying to do their very best under what seemed to be very challenging circumstances.

Derek's passion for the world of education and for teaching and learning really comes through in the book from start to finish. I truly enjoyed all the references that Derek makes to the curriculum and to the philosophy of education in the different times that he describes.

I found it fascinating that although there are some differences between then and now, there are also a huge number of similarities in terms of present day ideology and practice. I am very pleased to read that previous Headteachers of Balfour Primary School also placed a huge emphasis on developing the child as a person and as a learner. The description from the Scheme of Work from 1905 states that they wish to have a syllabus *'encouraging children to make full use of their powers to train them to notice, speak and discover what can be learnt in the ordinary phenomena of their lives'.*

in 1907 the syllabus even refers to values, thinking skills and habits of mind- all the things that I am particular passionate about and that as I write this we are working towards introducing into the everyday life of the school- *'The natural and free development of powers, physical, mental and moral of the scholars; to train them in the habits of thought, application, diligence, self-reliance and self-respect and to give the power and love for self-improvement and self-development in all stages of Life'*

This is incredibly similar to our modern day wish to ensure that all children develop into effective lifelong learners with a high level of esteem who take pride in what they do and who develop a deep love of learning.

There is an enormous amount of richness in the book as Derek includes wonderful photographs, archived information, fabulous quotes and stories of past events. To see all these records come together in a way that they can be appreciated and enjoyed now by some many people is what makes this book a truly invaluable piece of work.

I was very lucky to meet one of the former pupils last year, whose sole birthday wish when she turned 100, was to come to visit the school. It was fascinating chatting with her and hearing all the stories she had to tell. I am sure that Derek's book will now enable others to also feel that they have been able to have this 'first hand insight' into the history and life of the school and to also feel that we are all still contributing to its history and doing all we can to provide the very best education and experiences for all the children and families that become associated with it.

This book is a real masterpiece and a real work of love that will forever be treasured by all at Balfour Primary School and the local community.

Marcelo Staricoff - May 2015

Contents

Introduction

My personal seven-year journey through part of the history of the Balfour Primary School started on 13th September 1945 when I arrived at the school gates with my mother for the first time. This was when I opened a memory file marked 'Information on Balfour', which has stood a test, rather than the test of time, by providing episodic flashes of remembered happenings; I certainly do not have a full narrative with names and dates that can be relied on.

My inspiration to write a history of Balfour came as a result of the celebration that was held in July 1999, to mark the 75th Anniversary of Balfour Junior School, which opened on 27th February 1924. The centre-piece of the event was a display of all the available material that could be mustered, which included one very surprising and, for most of us, a totally unexpected pictorial piece of the School's history.

Amongst the many exhibits on show were two letters and two coloured pencil drawings that had been sent in. The letters contained a total of just three sentences but the two pencil coloured pictures were of a school building and the plan of its footprint and represented a revelation.

The picture was of the Balfour Junior School, which opened on 1st May 1905 and, like the building in which we were holding the celebration, was built on the corner of Loder Road and Balfour Road. It just happened to have been built on the opposite corner of Loder Road. Thus, one glance at the picture revealed that it wasn't the 75th Anniversary we were celebrating after all! It was the 94th year since the Balfour Road School had been in existence.

The two letters contained the information that confirmed the school building had been erected largely from sheets of corrugated iron and it remained in place for nineteen years until closing in 1924 when, at long last, the new building was opened.

Unsurprisingly, the first building was colloquially referred to as the Tin Hut or, as one of the letter writers said, it was the Tin Hutment. The local press sometimes called it the Tin School.

Officially, the building was a temporary one; this school, which was called Balfour Junior School from the start looked set, as time went by, to challenge the very definition of the word 'temporary'.

Also seemingly temporary, were the names given to both school buildings, which have been subject to many changes over time. It was called Balfour Primary School in 1955 at the end of its first 50 years and it was back to its 'Junior' title by the time I joined the governing body in 1999. Presently, it is again called a primary school.

Fortunately, I have been able to supplement the remaining fragments of my memory with a wealth of material that had been collected and stored at the school over the years together with yet more information that is held in the local East Sussex Record Office at The Keep. I do rely heavily on the extensive records of the Head teachers' Log Books and Minutes of the meetings of the Managers. One hundred and ten years ago, this School started out on an incredible journey and I make no apology for telling the story through their eyes and pens. Only a few people will now remember the Tin Hut. The Head teachers were praised at the end of their service at the Tin School, not just for their excellent work but for coping with the appalling conditions with which they had to contend.

Just as important, has been the information that came from many the past pupils who submitted a diverse set of recollections of their school days spent at the evergreen campus of Balfour Road School. These included contributions sent in for display at the earlier 60th anniversary celebration – well alright, the 79th anniversary.

Following the unexpected information that had been received about the nearly forgotten part of Balfour's history, the key to unlocking that past could only be determined by the sufficiency of reference material held at the Keep. Fortunately the first, and most significant find, was the Log Book of the Loder Road School's Infants' Department, in which the Head teacher, Miss E Mills started to record daily happenings from the opening day on 1st May 1905. She went on the fill nearly 500 pages with details of school life that must at times, have been very difficult indeed to manage. So much so, that the last few years of her time at the school were punctuated with periods of absence through ill-health.

By 1922, she must have known that the new building was soon to be opened but she also knew that it was unlikely that she would make the journey across Loder Road to work in it. As we will see, she had decided to seek a new appointment in an established school. Perhaps she felt that she should leave the challenge of managing the future development of the Balfour School in its new building, in the hands of a younger teacher.

Having found the second Log Book, which extended the Balfour School story through to 1937, it seemed that all the extant sources of information, specifically about the Tin Hut, had been located.

Not so, because while looking for documents unrelated to School Log Books, I came across a set of four Journals containing the Minutes of meetings of Managers of Schools in north Brighton (1903 – 1937). This was pure happen-chance, as I had not seen any reference relating to the local management of schools up to this point.

The Journals revealed that, in 1905, the responsibility for the management of Loder Road School was added to the work of this group of managers, who were already responsible for the Ditchling Road, Preston Road and Stanford Road Schools. As one would expect, their records mirrored many of the events and happenings that had been recorded in the Head teacher's Log Book.

Making use of this new information soon led me to read the Minutes of the meeting in 1922, when the Managers recorded their congratulations to Miss Mills on her successful appointment as the Head teacher of Lewes Road Primary School. I already knew that Miss Seward had been the Head teacher of Balfour Infants and mixed Junior School in the 1920s and 30s, but did not know when she had been appointed to the job.

The Minutes of the Managers' meetings tell us so much more than providing the evidence for the change of Head teachers in 1922. Without them, we would have almost no knowledge of the 'other' half of the Loder Road School, which was the Mixed Juniors' Department.

The plan of the school on the back cover shows that there were two sets of four classrooms – the Infants' Department, where Miss Mills was in charge and the Mixed Juniors Department. The Hall was in between the two. No Log Book has ever been found in relation to the upper school but much of what Miss Mills described in her daily round would have applied more-or-less equally to the other side of the Hall. The Managers' Minutes do fill in some of the gaps and cover issues that affected the whole school like the caretakers' duties and wages, HMI reports, use of playing fields and general awfulness of the conditions in which everyone had to work. Or, more accurately, simply endure at times.

We also know that the Mixed Department also had two Head teachers. Mr Down who started in 1905 and was soon replaced by Mr Weeks when he retired, having not been allowed to stay for an extra year after his 65th birthday. The Managers gave their support to his request but the Education Committee clearly didn't agree.

The other key witness with first-hand knowledge of the Tin Hut, who should get a special mention here, is Owen Williams who started school there in 1908 at 5 years of age. His account appears in an autobiographical book, "Those Were the Days", which he wrote with Doris Williams. There are just a few paragraphs at the beginning of the book that speak volumes about the schooldays of children at Loder Road during the years leading up to the First World War. I have quoted a short paragraph in which he reflects on the ending of his time at school towards the end of WW1; putting this at the end of Chapter 1 which marks the end of the Tin Hut's 'useful' life as a school building. It seemed an apt place to put it and, to me, it reads as though he had written it with the lyrics of Mary Hopkins' 1968 hit record in mind, "Those were the days my friend, we thought they would never end". But, they did end, as did the days of the Tin School in 1924.

In Chapter 2, we pick up the history of Balfour Junior and Mixed Infants and Senior Mixed School now in the new building and with a new name. In effect, there were two schools sharing the school building; not unlike the set-up at Loder Road but now with secondary school age children in the 'other half'.

It opened for business on 27th February 1924 with Miss Hilda Seward remaining at the helm. As the Managers' Minutes record, Mr Weeks was confirmed as the Head of the Senior School but, within a couple of weeks after the opening, he suddenly resigned. Sadly, the reason must have been health-related as Miss Seward mentioned him in one of her Log Book entries a year later, as the late Head teacher of the Senior School.

Section I of this Chapter is devoted to the 15-year period between the opening of the School and the start of the Second World War in September 1939.

During this time, Miss Seward maintained her Log Book and recorded several battles she had with the Head of the Senior School over the dual occupancy of the Hall. It was, like the Loder Road version, too small for the purpose. Like Miss Mills before her, she would write statements about what she saw as failings in the system and in doing so, would no doubt have the page of text open for any visitor to read and inwardly digest. She actually went further than did Miss Mills by underlining important points and even, on a few occasions, signed the statement in her own Log Book to add emphasis. If she was writing today, I am sure she would be making extensive use of **B**, *I*, <u>U</u> on her keyboard.

Also during in this period, the Managers were pressed by the Head teachers of the north Brighton schools to consider an investigation into the demography of families in the localities to determine the numbers of children and their ages in relation to the capacity in schools to accommodate them. This seems to have been an early initiative to develop what we would now call 'catchment areas', which have played a part in the organisation of admissions' policies ever since. Another innovation that was described in the meetings of Managers was the use of the Appointments' List from which a qualified teacher could be selected to fill a vacancy and could be confirmed in that post later, after an interview. This might have been part of a 'Supply' system as many supply teachers came and went at regular intervals. Finally, another word with which we are familiar, was 'secondment', was mentioned in the records in relation to requests that were made to schools to identify any teacher who might be 'surplus' to immediate needs. Such teachers could subsequently be seconded to another school for a period.

The records of this period in the Log Book and Managers' Minutes have been supplemented by the reminiscences of past pupils who recalled memories of their Balfour Days in responding to invitations to send in material for the celebrations of the 60th and 75th anniversaries of the opening of the new building. Additionally of course, new technologies were becoming more readily available at this time, so some of them were also able to provide photographs and copies of individual school reports and other items of memorobilia. When all these individual inputs are taken alongside other documents that remained stored in school cupboards and escaped being lost during WWII, we have a rich account of school life in the 20s and 30s, which was so different from that which the children at Loder Road had experienced.

Just how different these experiences were from those of children at school in the first two decades may be glimpsed through the autobiographies of Albert Paul (who wrote about his schooldays at Finsbury Road School) and Owen Williams when they are compared to the memories of Malcolm Hampton and John Booker who documented their school days by recalling the 1930s.

I refer in the book to Albert Paul's autobiography, the first QueenSpark book published in1974, as his record is a very full account of being a pupil at school in the first few years of the 20th century.

There is another way of looking at changes over the decades, rather than speculating on the significance of differences between the old and new schools. The alternative approach is to recall the 1849 epigram by Jean-Baptiste Alphonse Karr, "*plus ça change, plus c'est la même chose*", usually translated as "the more things change, the more they stay the same."

For me, this epigram was encapsulated by a comment made at an education conference a few years ago, when a speaker recalled an interesting comment made by the well-known scientist, Heinz Wolff, who offered his opinion on coping with, and planning for, the major challenges ahead.

Specifically, when asked about the likely changes that would be brought about by the impact of developing technologies, Wolff replied saying he thought that "the future is further away than you think. *I think that for the foreseeable future, we will have groups of between 20 and 40 students, with a teacher, and most of the learning is going to be in classrooms that are the size we have now, with some IT of course, but the quality of the learning is going to be dictated by what's going on in that classroom*".

The description he gave would have fitted the Tin Hut a hundred years ago with chalk & slate in place of keyboard & screen. The words being written will not have changed very much. And it is still not out of place in schools today many years after Wolff's prediction was made.

Section II covers the period of the Second World War, which began at the start of September 1939 when the school was evacuated, having been commandeered by the Ministry of Defence for use as a military hospital. On that day too, there was a personal co-incidence that you couldn't make up.

Eleanor Horsley, who, as a sixth-former at York Place at the start of the First World War in 1914, helped the younger children at the school to move to temporary accommodation following an order to evacuate the building for military use. Twenty-five years later, now the Head teacher at Balfour Senior Girls School, Eleanor Horsley again helped to evacuate a school building that was required by the Military for a use as a hospital.

The School's stock of furniture and equipment was transferred to the Varndean Boys School across the playfields.

However, the children were transferred in the opposite direction to the Ditchling Road School, which then meant that some of the stock had to be moved again quickly so that classes could function without too much delay. The move to Ditchling Road School proved to be a temporary one as some classes were then transferred to Varndean Girls School where there were air raid shelters (as there were also at Ditchling Road). Miss Seward then had to repeat her task of moving the material up the Ditchling Road this time rather than down it.

Unlike the WW1period at the Tin Hut, about which very little school-specific material has been uncovered, events relating to WW2 at Balfour Road were well reported. The Log Book contains the details of the many locations that classes of children, displaced from Balfour, were housed. They were mainly at Varndean Boys School and the Varndean Girls School. In addition, the Downs School in Ditchling Road was also used as were several Church Halls. Alongside all these arrangements (and re-arrangements), the Head had to organise a rota of teachers who maintained the education of the evacuated Balfour children who were sent to the Holme Valley and Holmeforth. I wonder how many of the evacuated Balfour children went on to watch the TV series, "Last of the Summer Wine"? None of the former pupils who were evacuated, and who wrote about their memories, mentioned the connection.

In addition to the Head's diary of wartime experiences, there are a number of very good oral histories from past pupils, including one wonderful piece by Rita Hollands about the day the German (armed) bomber flew over Havelock Road.

Now, to the last Section of the Chapter, 1945 to 1955, where I join the narrative but only in so far that I have added my own memories of the period alongside all the other past-pupils in the sections of reminiscences. Everything else that has been written in this section comes from the same combination of Log Book entries, pupil memories plus a mixture of photographs and a store of various school documents.

This section sees the start of the Mr Slater's 25-year service as Balfour's Head teacher. He was one of three Head teachers who shared the leadership role for 48 of the first 50 years in the school's history. He introduced yet another style of Log Book writing. His was modelled on what we might call, 'one-liners'. Certainly not along the lines of the stand-up comedian, more like the brevity of a text message.

Where Miss Seward had sought to maximise the opportunities for using the open air for as many (educational) activities as possible, Mr Slater concentrated more on sporting activities. As this period was much closer to the 60th and 75th anniversaries, there were many more personal histories to include alongside Mr Slater's Log Book record. The number of photographs sent in increased again when compared with the pre-war period.

Probably the most significant change during the period was the introduction of the 11-plus examination and a number of former pupils referred to it and the effect it had on them and their friends. It was a controversial system that was ended in 1965 when comprehensive secondary education was introduced and most schools converted to this system and the 11-plus was withdrawn. A small number of areas, Kent and the Wirral being two examples, have retained their grammar schools.

The history has been rounded off by a final miscellany of items that have appeared at frequent intervals throughout the period. The first item is a display of photographs of classes from 1925 to 1951, which confirm that the classes were much larger than today, together with two photographs of groups of the teachers whose names often appeared in Log Book entries. The second item is an analysis of the changes that were made in approaches to school discipline, which have been drawn from original sources. Thirdly, there is a group of School Reports that were sent to parents, which didn't change significantly in curricular content over the years. Lastly, there is a selection of images of sporting activities, which increased in volume and variety but only dramatically if one measures activity against the Drill lessons in the early days at Loder Road. But then, that would be a pointless comparison anyway given that the school didn't have a proper playground and playing fields over the road were 'out-of-bounds'.

Finally, I have realised that, in choosing to write about the first fifty years of Balfour Road School's history, the final event that happened turned out to be a rather coincidental one; not intended, but I did know the relevant date and remembered it only when writing this bit.

It is that, 50 years after Balfour Junior School opened at the corner of Loder Road in 1905, a new school was opened in 1955, on the campus and with an entrance in Loder Road. It was the Dorothy Stringer Secondary Modern School. Here, Miss Dorothy Stringer's name was associated with an opening ceremony. As can be seen on the last page of the Minutes of the north Brighton's Managers' meetings in 1937, she signed the letter as Chair of the Education Committee, which confirmed the closing of the system of the group management of schools across the town.

And in 2015, politicians are still re-inventing systems of management of schools not too dissimilar to the one that Miss Stringer abandoned nearly 80 years ago. We can just about cope with 'the more things change, the more they stay the same', so long as the 'things' aren't deck chairs being re-arranged on the Titanic.

However, my money is on Heinz Wolff's interpretation of Jean-Baptiste Alphonse Karr's epigram.

Derek Betts July 2015

Chapter One   The Tin Hut Years

Section I   Setting the Scene

It all started with a celebration of the 75th Anniversary of Balfour Junior School – but was it 75?

In July 1999, the Balfour Road Junior School celebrated its 75th Anniversary.

The school, built on the corner of Balfour Road and Loder Road, was the most northerly school in Brighton at the time. It was officially opened on 27th February 1924. The Log Book entry records the cost of the building to be £14,872.

However, what seems to have been unknown to many, if not all of the organisers of the celebration, was the existence of a school, also at the junction of the Loder Road and Balfour Road, which was built in 1905.

This was in fact, Balfour Road Junior School, which was opened on 1st May 1905 but on the opposite side of Loder Road, on a site that ran from Balfour Road down to what is now Loder Place. There is no doubt about the name that the Education Committee gave the new school. It was printed on the official Visitors Book that was provided by the local authority, in gold lettering and expensively bound.

The very existence of this school was demonstrated in pictorial form, as shown on the front cover, in a drawing by O. Williams. The drawing was sent in response to an article about the anniversary in the local newspaper calling for past pupils to send in their memories of school days at Balfour. It might have been sent in by a relative or friend of Mr. Williams because later research discovered that he died in 1988. In fact, two of his drawings were submitted; the second one is shown on the back cover. As will be seen later, Owen Williams provided us with more than his art work; he also recounted his days spent at the Loder Road School in a chapter of the book published by Doris Williams in 1991, "Turn Back the Years". His is the only significant description of life at this school that has been found and seems very likely to remain so.

His significant and revealing drawing showed that the school was constructed from sheets of corrugated iron, a construction that earned it the nickname, rather unsurprisingly, of the 'Tin Hut'. A second drawing outlined the plan of the school's footprint on the site. It seems that the 'Tin Hut' wasn't just a name used by locals, the Brighton and Sussex newspapers referred to Balfour Junior School as the 'Tin School'.

One official name and two nicknames but the variations didn't end there. It is referred to in archives at the East Sussex Records Office as Loder Road (Balfour) School (temporary) and elsewhere as Loder Road Mixed Infants and Seniors School. Whatever name we chose to call it, the 1999 celebration held at the Balfour Junior School was definitely its 94th Anniversary.

The School building that was made from bricks and mortar was indeed 75 years old in1999.

Photographs and Monographs

The collection of photographs and drawings below illustrate local scenes and buildings that would have been familiar to pupils at the Loder Road School or would have connections with the School's history.

The three schools shown were built by the Brighton School Board; Preston Road (1880), Ditchling Road (1890) and Stanford Road (1893). They were all managed by the north Brighton group of Managers to which the new Loder Road School was added to their sphere of influence, or they might have said, 'to their workload'.

As can be seen, Stanford Road School was requisitioned by the Military in the First World War as one of a number of schools that were used as hospitals, as were the York Place schools. Balfour Road School was similarly requisitioned at the start of the Second World War.

Pupils at the Loder Road School would have walked along these car-free roads around their school on a countless number of times.

Slightly further afield, the Diocesan Teacher Training College (now the Brighton Business Centre) at the corner of Ditchling Road and Viaduct Road was where many of the pupil-teachers came from to do their teaching practice at Loder Road and, more regularly as student -teachers, at Balfour Road School.

Down at the other end of Viaduct Road in 1909, a tram was at a standstill after a heavy fall of snow. It was parked opposite hoardings that were hiding the building of the Fire Station and the Duke of Yorks cinema. When not snowed up, the tram would be used to bring children down from Loder Road occasionally to be given boots, which the Fire Brigade gave to those who were found to be in need.

Lastly, a photograph of the York Place building, which housed both the Municipal Secondary Schools for Girls and Boys (their Art class is shown) and a Teacher Training facility for pupil-teachers (also shown).

Fig 1

Fig 2

2ND EASTERN GENERAL HOSPITAL   STANFORD RD   BRIGHTON

Fig 3
Stanford Road School (above)

Fig 4
Balfour Road

Fig 5
Loder Road

The Balfour Connection: The Diocesan Training College for Schoolmistresses was built in 1854. Its Principal in the early years of the twentieth century, was the Rev. G Corfield, MA (Oxon) who became a frequent visitor to the new Balfour Road Junior School, which opened in 1905

Fig 6
The Diocesan College in Viaduct Road

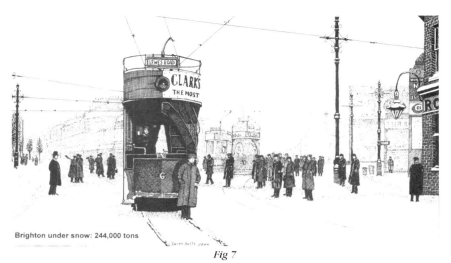

Brighton under snow: 244,000 tons

Fig 7
Stranded tram in snow at Preston Circus in 1909

Fig 8
Entry to York Place Schools

An Art Class at the Municipal Secondary School, about 1906

Fig 9

Teachers in training in 1906 at the Brighton
Pupil-Teacher Centre, York Place

Fig 10

Now the monographs

The pupils' view of their educational experience at the start of the 20th century

Any child, having started school at the Loder Road School in its last academic year 1923/4, would have been in their 80th year by 1999, so to obtain any first-hand recollections of the temporary building amongst the letters that were received from former pupils was a bonus. So, we will start the oral histories.

A recollection from Mrs Elms sets the scene perfectly because, as we will soon see from the seemingly endless references in the Log Book, which the Head teacher maintained from 1905 to 1921, that it was the condition of the building and its corrugated iron structure that dominated the entries that were made.

"I am 85 years old and was born in Bates Road. I went to the then Loder Road School and it had a corrugated iron roof and when it rained, it was so noisy we had a job to hear the teacher speaking".

Muriel E. Elms (nee Watts)

And here is yet another name that was given to the School (but was not repeated elsewhere.)

I am interested in your 75th anniversary, and as I have just reached 75 years of age you can reckon the School had only just moved up from the old Loder Road Tin Hutment. One family member recalled how she attended Loder Road during the First World War and walked home with candles in jam jars!

I was lucky to start at the newly built school and one of the teachers Miss Young was there to make me feel at home. She had been a training teacher with two of my aunts.

Nora Cox

Three witnesses, E. Marshall, Muriel Elms and Nora Cox, have given us just a few glimpses of the forgotten past. However a fourth, very important first-hand account, was found in the pages of the publication, "Past and Present – The Story of Blaker's Park".

In a section in this book about the schools and churches in the area of the Park, mention was made of the opening of the Loder Road Council School in 1905. It was seen as a temporary Balfour School to accommodate the burgeoning numbers of children seeking admission to the Ditchling Road and Preston Road Schools.

This information about the Loder Road School was drawn from another local history book, "Turn Back the Years", written by Owen and Doris Williams. It is Owen's description of his years at the corrugated iron school that provides us with a forth-right and blunt account, which offers a different perspective when compared with the Head Teacher's more measured descriptions of the highs and lows of life in the Loder Road School. She did have to be rather more diplomatic, of course.

Owen also offered an explanation of the origins of the Tin Hut – *"This structure masquerading as a school mainly consisting of solid sheets of corrugated iron, had, as we were told, stood originally on a site elsewhere. Not for education of the young, but to confine the mentally unstable".*

Owen Williams' account of his school days is reproduced in full at Appendix 4 and it is fair to say that, whatever he felt at the time about his *"ugly old school"* and being frequently called a *"Blockhead"*, he did praise his teachers by recalling that *"much can be said for their courage and expertise, when against all odds, they succeeded in the task"*.

Lastly, there is one more first-hand record of a pupil's school experiences at the beginning of the 20th century, but this is not one from the Loder Road School. Albert Paul, who started school at Finsbury Road School in 1907, wrote an autobiography for the series of QueenSpark Books. He went there aged 7 years and was therefore a contemporary of children in their first few years at the temporary Balfour School in Loder Road. It is perhaps reasonable to suppose that his experiences at Finsbury Road were similar to those of the Balfour children. In fact, the first school experience he recalls in his book, which involves the distribution of 'Boots', describes the same events that were taking place at Loder Road School a couple of miles to the north.

Fig 11

In an extract from, *"Poverty – Hardship but Happiness: Those were the Days"*, he writes

Boots
"Every year before the winter set in, the headmaster would come into the classrooms and ask all the boys with their fathers out of work, to stand up. 'Lo and Behold', nearly all the boys would stand up.

A good many boys went to school with no stockings or boots on, quite a common thing and nobody took any notice of this. These would have their names taken down; us other boys would have our boots inspected and if the headmaster considered they were beyond repair, he would put our names down.

The next thing was, all us boys were lined up on the pavement (four abreast) and marched out into Southampton Street, down Southover Hill, along by the Level, through St. Peter's Church grounds, over to Trafalgar Street and then marched up to a boot shop (named Lacey's) just above Sydney Street. We would line up on the pavement and into the shop went eight boys at a time. The assistants would fit us out with a heavy pair of hobnailed boots with metal toecaps and pelts on the heels and then, as we passed out of the shop, another man would punch a hole in the uppers of the boots. This prevented the parents from pawning them at the pawnbrokers".

(J. Lacey's shop was at 21 Trafalgar St. and he was a shoe and boot maker.)

Note on the photograph Fig 11 on the previous page:

In County Durham, where the photograph was taken, as in Brighton, there was a Boot Fund for the same purpose.

In addition to the supply of footwear, an Act in 1906 empowered local authorities to feed children in need. This followed a report by the Committee on Physical Deterioration, which was set up in 1904 and which took the view that it was "the height of cruelty to subject half-starved children to the processes of education".

Albert Paul was also familiar with this situation, writing in his autobiography about soup kitchens and being provided with tickets for meals at breakfast and dinner that were made available at several schools in the locality.

Discipline

"Discipline was very strict at school. We had desks with lift-up seats and tops with slots for the slates. The teacher would say, "Seats down by numbers." Number 1; hands on slates. Number 2; slates on desks and arms folded.

Once a week a monitor (or a very good boy), would go around the class carrying a wooden tray full of holes and collect up the inkwells, take them to the wash-room, give them all a good wash. Then fill them with new ink and place them back into the desks.

When the time came to use the slates, another boy would go around the class giving out round slate pencils. When these broke, we were given a 5-inch metal tube to push the short pieces of slate pencil in and so make them usable. We sometimes used these metal tubes as pea-shooters firing ink-soaked blotting paper balls to stick to the ceiling. My word, if the teacher caught any of us boys doing this, the punishment was to kneel on the rough floorboards, with your hands on the back of your neck, for a period of about 20 minutes. Should you lop over, aching all over, the teacher would slap you across the head with his hand and shout sternly:- "Get upright, will you."

Another punishment was, hold out hand and get the cane across one hand and then the other. It didn't 'arf sting. Should you be extra naughty, the teacher would make you go to the headmaster's room and fetch the tawse. (This was a leather belt slit up at one end into narrow strips to make it sting across your hand). You only wanted this once.

We had a very strict headmaster. Every Friday evening he would throw up the wooden shutters (which divided the classrooms) and have all us boys (350 to 400) assembled to say prayers, sing a hymn, and then he would say, "Now then boys. The dark winter evenings are now drawing in on us and this is the time the Devil gets busy. Please don't get into any mischief. Stop indoors and help your mothers and so keep yourselves occupied. When you return to school on Monday let's have you turn up early with your boots cleaned and a nice clean collar (and straight tie). Also, remember, a nice clean neck and no high water mark." (Meaning; wash your neck properly – not just to down to your collar.)

Standards not classes
Our various classes were not called form 1, 2 etc (as they might be today). They were called Standards 1, 2, 3, 4, 5, 6 and 7. As we passed our various annual examinations, comprising 10 subjects, which were Reading, Writing, Arithmetic, Spelling, Geography, Grammar, Nature Study, Composition, Dictation and Mental Arithmetic, we were given a possible 10 marks per subject, making a grand total of 100 (which no boy ever obtained).

At the end of the examination, the marks were totalled and those with low marks might have to remain in the same Standard until they improved enough to move on.

It was quite a common thing to see boys start in Standard 1 and leave at 14 years of age still in Standard 1.

(We will see later that this issue of age-related progress or standards being reached before further progress can be made irrespective of age, was debated at Loder Road and later at Balfour Road School in the 1950s where there were classes with a few children either held back or pushed forward.)

Fire Drill
Finally, Albert Paul recalls an event that was also very familiar to children at the Tin Hut.

"Every Standard had a fire whistle hanging on the classroom door-post. Without any warning the headmaster would blow hard on his whistle in the corridor and then the teachers in every class would rush to the door and open same, blow their whistles hard, all boys would be hustled out into the playground and lined up strictly. The headmaster would look at his watch and tell us how proud he was that we had beaten the last fire-drill turn out, by so many seconds."

From Monographs to the School Log Book

There is a much more detailed account of what school life was like for both children and teachers at the temporary Balfour Road School, through the records made at the time by Miss Mills, the first Head teacher of the Infants Department. She wrote most of the entries that were made in the Log Book between 1905 and 1922. When I arrived at this point during early stages of researching the history, I didn't know why Miss Mills had stopped writing the Log.

However, further researches at the East Sussex Record Office (The Keep) the archives revealed six volumes of Minutes of meetings of the Board of Managers of north Brighton schools. These included Loder Road School along with Preston Road, Ditchling Road and Stanford Road. One of the meetings held in 1922, provided the answer as to why Miss Mills had stopped writing.

Simply, it was that she had left the school. As the Managers were told:

It was reported that Miss Mills, Head Mistress of the Infants' Department had been appointed Head Mistress of Lewes Road Infants' School. A letter (17.7.1922) of resignation from Miss Mills was submitted.

Resolved:- That the resignation of Miss E. Mills, to take effect on August 31st 1922, be accepted..

> *Resolved:- That the Managers place on record an expression of their thanks and appreciation of the excellent service rendered by Miss E Mills during the 27½ years she has been connected to this Board of Management. After 10 years as a Assistant at Ditchling Road Infants' School, Miss Mills became the first Head Mistress of the Infants' Department of Loder Road Temporary School, where in spite of great difficulties and discouraging conditions, the results have been such as to evoke satisfactory reports from H.M. Inspectors. Whilst parting with her services with much regret, the Managers congratulate Miss Mills on her appointment as Head Mistress of Lewes Road Infants' School, where with the larger number of scholars and more convenient premises, the Managers feel she will have wider scope for her undoubted abilities.*

- Having read every one of the 17 years of diary entries made by Miss Mills, I can easily understand the sentiments that lay behind the Managers' assessment of a job well done despite the very difficult circumstances. There is more to be said about this change of leadership in the sections of a second Log Book and the Minutes of the meetings of the School's Managers during 1922.

As the pictures of the Loder Road School show, it had two sections of four classrooms separated by the Hall. The boys' entrance was in Bates Road but the Mixed Department, as the title suggests, held boys and girls together. By comparison, the Ditchling Road School (now the Downs Primary School) had a Girls' Department and a Boys' Department. In order to segregate the older boys and girls at Loder Road, there would need to have been more floor space than was available.

While it appears that there is no record of the existence of a Log Book for the Mixed Department, we can learn a lot about it from the many incidental references made in the Infants' Log Book and in the Managers' Minutes. To begin with, the first Head teacher was Mr Down who was nearing his retirement age in 1905 and was soon replaced by Mr Weeks who remained in post up to the opening of the new building in 1924. It can also be taken as read that the condition of the Tin Hut, the prevalence of serious illnesses, the weather conditions that were often severe and the absence of a playground with a tarmac surface were all circumstances that were common to both Departments.

So, the scene is set at the start of the Balfour School's journey through history with Miss Mills and Mr Down in charge of the Infants and Mixed Departments respectively. We know which schools in the district were being overseen by the Board of Managers and that the journey was being chronicled in the Infants' Log Book and Managers' Minute Book. We have already seen evidence which, when compared with today's standards, would suggest that the children's educational experience was taking place in very tough times. For anyone with a sensitive disposition, we would probably have to say, euphemistically, that it took place in challenging times.

The start date of the School Managers' meetings in 1903 was as a consequence of the transfer of responsibility for education provision in Brighton from the local School Board, set up following the 1870 Education Act, to the new Local Education Authority.

In his book on the 100-year history of Middle Street School, George Haffenden, its Head teacher, referred to 1st April 1903 as the "Appointment Day" when under the 1902 Education Act, all powers and duties of the Brighton and Preston United District Board were transferred the County Borough of Brighton. Its Education Committee became the Education Authority for primary, secondary and technical instruction in the Borough.

In taking over in 1903, one of the first duties that the Brighton Education Committee had to shoulder was the responsibility for providing additional capacity for the growing number of children in the Borough who needed a place in school.

Developing a new system of administration while, at the same time, organising the construction of a temporary building with the attendant requirements for stock, interior furbishing, teachers and the rest, in a relatively short timescale, may not have been the ideal formula for a smooth, trouble-free transition.

This is mere conjecture, of course. However, what isn't guesswork is the cumulative record of information about the difficulties experienced at the school in its first few months.

Opening Day arrived on 1st May 1905 but the Loder Road School building wasn't finished.

In the event:

- There wasn't a full complement of trained teachers available

- The materials that were needed for needlework (girls) and handiwork (boys) were not available. Both of these subjects played a significant part in the school curriculum in those days.

- The building wasn't finished until the end of June.

- The roof of the second-hand building was leaking 18 months later – the first sign of what became a catalogue of serious building-related problems.

- The Head teacher was moved to write to the Education Committee about the need for the construction of a flight of steps linking Osborne Road with Balfour Road to improve access to the school – a request that took 15 years to bear fruit, finally being constructed in 1920

- The full complement of qualified teachers was not achieved until 1907

Before we delve into the first of Miss Mills' Log Books, we can view the outcome of her immediate task on Day One; the enrolment of the children (the scholars, as they were often called at this time). As her Log Book entry records, she enrolled 54 children on that day. Just before finishing writing this book, I was given a copy of the first two enrolment forms that a parent of the current generation of pupils had sent in to the school. The first completed sheet dated 1st May 1905, is shown below.

The admission sheets would have been retained on file until the last pupil on the list had left the Infants' Department. All the forms were sent to the Education Department of the Council and ever since, have been kept stored at the East Sussex Record Office, which is now at The Keep in Brighton.

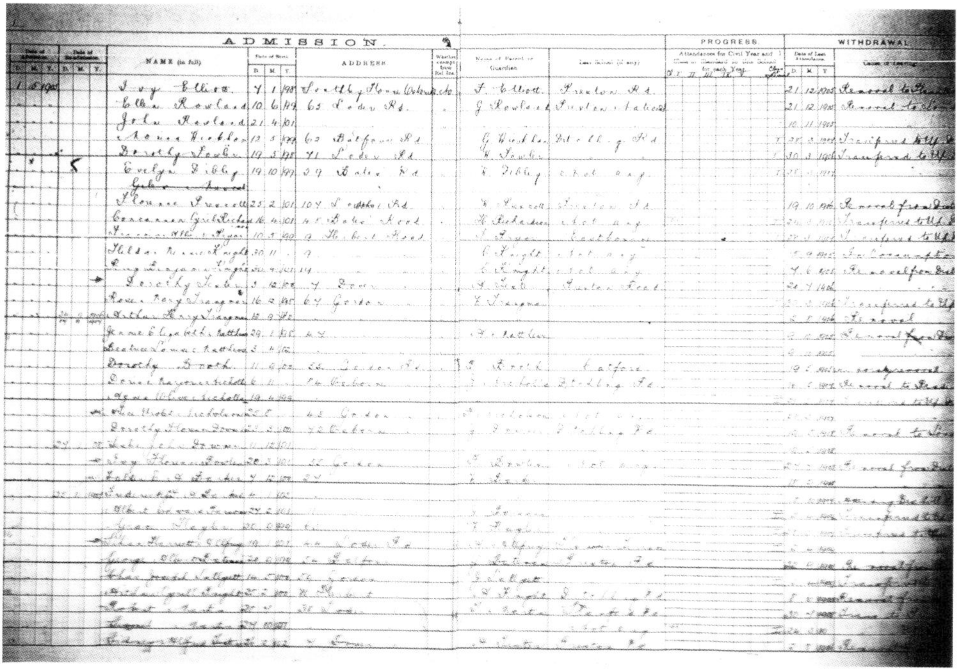

ADMISSION.

(handwritten admission register — largely illegible)

Fig 12

The two sheets show that about a third of this group of scholars were transferred to the Upper (Mixed) Department in due course but nearly as many were removed from the Loder Road School by their parents in moving to another district or to another local school. A small number were removed on grounds of ill health, including one with TB and there was one death.

Amongst the first 70 children enrolled, there were 56 different first names, including one "Ebenezer" and, 110 years later, a pupil in Year 6 at the school today said that she could identify at least 50% of these names in her circle of friends.

> Ivy, Ellen (2), John, Monica, Dorothy (4), Evelyn, Giles, Florence (2), Connanon, Hilda, Francis, Benjamin, Rose Arthur (2), Jennie, Beatrice, Doris, Agnes (4), Alice, Leslie, Joy, Walter, Frederick, Albert (2), Grace, Lillian (3), George (2), Chas, Robert, Lionel, Sidney, Cyril, Bertha, Cecil, Ethel, Flora, Eva, Dorothea, Winnifred, Ebenezer, Margaret, Frank, Rose, Alexander, Eleanor, Mary, Harry, Edwin, Thomas, Elsie, Louise, Gladys (2), Reginald, Emily, William, Edith

Their addresses reveal, as might be expected, that they lived in close proximity to the Loder Road site. The majority of them came from Balfour Road and the four adjacent roads, Loder, Bates, Gordon and Herbert Road and from Osborne Road. A family in each of Havelock, Dover, Ashford and Sandgate Road also sent their children to this school. On a map, the catchment area could have been illustrated by a circle of radius ¼ mile being drawn around the school that would have enclosed every child's home.

So now, with children being enrolled and recognising that there were some start-up problems, the School's Log Book entries show what one might expect, which is that many things occurred regularly every week, or every month or so, with a few that appeared annually. Some of this information will be much the same as in today's schools, though not recorded in the same fashion.

Rather than include all the nooks and crannies of 19 years of Log Book records, I have picked a representative selection of the normal day-to-day entries covering the first two years, after which we can take them as read without repeating them here again each year. The selection forms the first part of the study.

The second part of this study of the daily life at Loder Road School, as witnessed by Miss Mills, will look at a broader selection of records that would often challenge a definition of normal circumstances. They will collectively, demonstrate that a school built of second-hand sheets of corrugated iron was anything but normal.

Section II

Infants' Department Log Book, 1905 -1907
Minutes of Managers' meetings held between 1903 and 1907

Extracts from the Log Book kept by Miss Mills

There are six main groups of records that appeared regularly in the first two years: Attendance, Illnesses, Boots & Fire Drills, Annual Events, Schemes of Work and Teachers.

1. **Attendance**
   - *Low attendance; still much sickness amongst the children*
   - *Very low attendance*
   - *57% attendance; the lowest since the school opened – severe weather and the exceptionally bleak district surrounding the school*

The focus on attendance levels (always a matter of concern to this day), was, in 1905, probably more to do with a throwback to the Victorian period and payment by results. As can be seen in Fig 13, in 1876, a School Board School in Lewes Road charged 3pence a week per pupil but if attendance had been one of the full 10 sessions in a week, the charge was reduced to 2 pence.

Later, in 1911, Ditchling Road School rewarded pupils with book prizes for good attendance records; a different kind of incentive. A hundred years on, maintaining good school attendance levels remains an issue to be dealt with.

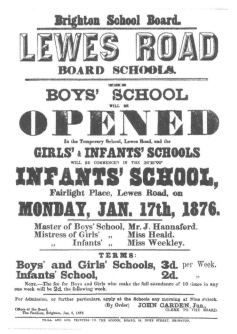

Fig 13

Fig 14

Now, instead of the weekly incentive that was offered to parents in 1876, there is the disincentive of a fine that can be imposed on parents who take their children away on holiday in term time.

In the first year at Loder Road, attendance reports were often coupled with the number of children admitted to the school at the same time. On the opening day, 54 children were admitted. During the year, more groups of children joined. Some were of school age but had not been attending school anywhere or had attended but then dropped out. This left the Head teacher having to determine which Standard to place the child in irrespective of their age, which in some of these cases, meant that the child would be in a class with younger children.

The last Log Book entry of the three quoted above showing 57% , was recorded in 1906 when there were sufficient children attending regularly to establish a steady roll number against which a meaningful percentage of attendance could be stated. Thereafter, low percentages of attendance would simply mean two things; high levels of illness or extreme weather conditions, or both at times.

2. **Illnesses**
    - *Whooping cough is still keeping many children off school*
    - *Severe colds and influenza Low attendance – chicken pox and measles*
    - *Notice received from the Health Department warning of suspicious cases of whooping cough, diphtheria and measles*

These are just a few of the recorded entries indicating the range of illnesses that children were suffering from at the time. Later on, an additional illness appeared which extended this range – scarlet fever. Worse was to come; not so much about the range of illnesses but in the epidemic nature of the outbreaks.

3. **Boots and Fire Drills**
    - *Pupil-teacher, Florence Wells out for the morning in charge of 15 children who went to receive boots by means of the New Year Fund*
    - *The Fire Brigade carried an inspection and there was a Fire Drill (38 seconds)*

As we saw earlier in Albert Paul's memories of school life at Finsbury Road School, children were being fitted for boots if it was found that they had inadequate footwear. This event was, like fire drills, a recurring event at school. By coincidence, these two events were 'connected' at Balfour. The closest source of boots to Loder Road was at the Preston Circus Fire Station where the Fire Brigade had established a distribution centre. The fire service would also keep a check on the fire drills held at Loder Road.

4. **Annual events**
    - *Empire Day – afternoon off by the desire of the Education Committee and School Managers but only after an assembly for the purpose of a 'little talk' on the meaning of Empire Day (and ended with the singing of the National Anthem)*
    - *The celebrations for St George's Day and Empire Day have taken place and the children have been sent home for the rest of the day.*

In addition to these national celebrations, the school was able to gain extra, often half-day holidays, for good attendance – even, as far as one can tell when the levels of attendance had been self-evidently very low. However, we will see soon one example of a requested holiday that was refused. Perhaps that was a warning that had the desired effect as no such further refusals were recorded.

5.   **Schemes of Work**

At the start of every year, the Head teacher would publish the Scheme of Work to be undertaken in the coming year. It would be only a brief summary as most of the detail would have been written into individual teachers' Record Books. The full version would be copied into a document, which would then be sent to the Education Committee for approval. So, for 1905, the Scheme that appeared in the Log Book was as follows:

The year's Syllabus – Observation of surroundings and Simple facts of Nature; encouraging children to make full use of their powers, to train, then to notice, speak and discover what can be learnt in the ordinary phenomena of their lives.   Details of the Scheme will be found in the Teachers' Record Books.

1.   Natural History lessons

1.1   Duck, Swan, Pig, Sheep, Fish (round, flat and shell), Dog, Fox, Squirrel, Mouse, Cow, Goat, Cat, Robin, Donkey, Sparrow, Rook, Fowls – bird life in the spring

1.2   Observation lessons: A pond and nests, a summer ramble, flowers in season, the seashore, boat and ships, fruits, the harvest, nuts and berries, milk, water, lemon & oranges, Christmas plum pudding, the stable (blacksmith), snowdrops, circus, windmill, baker, bread, talks about stems and leaves, trees, talks about the Home.

These lessons will be taken in connection with the help of definite Nature/Home observations, or as an opportunity arises.   As children are fresh to school routines, the same scheme has been prepared for all and can be adapted to the capabilities of the children.   Continuity and proper development will be attainable as children reach upper classes.

1906

Education Committee agreed the Scheme of Work:

This is based on the fundamental principle of true development, viz.:

"The cultivation of the exercise of individual powers, and the right direction of the activities into channels leading to true progress being made."   The details of the Scheme are in the Teachers' Record Books

All subjects will be linked together as much as possible so that all aspects, uses, etc. can be brought before the mind for the promotion of good intelligence, active interest, and the growth of memory

For the Standard, simple History/Geography leading to broader ideas of the World in general.

1907

The same Scheme of Work ie.

The natural and free development of powers, physical, mental and moral of the scholars; to train them in the habits of thought, application, diligence, self-reliance and self-respect and to give the power and love for self-improvement and self-development in all stages of Life.

Details are set out in the Teachers' Record Books for all branches of the curriculum.

It can be assumed that the syllabuses for 'Reading, Writing and Arithmetic' – the 3Rs with which children were so familiar – were included in all Standards and therefore not repeated in the Log Book. The same may have been true for needlework (for girls) and woodwork (for boys), which were also part of the standard curriculum

The term 3Rs, to describe some of the fundamentals of English and Mathematics, was well understood by the pupils in 1905 and is still familiar now as shorthand for key basic subjects. Perhaps it was a quirk of the English sense of humour that only one 'R' of the three was the initial letter of the relevant word – but then, using the acronym WAR or RAW might not have captured the same lasting attention. (Perhaps this is debatable, given our addiction to using a pea-soup of acronyms in all walks of life and professions.)

It is worth noting that while the "3Rs" remain central to the school curriculum, the Aims of education as defined, especially in the 1907 Scheme of Work, would, like the 3R's, certainly not look at of place today. In fact, a modern version of the second half was used nationally a few years ago to emphasise the value of adult education by defining the sector as 'Lifelong Learning', a personal development process that shouldn't stop when you leave school.

6. **Teachers**

1905 Opening Day

1. Head teacher Miss E Mills 1st Class Certificated teacher (Homerton College)
2. Mrs M Churchill (Certificated) – classes 2/3 Upper Division
3. Miss L Grinstead (ex pupil-teacher) – classes 3/4 Lower Division
   [Both on supply as no permanent staff yet settled]

By **1906,** the staff complement stood at:
1. Head teacher Miss E Mills 1st Class Certificated teacher (Homerton College)
2. Mrs M Churchill (Certificated)
3. Miss L Grinstead (ex pupil-teacher)
4. Alice English (senior pupil teacher)
5. Lilian Bosworth (pupil- teacher)
6. Florence Wells (pupil-teacher)

[See the Footnote (Appendix 1) on the development of the teaching profession following the 1870 Education Act.]

By **1907**, there were four qualified teachers in post supported by a number of senior pupil-teachers and pupil-teachers in assistance. The *"Rev Corfield MA (Oxon) Principal Training College"*, as he always signed himself in the Visitors' Book, would have been attending to observe, monitor and assess the pupil-teachers who would have been receiving further tuition at the Training College.

The groups of Log Book entries, ('Attendances', 'Illnesses', 'Boots & Fire Drills' and 'Annual Events') shown above, continued to appear regularly in the Log Book although the incidence of children requiring boots did seem to decline after the First World War.

References to the 'Schemes of Work' and the lists of teachers didn't reappear after 1907. As the Schemes had to be approved by the Education Committee each year, the visiting inspectors didn't need to see a record in the Log Book to which they already had access via the local authority.

After 1907, teachers were only named in the Log Book when they were appointed or resigned; or when they were ill or out on business, although this practice was altered by Miss Seward when she took over in 1922. She favoured setting out the list of teachers and the class for which they would responsible, at the beginning of the year. By then, the pupil-teacher role had, at last given way to qualified or probationary teachers with a system of supply teachers available to cover for absences – not unlike today.

By the third year, the pattern of entries was largely repeated but, at the same time, it was becoming apparent that there were underlying difficulties related to the infra-structure and the level of available resources.

Perhaps Miss Mills was an optimistic person who considered the additional problems to be the initial teething pains of a new school on a new site.

However, if she thought that "things could only get better", Miss Mills was soon to discover that they didn't. She continued to record the 'normal' information that we have seen above but this was increasingly mixed with the unexpected, and worse still, the unwanted.

So in the Section II, the spotlight will be on the Log Book entries that Miss Mills made where she often went further than just recording a problem but she also sought to draw the Education Committee's attention to the consequential harm being done to the school's reputation in the community. This next set of entries will focus specifically on the Buildings, Attendance, Sickness, Events and Miscellaneous Items.

It was to become a very long drawn out process.

Before we continue to find out more about the daily life of the Infants' School through Miss Mills' record of events, we will look, in the same time-frame as above (1905-07), at the record of business dealt with by the Committee of Managers of the Schools in north Brighton.

Extracts from the Journals of Minutes of Proceedings of the Governing Body of School Managers (1903 – 1937), who were responsible for overseeing the work of a group of schools in the north of Brighton.

In 1903, following the 1902 Education Act, local authorities assumed the responsibility for the provision of education in their areas. They replaced the School Boards which had been established for the same purpose in 1870. Under the Act, the authorities were given the option of creating a Board of Managers to be responsible for a group of schools. In the context of Balfour's history, a group of Managers was designated to look after schools in the north of Brighton, specifically those in Ditchling Road, Preston Road and Stanford Road.

The Act did provide for an alternative school management structure which was similar to the current system of school governors. Thus, individual schools could be governed by a group of Managers including up to four LEA representatives. Church leaders were also well represented on the school groups.

We will see later that Brighton's Education Committee decided to abolish their initial system of managing groups of schools with a committee of managers, in favour of each school having its own managers or governors.

> In **1905** – The Managers take on the new Loder Road (temporary Balfour) School and the rest of this year can be seen as a settling-in period as described below.

In the week after the Loder Road (temporary Balfour) School opened on 1st May 1905, the Managers met but no mention was made of the new school that had just opened on their patch. The Chair at the time was Major J. O. Bloomfield, who was to become a fairly regular visitor to the new school.

Mr. E. B. Lethbridge was also a member of the Committee whose name was also often found written in the visitors' book and who frequently gave good advice in support of the Head teacher at Loder Road. He had been the first Head teacher of the York Place secondary school in 1884, which went on to become Varndean School for Boys when the new building opened in 1932 on the Balfour campus. He was forced to retire early on health grounds in 1901 but remained active and died in 1932.

Boys who went on to Varndean after leaving Balfour from the 1930s onwards might remember his name, as I do, because the School named the sixth-form Library after him in recognition of the substantial contribution he had made to education in Brighton.

Having apparently ignored the presence of the Loder Road School at its meeting in May, the Managers gave the new school a less than fulsome welcome at its next meeting when a Resolution from the Education Committee was reported to them.

> *"Resolution of the Education Committee as to the appointment of Managers to Ditchling Road, Preston Road and Stanford Road Schools as the managers of Loder Road School, was submitted and considered".*
> *It was Resolved "that the Elementary Schools Sub-Committee be informed that the managers of Ditchling Road, Preston Road and Stanford Road Schools are only prepared to the undertake the management of Loder Road School as a temporary measure."*

In making this decision, the Managers revealed the existence of the "Elementary School Sub-Committee". By the time their work as School Managers was brought to an end in 1937, they will have regularly encountered a multi-layered system of bureaucracy, which included:

Board of Education – the Government Department for Education

Brighton Borough Council
Education Committee, linked to:

Elementary Schools Sub-Committee, Sites and Works Sub-Committee, Evening Schools Sub-Committee, Canteen Branch Sub-Committee, Improvements Committee, Requisition Branch Sub-Committee. School Staff Branch Sub-Committee, Special Branch Sub-Committee, Secondary School (Appointments of Head Teachers) Sub-Committee, Higher Schools Sub-Committee, Finance Sub-Committee, and the Schools Attendance and Accommodation Sub-Committee

At the next meeting on 10th July 1905, the Managers dealt with a Loder Road issue for the first time:

"Resolved to recommend that Miss A. English, an Uncertificated Assistant Teacher in the Infants Department be appointed at a salary at the rate of £50 per annum according to the Scale of the Committee, the engagement to date from the 1st August 1905, and to be subject to one month's notice, such a notice to expire at the end of any calendar month. This appointment is made in accordance with the terms of Art 15(a), Clause 1, of the Code of Regulations for Public Elementary Schools."

The way in which Miss English's appointment has been recorded is repeated for all such appointments that were made by the Managers. It is recorded here as an example of the form and style of Minute-taking. As a matter of interest, in the archives of documents relating to East Sussex held at The Keep, there are volumes of Minutes taken at meetings of other managers' groups covering this period of time. In one such set of journals which included the Finsbury Road School, the Minutes were so similarly set out it was almost as though there was a Brighton 'house style'. I recognised the handwriting in some sections and it would not be too big a stretch of imagination to think that the Education Committee had organised a small group of trained minute-takers to be available when needed. Perhaps they were also employed at other Council committee meetings. As we saw above, there were a dozen sub-committees that the Loder Road Managers were in contact with, some on a very regular basis.

The Minutes taken at the Finsbury Road School group meetings were full of staffing records like that of Miss English's appointment above. It can be presumed that there were just as many such staff appointments and resignations made over the 19 years' life-time of the Loder Road School. Only a few will be recorded here because it is going to be more illuminating to display the very wide range of other decisions that were made by the Managers over the period, 1905 to 1937.

That said, the next entry is of another rather repetitive committee response, which is still familiar to us nowadays whenever a meeting decides that the best 'action' to take on an issue, is to defer taking it until later or to refer the problem to another committee. So:

"After the summer break, Miss Mills and Mr Down wrote to the managers asking for additional staff to be appointed.

Resolved:- It was agreed to further consider the matter at the next meeting"

This is first mention of Mr Down in his role as the Head teacher of the Mixed Department.

Later in September, Miss Mills contacted the Managers about getting temporary assistance for the caretaker and it was agreed that this could be granted for two weeks, ending on 23rd September. Apparently, the caretaker had met with an accident. The cost of the cover was said to be 15 shillings

Note: !5 shillings would translate to 75p in today's money but not in value, of course.
The National Archives' website carries a currency converter from past values between 1270 and 1970 compared with 2005 (This site is no longer active but knowing a rough comparison of a payment of £1 in 1915 converts to a face value of £43.06 in 2005, permits us to make an estimate of the wages of the temporary caretaker's two week cover, reported to be 15 shillings, which would now be approximately £30.75. The missing aspect in making these comparisons with the past is that the conversion doesn't match up to the changes in the spending power of the money. That is more difficult. Nevertheless, the payments made to the monitoress, caretaker, supply teacher, senior teachers and head teacher quoted here in old money, can still be used to make comparisons of the relative financial values of different employment grades.

The Managers were responsible for authorising payments to be made to all grades of staff and for items of equipment, etc, although, with the somewhat Byzantine structure of Boards, Branches and Sub-Committees with differing powers of authority in the system, it is hardly surprising that many requests from the Head teachers resulted in being deferred or referred to another committee.

As an example, the next meeting received another request from Miss Mills also about staffing, which was referred to the School Staff Branch Sub-Committee.

A letter dated 9th November from Miss Churchill was received. It was a request for an increase in salary, which was held over to the next meeting, allowing time for Miss Mills to furnish a Report on Miss Churchill's work.

At the same meeting, there were two Reports; one about the Mixed Dept. of Loder Road School and the other concerning the Infants' Dept. As no Log Book or any other contemporary record of daily life at the Mixed Dept. has been found, this history of the Loder Road School is inevitably skewed in its focus on the Infants' Dept. Nevertheless, the considerable benefit that has been derived from discovering the Minutes of the Managers' meetings is clearly demonstrated by this entry because the Reports received relate to both the Infants and Mixed Departments.

Note: The two halves of the Loder Road School, four Infants' classes and four Mixed classes approximate in today's terminology to Infant and Junior Schools. The Infants' Dept. would be where today's Year 1 and 2 would be found but progress to the Mixed Dept. would depend largely on reaching Standard 1 not on reaching 7 years of age. Albert Paul, in his autobiography, describes the situation where a boy could start in the Standard 1 and leave school still in Standard 1 at the age of 14.

The term Mixed was applied to schools where boys and girls were educated together. Ditchling Road had Boys and Girls sections in the Junior stage. Secondary schools in the area were generally single sex.

Report to Managers:

> Brighton: Loder Road Council School
>
> Mixed
>
> "This new school has had its full share of unpromising scholars, but in classifying the children, a somewhat low estimate has been taken of their capacity for progress. The instruction has been given with much diligence but with methods that are rather antiquated".
>
> Infants
>
> "When this school was opened in May last many of the older children who entered were decidedly backward. The progress these have made is creditable to the Teachers. The younger children are being carefully trained".

It might be gently pointed out here that this Report to the Managers towards the end of 1905 refers to a school that had been open for less than 8 months. The building was unfinished at the start, the staffing levels were incomplete and many of the children, who were well over the age when children normally started school, had never been to any school before. The author of this rather shallow analysis could surely have been a bit more understanding of the new

> By **1906** – The Loder Road School has been incorporated into the Managers' area of responsibility despite an earlier reference to a temporary period and there is a good example of their modus operandi in the structure of the meeting on 6th October, which is set out below.School's obvious teething problems.

The year began with the Managers giving an instruction that would not be acceptable today (and having seen some parental responses in the Log Book that were reported to Miss Mills in the Infants' Dept., it wasn't acceptable in 1906 either.)

Miss Ansell and Miss Comley (Heads of the Ditchling Road Boys and Girls Departments) had an interview with the Managers with reference to the scholars who will shortly be ready for transfer to the Boys and Girls Departments.

<u>Miss Ansell was instructed to request parents, by means of a circular letter, to send the boys to the Loder Road School.</u>

The concern here about the lack of school places, was a recurring issue throughout the period of the temporary school at Loder Road.

Also at this time, the Managers dealt with another kind of recurring problem - absence of a teacher at Ditchling Road School on the grounds of ill-health. At first, they granted her an extended period of leave, and then she was transferred to Loder Road Mixed Department (for a reason that was not made clear). Finally, she was granted full pay for another limited period followed by half pay for a shorter period before ending her contract.

A similar construction of tapered payments made to seriously ill teachers who are facing having to leave the profession, remains in force today.

During the absence of this teacher, a supply teacher was appointed at 30/- a week.

A second supply teacher was appointed to the Infants Department at a rate of £22 per annum.

Also at the same meeting, Miss L Haffenden a trained and certificated assistant was appointed to Miss Mills' staff and she was to play an important role at Loder Road School before moving on following promotion, finally reaching Ditchling Road as Head teacher. Her initial salary was £75 per annum to start on September 3rd 1906.

I discovered her name was mentioned thirty-three years later when she was listed in the published list of people who were involved in the organisation of Brighton's Education Week in 1939. She chaired the committee that was responsible for arranging a series of concerts that were held during the week's celebrations.

By September 1906, the meetings of School Managers had clearly incorporated Loder Road School on a permanent basis despite the temporary nature of relationship that was expressed a year earlier at the time the new school was opened.

The record of the meeting held on 8th October 1906 (see below) was a good example of the structure and processes of this form of school management. It doesn't compare with majority of schools today where local authorities still do stand between the Head teacher and the Department on Education

However, the role of the local authorities is now more variable in different areas of the country. The significant difference is that the responsibilities for much of the delivery of education have been transferred to schools in concert with their school board of governors.

Managers From:-
Ditchling Road
Loder Road,
Preston Road &
Stanford Road School

At a meeting of Ditchling Road,
Loder Road, Preston Road &
Stanford Road School Managers
held at the Offices of the Offices
of the Education Committee at 54 Old Steine

8th October 1906

Present: Major J A Bloomfield (Chair)
Mrs Miller. The Revs Hugh Shearer and
S B Lane, Councillors Brown, Campbell
and Whittone, Messrs E B Lethbridge and
J W Penfold

The Minutes of the last meeting having been read were signed by the Chairman

1. *Managers who had visited reported as to their visits*
2. *Caretakers and Punishment Report Books were submitted and examined*
3. *Quarterly Reports and Time Books were submitted and examined*
4. *Pupil teachers' 'Record' Books were submitted and examined*
5. *Calling of Manual Instruction Registers was considered*

   Major J A Bloomfield and Coun. J Whittome undertook to call these registers during the coming quarter.

6. *School Staff*

Loder Road School

Application for a School bell was considered

Resolved to Recommend:-

That a bell be supplied to Loder Road School

Ditchling Road School

Appointment of Monitoress in the Infants Department was considered

Resolved to Recommend:-

That Mabel Antram, a Monitoress in the Girls' Department be transferred to the Infants' Department and that her salary is hereby increased from 1/- to 2/- (10p) per week, to date from September 1st 1906.

At this meeting, agenda items from only two schools were considered. The first five items are effectively 'standing' items of report that would always be dealt with at the quarterly meeting and would be expected to take up most of the time. As might be guessed at now, the time taken to agree to supply a bell to Loder Road and agree to appoint a monitoress for Ditchling Road would not amount to more than a few minutes.

Also noteworthy in this Minute, is the list of committee members containing most of the names that regularly appeared in the Loder Road School's Visitors Book. It would seem that all four schools under their supervision were visited by all members. If there was any degree of specialisation, it was in areas of the curriculum such as Nature Study, Handicrafts and Painting. Checking Registers was another purpose that the members frequently signed-in to undertake.

> In **1907** – We meet Miss L Haffenden again and will do so on a number of other occasions. We discover that the Managers can award 'occasional' school holidays and support a Head teacher who wants to carry on beyond the retiring age.

In the New Year, we find that Miss English did get that wage increase she was seeking last year but not very quickly at all.

It was resolved that the salary of Miss A. English, an Assistant in the Infants' Department, be hereby increased from £55 to £60 per annum, according to the Scale of the Committee to date from 31st August 1907.

And there was still more largesse to come during the next committee meeting of the managers when a number of teachers in all four of the north Brighton group of schools, were awarded increases in salaries, which was normally another £5, to take effect on 1st September 1907.

The Loder Road Infants' teacher, Miss L Haffenden was awarded a salary increase from £75 to £80 per annum.

At a subsequent meeting, Miss K Haffenden was appointed 'on Supply' to the Preston Road School (not a concern for Loder Road School but simply a matter of interest here as Miss K Haffenden must surely be a sister of the Loder Road Infants' teacher). Also, their father may well have been the Head teacher of Middle Street School, George Haffenden, who wrote that school's 100-year history book, which was published in 1905.

What follows, is another example of the many recurring decisions that managers had to make. This one was the granting of occasional holidays at the request of Head teachers. They always seemed to have been granted. Always that is, until the next letter was received from the Loder Road School:

In October 1907, the Head teachers of the Infants and Mixed Departments wrote to the Managers asking that the school might close for a holiday on the next Friday, 25th October. As the attendance in the Mixed Department had not been as high as might have been expected, it was decided to grant a holiday to the Infants' Department only. Whoops

Now for a request to the Managers that may not be seen very often, if at all, today.

Received letter from Mr C Down of Loder Road School, dated September 6th 1907, asking to be allowed to extend his services after August next when he will be sixty-five years of age, for a further period of 12 months.

Resolved:-

That the Managers do support Mr Down's application to the Board of Education to be allowed to extend his services as Head Master of the School under the Elementary School Teachers Superannuation Act 1898, for one year from 1st September 1908.

Section III

The Log Book's record of daily life at Loder Road as seen by Miss Mills [1908 – 1914]
Minutes of Managers' Meetings (1908 – 1914)

Selected items from the Log Book

These are Log Book entries that could not be regarded as 'normal' or commonplace. Specifically, they cover the areas of;

1. The school building and playground,
2. School Attendance,
3. Sickness and Injuries and
4. Events.

1. The School Building and Playground

While evidence of defects in the school building had started to appear early on with the leaking roof, it was the state of the playground that gave rise to much early concern. As the diagram on the cover shows, with just eight classrooms between the two departments, each designed* to hold 60 children and sharing a single Hall, the playground was seen as a vital alternative space for a range of activities to take place.

A permanent record of the accommodation provided by the various classrooms in this Department is desired by the Education Committee. The four rooms provide an accommodation of 240, i.e. each room is sufficient for 60 on the 10ft scale. Log Book 10.1.13

The school was built on waste ground and the playground was not really fit for purpose and something that was never properly rectified. Its condition was largely determined by the weather and there was no way of avoiding that situation. However, seeking to avoid using the playground by going 'in doors,' wasn't always a solution either, even if there was available space in the Hall. All of which flew in the face of the 1890 Code of Regulation that had stressed the need to focus on the physical welfare of children as a duty of the State to ensure.

As the building was made of corrugated iron it was a very good conductor of heat energy – drawing it into the building in summer and out of it in winter. As a result, the classroom temperatures could be low as 40°F (or 4°C) and as high as 87°F (or 30°C). A situation in winter that wasn't helped by repeated failures of the boiler or coal/coke shortages. Even when there was a working boiler with sufficient coal and coke available, the very construction of the building failed to contain enough heat energy to keep the children warm in very cold weather.

Here are few of the Log Book records:

1908

- *Owing to the extremely muddy state of the playground, caused by frost/rain during the last 3 weeks, children are unable to go out to play. The Hall is used as often as possible at such times, but as the two departments use it for general work, it is not always available. The caretaker of the school has utilised the gravel to the best advantage but much improvement to the outside ground cannot be affected until a drier state of weather prevails.*

1909

- *Surveyor has had a look at the playground*
- *The condition of the playground has been so bad that no play could be allowed in the Infants section. The interior was rendered extremely unpleasant and dirty by reason of the same, as the small stones or chippings and mud were so difficult to rub off the boots on to the mat.*
- *Some beach stones have been thrown down in the playground today and are to be rolled into the surface*

1910

Now something completely different:

An instruction that Miss Mills really did not want to receive

- *Information has been received from the Clerk to the Education Committee – that the children of this school **may not use the Loder Place Field**, as the ground has been allotted to the use of the Municipal Secondary School.*
- *As the use of this field (owned by the Education Committee) proved invaluable to the children of this school – by reason of the rough surface of the Playground – the effects will be keenly felt.*

This decision to allocate the playing field had been made possible following the acquisition of the land north of Loder Road, in 1909. Given the large area involved, it is unfortunate that some arrangement couldn't be found to share part of it with the Loder Road School. Alternatively, perhaps the Education Committee should have paid a bit more attention to the number of requests made by Miss Mills to produce a useable Playground. Also, the point that was made earlier about the education committee not being sufficiently responsive to children's physical welfare, can be repeated here.

1911

- *The moisture from the snow is leaking into all classrooms from numerous points on the roof. In room IV, the leakage is especially bad, a portion of the room being flooded.*
- *Babies' room still damp throughout as the snow continues to leak through the roof and ceiling.*
- *The temperature of the Babies Room during this afternoon has been 87°. During last week, 85° was reached on two afternoons.*
- *The Playground is impossible for work today owing to the high wind and dusty conditions prevailing.*
- *The other classrooms had temperatures of 85°, 85° and 82°.*

1913

- *The use of the Hall is very restricted again, by reason of the Open-Air arrangement proving uninhabitable for the Upper Classes – Mixed Department. This restriction is very detrimental to the wellbeing of the children (Physical work, etc.) and to the general work of the school, especially so, as there are no means of separation between the two Departments.*

- *The Hall is now continually used by a class, formerly accommodated in the Playground. The desks are now placed in the Hall, thus taking up much of the floor space.*
- *By means of screens, a portion of the Hall is reserved for free space for Physical exercise, games, etc. The restricted room is very disadvantageous to this section of the Infants' work however, and precludes much freedom and beneficial effects.*

1914

- *The weather is very wintery this morning, with a searching NE wind. The heating apparatus is working well, but the classrooms are at a very low temperature (42° at 10am). The Infants' Playground, being so exposed to the sharp wind, is not used unless really necessary – recreation being taken in the Boys' Playground, which is facing the south.*
- *A letter has been sent to the Secretary of the Education Committee concerning the cold and draughty nature of the school Hall. The temperature has been between 40° and 42° for several days and the draughts are excessive and injurious to all.*

At this point, the First World War was on the horizon. During this war, there were far fewer Log Book entries as it was a period of great disruption and disorganisation and this will be dealt later in sections covering the World Wars.

2. School Attendance

This section will not attempt to convey the records of attendance in the way information is collected today – schools now have target percentages to meet and will report the actual figures at the end of the school year. This is not to say that the Head teacher of the Infants Department didn't have similar statistics to calculate and report.

As we will see, the percentages she published have little in common with today's aggregations. For one thing, most comparable schools now have a pupil number on the Roll, which normally remains fairly constant throughout an academic year, save small changes usually related to parents moving in or out of the area.

At Loder Road, the Roll could change significantly on a weekly basis, leaving a monthly attendance figure somewhat academic. All will be revealed later with some worked examples.

Here is a selection of some of the ways in which school attendance was handled and reported. The first one appears to relate to cleanliness, something on which the school nurse had the power to act. There are other similar reports below where the reason for the exclusion is made clearer. As with many Log Book entries, the Head teacher is making a brief outline of an issue in the knowledge that the context of the report is generally understood at the time by those reading it. We may now have to make educated guesses as far as an interpretation is concerned.

The first entry is not, as it happens, a report from the Head teacher, but copy of an HMI Report. It is full of concerns about the effects of a migratory population, which will be seen as a recurring theme of a number of reports, both by the Head teacher and from observers.

Report of HMI (Mr Harrison) after visit of 22nd March 1910

"INFANTS"

The migratory character of the population round this school is probably the cause of many children coming to school after the usual age. It is certainly not satisfactory to find that a large number are at present, backward for their age. The First Class has been without its regular teacher since Christmas and is therefore seen at some disadvantage. The children in it read and write fairly well, but are not very alert when questioned in Number, and their attempts at Drawing show less than ordinary facility and power of observation though, in modelling with clay, they are rather more proficient. The Second Class contains children of varying attainments, and has a distinctly weak section; the reading books in this class might be better graded; those in use at present are too difficult for many of the children. The teaching in the Third Class is animated, the methods are generally suitable, and the progress made by the children is satisfactory. Some of the Physical Exercises** appear to be too formal for very young children.

Signed on behalf of the Local Education Committee – J. Herbert Toyne

The Physical Exercises** the HMI probably had in mind were the ones that were standard practice at the turn of the century and shown below in a photograph taken in Brighton.

A typical 'drill' lesson at the beginning of the century. Physical education now embraces a much wider scope of activities

Fig 15

Four children are excluded from school until Thursday by order of the School nurse. The cleansing process at the Sanatorium is to be applied in the case of each of the children. The School nurse attended yesterday afternoon.

The next entry, 105 years later, may bring the term déjà vu to mind

An application for two transfer forms has not been complied with owing to insufficient reason for such a request. The reasons given by the parent were:

1. *Exposed situation and district of the school*
2. *Imperfect nature of school building*
3. *Inability of small and temporary building to provide means of efficient training for scholars*
4. *Better class of children will be found*
5. *A friend, attending the proposed school, will provide company to and from school*

The elder girl in question has now attended this school for 12 months and much appreciation has been shown for work done on several occasions. The matter is now to be placed before the Education Committee.

In refusing the application, I have endeavoured to carry out the instructions of the Committee regarding the transfer of the children.

- *E Hackforth, Esq. M.A. visited the school this morning to discuss the case referred to above. An acknowledgement of the extreme disadvantages under which this school is working, owing to its nature, reasons for withdrawal from roll, and much outside prejudice, was freely made by the Clerk to the Education Committee. The expression of the legal phase of the case was, however, brought to the front, and the opinion was expressed that such would necessarily decide the question – in spite of the fact that full sympathy and desire to support the means of progress in connection with this school, were earnestly felt.*
- *The utmost will be done, however, by the Committee to decide the matter in support of the school.*

(A few days later)

- *The Clerk of the Education Committee has decided not to oppose the request for the Transfer Forms, the verdict being necessary from a legal point. The forms have, therefore, been transferred to the Head teacher of Ditchling Road Infants' School*

This next entry is another from the wise Mr Lethbridge, who touches on what was then, the thorny question of whether children should be moved up a class each year or kept back until they have reached the accepted standard.

Albert Paul made the point from his own experience at Finsbury Road School – *"It was not uncommon for boys start in Standard 1 and leave at 14 years of age still in Standard 1".*

- *E B Lethbridge Esq. visited the school this morning. An expression of the difficulty which is being felt at the present time in Infants' schools – arising from the late age of admission of many of the children – was made. The stage of development of each child must be considered greatly before the age in point of years, which fact renders the organisation increasingly difficult.*

41

1911

- *The increase in the Average Attendance is 1; this number would have been much improved if December's totals had not been so adversely affected by reason of the epidemic of measles.*

- *Eighteen children, in the charge of Miss Bartholomew, have been taken out of school for a short time, to be fitted with the 'New Year's' Gift of Boots. By arrangement with the Superintendent of Tramways, these children have been permitted to travel to and from the town – by reason of the great distance. J. Carden Esq. suggested that such an arrangement should be made, if possible, on the same terms as were allowed for the scholars to and from the Baths. This has accordingly been done. (Half fares were charged.)*

Hence, a very early example of discounted student bus fares

The next two entries from January 1912 and 1913 have been put together as they demonstrate the point made earlier that the attendance percentages need to be treated with caution. Two consecutive years where the end of year Rolls were 221 and 218 yet during the two years a total of 229 children were admitted. Clearly, a similar number must have left. Reasons – not given, but already Miss Mills is writing shorthand messages for the "many difficulties" that don't need to be listed yet again, merely "called to mind".

The 1910 HMI Report expressed the same concern about the migratory nature of the school population.

10.1.12

The attendance totals have been considerably reduced in the 1st Quarter; numerous isolated cases of Whopping Cough, Diphtheria and Scarlet Fever throughout the year, and a serious outbreak of Measles amongst the children in the last quarter of the year.

A fluctuating and ever varying Roll and the migratory nature of a large proportion of the population may be judged from the fact that from a roll of 221 at the end of the year, 115 scholars were admitted during the year. The many difficulties, attendant on the above, can readily be called to mind.

8.1.13

The number in average attendance during the year totals at 181, which is an increase of 4 on the number in the previous year.

The roll is still of a very fluctuating character. The number on roll was 218, out of this number, 114 children were admitted during the year.

1913

- *Six children are attending the school clinic this afternoon in the charge of the Monitoress, by request of the Nurse whilst on her visit of the inspection of the 15th January. These children have given much trouble lately, by reason of a lack of cleanliness (2 families – 3 children each).*

- *The School Doctor has ordered the exclusion of 3 of the above mentioned children (members of the same family for 2 days to give an opportunity of greater cleanliness.*

- *20 children, in the charge of Miss Guildford are out of school during part of the session as they have to be fitted and provided with boots by the New Year Boot Fund.*

1913

> Attendance Officers and myself; also with the District Attendance Officer regarding cases of children waiting for school accommodation in the district, yet not availing themselves of the accommodation offered at this school. Two scholars – one aged 6¼ yrs, and the other aged 7¼ yrs – have been admitted into this school in this week, have lived in this district for 5 months but have not been attending school, by reason of the above cause. These children are now compelled to work with very young children owing to their lack of development.
>
> The reason giving by parents for not using this school is wholly concerned with its temporary nature, the frequently unsatisfactory condition of the Playground and the inaccessibility of the school. 7.1.13
>
> Later: Regarding note of 7.1.13. An investigation has been made by the Superintendent of the Attendance Officers into this matter, with the result of supplying the necessary accommodation. Many parents have chosen Private School accommodation in the district, in preference to this school.

1914

- *The annual returns have now been compiled. The number in Average Attendance during 1913 totals 152, a decrease of 29 by reason of the epidemic sickness (Whooping Cough, Scarlet Fever and Measles), which was prevalent throughout the year. The average number on the Roll is 192, a decrease of 12, owing to the fact that no new admissions were allowed for the greater part of the last term of the year*

- *The Superintendant of the Attendance Officers visited during the morning, and some time was spent in the consideration of several cases of children who are not attending any school and have been on a referral list for some time. The parents of many of them have been visited and in the majority of cases, a Private School will be, or has been selected in preference to this building. In other cases, the distance precludes compulsory attendance at this school. Until there is more suitable accommodation for this district, and the cutting and flight of steps is made to lessen the distance, the parents will not make the use of this school as should be expected.*

Another reminder here by Miss Mills about the lack of a new school and the need to make the location of the Loder Road School more accessible for children travelling to school by building a flight of steps between Balfour Road and Osborne Road. With the War just starting, we now know that this reminder needed repeating in 1919.

3. Sickness and Injuries

Like the first two sets of entries, 'Buildings' and 'Attendance', this one was also dominant in the pages of the Log Book. The classification of topics rather breaks down here because many instances of sickness were recorded in references to attendance.

As we saw from the early months of Log Book records, there were instances of illness reported, including whooping cough, diphtheria, measles, chicken pox, scarlet fever and influenza. When outbreaks of any of these occurred the attendance went down very significantly. As we will see later, sometimes the drop in attendance was exacerbated by some parents who kept their children at home for fear of exposing them to illness.

What now follows are some of the references to the more serious outbreaks sickness and to some injuries that occurred after 1909, which show, not just the instances of epidemics of measles and scarlet fever, but ways in which attempts were made to control the spread of disease and some rather novel ways to treat injuries.

While we would not find it too surprising to come across old school buildings still use today that present environmental difficulties for the users, the Log Book entries that follow leave little doubt about the gap of 100 years that exists between us and the population of the Tin Hut.

1910

- *One of the Class I girls sustained a bad cut on the side of the forehead, by reason of a fall whilst playing in the Playground. The case was attended to at school; a teacher then took the scholar home and explained how the cut was caused. A simple game was being played by the children and a slip on the rough gravel was the cause of the nature of the injury.*

This accident was in July and first aid supplies arrived a few months later in November.

An Ambulance Chest has been received from the Education Office for the use of the Mixed/Infant's Departments; to be fixed in the Infants' school in the most convenient and accessible position for good use.

The contents:-

5 Rolls of Bandages

I Triangular Bandage

1 Packet Cotton Lint

The Packet Boracic Lint

1 Packet Cotton Wool

Surgical Safety Pins

I Box Boracic Ointment

1 Box Adhesive Plaster – 5½ yards

1 Pr Scissors

1 Measuring Glass

1 Bottle of Antiseptic Soln. Carron Oil

Sal Volatile

Liquid Ammonia

Friar's Balsam

Card of Instructions

1913

The following records appeared in the Log Book from the middle of July and the middle of October. They read like the 'Diary of an Epidemic', which includes references to children being kept at home for fear of catching the illness and the Attendance Committee declaring itself "helpless in the matter". Scarlet fever serum from horses was used at the beginning of the 1900s as a treatment and had contributed to a lowering of mortality rates. The discovery of penicillin was still 15 years away and the National Health Service even further, at 32 years

- *A letter has been received from J.H.Toyne Esq., stating that the MOH considered it advisable that, for the next three weeks, no fresh children should be admitted to the school by reason of the prevalence of scarlet fever.*
- *Notification of the necessity to close the two Departments of this school, owing to the prevalence of scarlet fever and whooping cough, has been received from the Education Committee on the advice of the MOH. This school will therefore close this afternoon until September 1st for the midsummer vacation.*
- *The above holiday has been extended by one week by reason of the continued sickness in the school district. The school building has been disinfected and during this week, the cupboards and various items of stock are being thoroughly cleaned.*
- *School has re-assembled this morning. Information from the Health Department has shown that 7 cases of scarlet fever have been notified to the Health Authority. One child suffering from a "skin" outbreak has also been excluded.*
- *Visit of the Health visitor from the Town Hall. A suggestion has been made that children should be kept rigidly to their own classes; no general inter-mingling, or as little as possible. Also no new admissions are to be allowed at present.*
- *Following on from the advice, the usual arrangements of the school have been modified slightly, to allow for as little risk of infection as possible.*
- *Slates and pencils have been washed in disinfectant. By reason of the sunny morning, children are spending much time in the open air.*
- *The majority of children attending this school and living in Loder Road are being kept at home by their parents, by reason of the prevailing sickness. The attendance Officer will bring this matter before the Attendance Committee today.*
- *Visit paid by Dr Forbes, MOH. The premises have been thoroughly inspected and the children well examined, all taking off their socks and shoes for the inspection of feet.*
- *The school has been thoroughly cleaned since Friday; all windows have been open throughout the time and the Committee have ruled at the same may remain open night and day for at least a month. As there are no fanlights in the building, all window ventilation has been rendered impossible at night, up to the present time. This defect, which has proved very injurious, will now be remedied by keeping some at least, of the windows open during the nights (By Permission).*
- *Many children are still absent for no other reason than the fear felt by parents re. scarlet fever in the district.*
- *The Attendance Committee have expressed themselves helpless in the matter.*
- *All pencils, etc are disinfected daily. Two fresh cases of scarlet fever have occurred.*
- *The MOH will not yet grant permission for the admission of the children who are waiting to be entered on the roll.*
- *There are now 15 cases of scarlet fever; also 8 'contact' cases.*

- *Two more suspicious cases in Class II. The room used by this class has been cleared ready for spraying, which was done immediately. All wall hangings have been destroyed and everything possible has been washed in disinfectant and the whole of the stock will be left in the open for 3 days. Work is proceeding in a disorganised fashion*
- *There are 120 present, 22 actual cases, 11 contacts and 10 suspicious cases. In addition, all children with sore noses and severe colds are excluded for a fortnight.*
- *The classroom mentioned above has been thoroughly sprayed and will not be fit for use until next week. I have not allowed the Student Teacher to be in school today, until the advice of the Education Committee has been obtained.*
- *Information has been received from Mr Toyne to the effect that no fresh children may be admitted yet owing to the odd cases of scarlet fever continuing to occur.*
- *The Student Teacher must also delay her return to her duties in this school by reason of the above.*
- *One suspicious case has been sent home this morning.*

After which, the incidences of scarlet fever seemed to be on the wane. Two more Log Book entries in this year just before Christmas, was something of a Postscript to the Epidemic – Gone but not yet forgotten

- *Several children are still kept at home by reason of the fear of the parents about scarlet fever. For a similar reason, no fresh children have been admitted.*
- *The numbers in attendance during this week have been much reduced (Colds and general debility amongst the children; also the fact that two other schools in the district have closed, owing to epidemic sickness that has caused a nervous feeling amongst parents and numerous children have been kept at home).*

There is little doubt that 1913 had been a very bad year as far children's health was concerned

1914

- *The annual returns have now been compiled. The number in Average Attendance during 1913 totals 152, a decrease of 29 by reason of the epidemic sickness (whooping cough, scarlet fever and measles), which was prevalent throughout the year. The average number on the Roll is 192, a decrease of 12, owing to the fact that no new admissions were allowed for the greater part of the last term of the year.*
- *A girl in Standard 1 has just reached her ninth birthday. She has not been able to attend school until a fortnight ago, for the past 5½ months, by reason of a serious heart trouble, resultant on rheumatic fever. She is now attending school, but her health is precarious, and great care needs to be exercised over her condition. By means of the above, this scholar is being retained in this Department until March.*

Two entries in 1914 that continued to report on the poor state of the health and now the children faced even more difficulties with the outbreak of War

4. Events

The events that were recorded earlier were the annually occurring ones like Empire Day

In this section are the few that were one-off celebrations, often including a day or half-day's holiday and some were linked to the First World War.

- On 20th October 1905, children assembled for a talk about Lord Nelson's centenary. And they *sang patriotic songs with "the Union Jack in their midst"*.

- In 1910, one normally reoccurring event was the Empire Day celebration, which *was curtailed (no outside demonstrations (e.g. dancing, gymnastics, etc) on account of the death of King Edward.*

- Another event on 18th July 1910, involving several other events that were very popular in early part of the 20th century, resulted in a day and a half holiday *Owing to the Police Sports taking place in Preston Park this afternoon, also to the fact of the annual excursion of the Preston Parish and also of the St. Matthias Sunday Schools' being arranged for 19th inst., this school must be closed from the end of this morning's session until Wednesday morning – by permission of the managers and of the Education Committee.*

Finally in 1910, Miss Mills recorded an event that was to prove a harbinger of things to come.

- Owing to the passage of the Lebaudy Morning Post Airship over the neighbourhood yesterday afternoon, all work was suspended for 10 minutes and the children allowed to assemble in the Playground to obtain a good view.

The French company, Lebaudy Frères specialised in building semi-rigid airships but the children watching it pass overhead wouldn't have had a notion that airships like this were destined to play a part in the Great War just 4 years hence. Before we get to that War, we will get up-to-date with the activities of the Managers over the period of 1908 – 1914.

Now to the Minutes of Managers' Meetings from 1908 to 1914

> In **1908** – There was an unusual start of a process to appoint a teacher before receiving a resignation from the one who was apparently leaving, which seemed to be a bit 'back to front' while the Managers' support for the Head to carry on after reaching retiring age proved to be unsuccessful.

In January, the Managers agreed that the Requisition Sub-Committee should be informed that they are strongly of the opinion that the new reading books, which have been requisitioned by the Headmistress of the Infants' Department, but refused, should be supplied as soon as possible.

The next entry recorded is an example of the handling of a resignation and the appointment of another member of staff. We know what decisions were taken but there are few details of the processes that led to the decisions. It would not be possible today, because we would not start to fill a post merely on the assumption of a resignation.

A question of resignation of Mrs Churchill was considered.

It was reported that Mrs Churchill would shortly resign her post in the Infants' Department, but that her resignation had not yet been received. It was agreed to hold a Special Meeting on Monday April 27th, at 3.30pm, to consider the question of filling the vacancy. It agreed to interview the following candidates:

Miss Anscombe, Miss English, Miss Guildford, Miss Harrison and Miss Powell.

The Minutes of the meeting that followed, at which the interviews were held, record a result and the action that was then taken. The recorded Minute was:

Appointment of a successor to Mrs Churchill was considered and the following candidates were interviewed by the Managers, viz:- Misses Anscombe, English, Guildford, Harrison and Powell.

On a vote being taken, there appeared;

For	Miss Anscombe	3 votes
	Miss Guildford	3 "
	Miss Harrison	1 "

It was agreed to send the names of Misses Anscombe and Guildford to the Elementary Schools Sub-Committee.

So, what happened next?

In May, the Managers met with an Agenda that included a reply from the Elementary Schools Sub-Committee. The outcome of the Managers' discussion was thus:

(a) Resignation of Mrs Churchill was submitted

Resolved:-

That the resignation of Mrs Churchill of the post of Assistant in the Infants' Department, to take effect on May 8th 1908, be accepted.

(b) The Clerk reported that the Elementary Schools Sub-Committee had recommended Miss Guildford as a successor to Mrs Churchill, which was noted.

Did the Elementary Schools Sub-Committee re-interview the candidates and did the Managers automatically accept their recommendation by 'noting it'?

In July, the Minutes recorded the annual round of salary increases and, as last year, the increases were for an additional £5.

Loder Road School

Miss L. Haffenden	*Infants' Dept.*	*£80 - £85 per annum*
Miss A. English	" "	*£60 - £65* "

In the new term after the summer holiday, the Committee awarded more salary increases

Miss M. Guildford	Infants' Dept.	£75 - £80 to take effect from 1/9/08

Also in July, the Managers reported *that they were seeking to appoint a successor to Mr Down, who was put on 'Supply', at his normal salary until a new Head was appointed.* You may remember that Mr Down had earlier, in September 1907, requested an extra year's employment beyond the normal retiring age. Clearly, he his request had been turned down. He would have been disappointed not to be allowed the extra year in post, despite the earlier support he had been given by the Managers to his request.

In November, the *"question of application to the Board of Education to retain Standard 1 in the Infants' Department was considered"* and it was resolved to make such an application for retention of the Standard

---

In **1909** – There was a very different mix of issues to be dealt with, which included a Flagstaff, a smoky chimney, lavatories that weren't called lavatories and a new job for the Caretaker that he probably didn't anticipate getting. In addition, we are acquainted with a phrase that will be repeated from time to time when the authorities do not what to spend money on improvements, however pressing the needs might be, because the school *"is only a temporary one"*. In 1909, it was still years away from being replaced. Finally, an issue that will be familiar in today's schools – the expulsion of pupils for varying forms of misbehaviour.

Now, the Managers' attention was moved away from the recent run of staffing matters and on to a more eclectic mix of issues to resolve.

Although the next entry relating Loder Road School is probably about the Mixed Department, the second sentence could well have related to both Departments.

The Clerk reported that he would endeavour to arrange for a number of girls to take up a course of Cookery Instruction from January next.
It was agreed to consider the question of a School Library for the above School at the next meeting.

The next letter from the Mixed Department carries a bit of unexpected information in as much as the Head teacher, who drew attention to a smoky chimney and the need to remove the desk rests, was Mr Weeks. The appointment of a new Head teacher must have been handled exclusively by the Education Committee or one of its sub-committees and Mr Weeks replaced Mr Down.

Letter from Mr Weeks dated December 10th 1908 with reference to a smoky chimney and the removal of desk rests, was submitted.

Resolved:-

That Mr Weeks' letter be forwarded to the Sites and Works Sub-Committee with the request that the matters referred to may receive attention

A second letter, this one from *"the Surveyors dated December 12th 1908, with reference to the provision of a room for the Head teachers, was submitted".*

It was agreed to defer the consideration of the question until the next meeting. In the meantime, certain of the managers undertook to make enquiries with regard to the matter.

At the next meeting, the last sentence was re-visited –

"Question of erection of room for Head Teachers was considered"

Resolved to recommend to the Sites and Works Sub-Committee that a room be provided for the use of the Head teachers of the School at an estimated cost of £55.

Application from Miss Mills dated January 14th 1909 for the school to be recognised as of the 2nd Grade.

Resolved:- That the Infants' School be now recognised as of the Second Grade, under the Scale of the Committee; the average attendance for last the School Year having been 178 and that the salary of the Head Mistress, Miss E Mills, be increased from £130 to £135 per annum, to date from January 1st 1909.

At the same meeting, *"a letter from Mr Weeks dated February 2nd 1909 reporting the gift of Story Books by Mr. Counc Campbell, and a Union Jack by Mr Counc Yates was submitted".*

[An unusual way of addressing the benefactors – but the Clerk then changed the style in the next sentence (below) to one that is now more familiar, but then promptly changed it back to the previous style]

Resolved:- That best thanks of the Managers be tendered to Councillors Campbell and Yates for their recent gifts to the School.

A further Resolution was made:

That a Flag Staff be erected at the School for the Union Jack, which has recently been given to the School by Mr Counc Yates.

More on the Smoky Chimney problem at the next meeting:

The Clerk reported that the Sites and Works Sub-Committee had decided not to take any action in the matter of the smoky chimney of the furnace and also the Managers should be informed that the Committee regrets that they are unable to entertain the application for the provision of a Head teachers Room at the present time.

[The last word though, goes to the Managers in their search for cleaner air]

Resolved to recommend to the Sites and Works Sub-Committee that an extra chimney or cowl be fixed to the chimney of the furnace at the above named School (Loder Road)

[Now, another request from Miss Mills, this time using terminology not normally associated with the particular room named.]

A letter from Miss Mills dated February 23rd 1909 with reference to the Teachers' Sanitary Office was submitted and referred to the Surveyors for enquiries and report.

By calling the toilet, an "Office", Miss Mills used the same word that Mr Slater, Head teacher at Balfour Primary School, used after he started there in 1947. I do not remember him saying it and I probably wouldn't have recognised the significance of its use in this Minute if I hadn't read the memoire of Paul Clark, one of my contemporaries, who wrote the following:

> *"Mr Slater used to refer to the toilets as "the offices", as in "Have you all been to the offices"? It's a wonder that ex-Balfour Road pupils of the era didn't engage in anti-social behaviour in their later business life".*

The Surveyors responded to Miss Mills' letter about the "Office":

A letter from the Surveyors dated 29th March re: Teachers Sanitary Office was submitted and considered.

The Minutes do not record their deliberations (and, it seems that they never do) but the Clerk was given a task to ask the Surveyors to furnish the Managers with the probable cost of carrying out the suggestion made in their letter.

Having advanced the question of sanitation, the Managers returned to flags and flag-poles.

An item involving Loder Road and Preston Road

The question of flagstaffs was considered
Resolved:-That the kind offer of Mr Counc Yates to present a flagstaff to Preston Road School be accepted and that the best thanks of the Managers be tendered to him for his gift.
It was further resolved to recommend to the Sites and Works Sub-Committee that the flagstaff at present at the Preston Road School should be erected at Loder Road School and that a new flagstaff that has kindly been presented by Mr Counc Yates be erected at the back of Preston Road School.

So, it looks as though Loder Road School got the second-hand flagstaff.

Back to the sanitation saga:
Question of Teachers' Sanitary Office was considered.

Resolved to recommend to the Sites and Works Sub-Committee that a lavatory for the use of female Staff be provided at the above named School and that estimates be obtained for carrying out the work.

The items on the next set of Minutes are mainly about the Mixed Department but have wider implications for the School.

A letter from Mr Weeks dated May 3rd 1909, with reference to the provision of a (Head) Master's chair and a Museum Cupboard, was submitted.

Resolved to recommend to the Requisition Branch Sub-Committee that in the opinion of the Managers, it is desirable that a Master's Desk should be supplied for the use of the Head teacher of the Mixed Department of Loder Road School and that the Requisition Branch Sub-Committee be requested to reconsider their decision in the matter.

Clearly, the Managers had already been told that no Desk would be forthcoming because they simply *resolved to recommend to the Requisition Branch Sub-Committee that a Museum Cupboard be supplied for the Mixed Department of the Loder Road School.*

The Clerk reported that the recommendation of the Managers with regard to the following matter had not been approved by the Sites and Works Sub-Committee: That is the erection of a Flagstaff.

So, there would be no new chair or flagstaff and in the next Minute, another negative on an even more pressing issue.

The Clerk reported that the Sites and Works Sub-Committee had agreed that the Managers should be informed that, in view of the fact that the School is <u>only a temporary one</u>, they are unable to recommend that a lavatory should be provided for the female staff.

Well, this was in 1909, and the women were in for a very long wait for their own toilet facility – 15 years to be exact. That they outnumbered their male colleagues on site, made no difference. But at least they were getting their annual £5 increases in salaries.

Miss L Haffenden	*Infants Dept*	*£85 - £90 per annum*
Miss M Guildford		*£80 - £85 per annum*
Miss A English		*£65 - £70 per annum (Aug 1st)*

Another Minute about the Mixed Department, which would have affected the Infants as well, was seen in a letter from Mr Weeks dated November 25th 1909 re: the improvement in gas lighting, which was submitted and duly considered.

It was resolved:- That Mr Weeks' letter be forwarded to the Sites and Works Sub-Committee with a request that incandescent gas lighting may be installed in the School.

The Clerk reported that Sites and Works Sub-Committee had agreed, (a) that the Managers should be informed that, in view of the fact that the School is <u>only a temporary one</u> the Committee are unable to recommend that playsheds should be erected and (b) that 15 dual desks should be supplied for the Mixed Department.

In reply, it was resolved to recommend to the Sites and Works Sub-Committee that Managers are informed that there is a good amount of used material on the School premises from which playsheds might be constructed. The managers beg respectively to renew their request that these may be erected.

Following this request, Major Bloomfield reported that he had arranged for scholars to use the Hall during lunch-time <u>and that the Caretaker would look after them.</u> He seemed to have assumed that the Sites and Works committee would not reverse their decision on the playsheds. This would not be the last time that the Caretaker's work would be directed by managers.

The School is only temporary!

The last few entries in the Minutes have shown a tendency of the Managers to question the Sub-Committee's negative responses and seek further consideration. It should be noticed that, in the answer that was received in respect of the playshed, the reason given was the temporary nature of the building. This is exactly the same answer that was given when the question of providing a female lavatory was raised earlier in the year. And there are still 14 ½ years to go before 'temporary' becomes 'permanent'. And this excuse was to be repeated regularly until the new school was built.

A pupil is expelled

In November 1909, *the case of the lad* (named in the Minute Book) *was considered: Resolved that the Elementary Schools Sub-Committee be asked to issue instructions to all Head teachers not to exclude children from attendance for disciplinary reasons but, if necessary, to report the case to the Clerk to the Committee who will take such steps as he deems to be expedient.*

The action that was taken over the suspension of this pupil perhaps heralded the beginnings of formal rules and procedures being developed to deal with situations of misbehaviour, which up-dated versions are still required today.

> In **1910** – We can see that the sanitation question hasn't gone away nor the state of the building, in this case, the playground but, on a more positive note, the Managers, rather unusually, turned their attention to curriculum development. Specifically, cookery lessons for girls and gardening ones for the boys. Cookery wasn't mentioned again as far I could see but there was no doubt about role that gardening played in the school curriculum and did so right through to the Senior School in the new Balfour building. This year drew to an end with a reminder about the need for steps to be built connecting Osborne Road with Loder/Balfour Roads, and about the thorny question of why children couldn't use the playfields over the road.

A new year and an old problem re-surfaces when the "question of the sanitary 'accommodation' for Teachers was brought forward by Mrs Lawson."

It was resolved:-That the Managers beg again to urge upon the Sites and Works Sub-Committee the necessity for a lavatory being provided at the Loder Road School, as they are fully persuaded that the health of the female teachers has suffered in the past owing to the unsatisfactory arrangements presently existing.

And the never-ending problem – the state of the Playground – exercised the Head teacher of the Mixed Department yet again:
Thus, two letters from Mr Weeks with reference *to the dirty state of the playground were submitted.*

It was reported that the Surveyors had arranged for playground to be repaired and the work was being preceded with this very day. [Also, this meeting heard that an earlier decision not to erect playsheds would not be reversed much as Major Bloomfield had expected]

Miss Mills receives a rather Delphic response to a letter she sent regarding Miss English:

The letter from Miss Mills dated February 7th 1910 was submitted asking that Miss English might be promoted to the rank of Certified Assistant.
Resolved:- It was agreed not to take any action in the matter in view of the fact that the general question of the position of Miss English and certain other teachers was receiving the attention of the Staff Branch Sub-Committee at the present time.

So, that was information that didn't provide Miss Mills with much information but there was nothing Delphic about the next decision, which was from the Sites and Works Sub-Committee:

It was reported that the Sites and Works Sub-Committee had agreed that the Managers should be informed that the Committee regret that they are unable to reverse their decision about the provision of lavatory accommodation for the female teachers. Again!

Two letters that follow were dealt with briefly with answers of 'no' and 'wait' respectively

A letter from Mr Weeks applying for some trees to be planted round the playground was submitted and considered.
It was agreed to take no action in the matter.

A letter from Miss Mills dated June 8th 1910 applying for the provision of a canvas awning for a portion of the playground was submitted.
It was agreed that this matter should be considered again at the September meeting and that, in the meantime the Surveyors to the Committee should be requested to prepare an estimate of cost for providing the covering.

At the next meeting in July, a new issue emerged.

The Clerk reported that the School Attendance and Accommodation Sub-Committee had agreed that Managers should be informed that before taking any action in the matter of enlarging the School the Committee were of opinion that the question should remain in abeyance until the effect of the new School at Coombe Road is ascertained.

It seems likely that the Managers might have been using the tactic of pressing the Attendance Sub-Committee to support the case for greater capacity being provided in north Brighton. Or, put it another way, when is the new Balfour school going to be built here?

And now another new issue:
This one drew the Managers into the realm of curriculum development, which was a territory that was not normally on their agenda.

The question about introducing the subject of gardening was raised at the next meeting, something that Miss Mills also touched on in her Log Book entries.
It was in a letter from Mr Weeks on the subject of instruction in gardening that was submitted.
(Report from Mr Weeks attached below)

It was agreed to hold a Special Meeting on Monday next at 4 o'clock to consider the matter.

EDUCATION COMMITTEE FOR THE COUNTY BOROUGH OF BRIGHTON

LODER ROAD SCHOOL

TO THE CHAIRMAN AND MANAGERS OF THE LODER ROAD SCHOOL

Dear Sir, Ladies and Gentlemen,

At your request, I have considered your suggestion for combining the ordinary school education with manual instruction in the shape of gardening, and I am heartily in sympathy with the idea.

I have inspected a scheme which has been in existence at a rural school for some years, and which has proved very successful. Here the boys spend two hours per week as in the ordinary course of wood-work, and grants are earned according to the hours worked each term of twenty or forty hours. However, if I read your instructions correctly, you would prefer a scheme for children who are not up to average ability and, as a consequence, would spend more time in the garden, and less upon actual theoretical work in the classroom.

Under ordinary circumstances, I believe that the department regulations define the maximum number in a class to be fourteen; but when working on similar lines in the Sussex Street Centre one teacher would be responsible for a larger number.

I found that twelve plots were being cultivated by twelve lads, and every one similarly laid out. This ensures the best method of instruction, and excites competition. Narrow paths separate the plots. These latter are roughly about in size 8½ yards by 5 yards and, at present are planted as follows:

1 row each of shallots, broad beans, parsnips, carrot, beans

2 rows of potatoes – early and late – 1 row of runner beans

A good space is left between each row to enable other crops to be added in season, as first crops ripen, and as the ground is freed.

Intensive cultivation is thus taught.

A bed in common for cabbage, cauliflower, kale, etc. is provided, and plants extracted when necessary in season.

Lettuce, marrow, cucumbers and others are also grown.

The course includes only vegetables, but with the amount of ground at our disposal, flowers – which could be used for drawing and Nature Study in the Schools – and the common fruit bushes such as currants, gooseberries, raspberries, should be added. The proceeds could be sold to the children, as in the case of garments made, and seeds and plants bought with the money. Thus, only the initial cost of the tools, need to be considered. Each boy would measure his ground, dig and manure it, set it out by line and tape, plant and weed it, etc.

He could make and maintain the paths in order; keep his note book sketching and dating plants and crops; and learn something of the rotation of crops.

The instruction in School would, to a certain extent, correspond to the outdoor work. One reading book should certainly deal incidentally with gardening. Cassells are issuing a book in story form, which I imagine would be suitable (price 9d) Simple calculations might also deal with their work; estimate profit and loss; cost of seeds; mensuration; making out invoices; writing out simple business letters. The curriculum could be speedily adapted to the ability of the children.

COST OF SCHEME

The children would require a complete set of tools. These are as follows:- Prices quoted being those I ascertained from Messrs Adams, Ironmongers, 11/12, Trafalgar Street. I find that these are generally below the prices given to me by my friend.

Spade	2/6d
Fork	2/6d
Dutch Hoe	1/s
Rake	10d
Trug	1/s
Trowel	7½d
Small fork	9d

In addition for a class of twenty or thirty, four shovels at 8/s each; 6 watering cans at 2/s each; 1 zinc wheelbarrow 16/s; lines for setting out plants, wooden labels; these could be made by boys at the Sussex Street Centre; and a tape measure.

Thus the gardening outfit would be more than covered by the allowance of 7/s per boy.

There is already a tool house on the ground, so no expenditure would be necessary in this direction.

An ordinary Class Teacher, with a liking for this class of work should be in charge.

When we consider the number of unemployed, who are also unemployable, because of the lack of any technical training, I am sure that a small outlay should not be allowed to stand in the way of this development.

One great colonial authority was recently deploring the fact that our great inheritance was passing into the hands of foreigners, because the type of emigrants we are sending knew little or nothing of agriculture. In such experiments as these we are making, we are doing a little to help solve this difficult problem.

I may say, in conclusion, that I have studied agriculture and botany, and hold certificates for the same.

> Yours faithfully
> (Signed) V. WEEKS.
>   Head Master.

I might also suggest that the cookery school could be supplied with vegetables

The Managers did not record their deliberations at the Special Meeting but various references that were made in future Minutes about gardening lessons and the teachers who were in charge of them, indicated that Mr Weeks' proposals had met with their approval.

We will never know just how successful the gardening initiative was in practice. However, we do know that Owen Williams, whose account of his time at Loder Road is the only significant pupil voice we have, wrote a short paragraph about his final days at school. His story touches on gardening. Having been frequently called a 'blockhead' while at school, which may have put him in the group of boys that Mr Weeks considered to be below average as scholars, he recalled his thoughts on leaving school:

> *"However, in the summer of 1918, all this was behind me, my schooling such as it was had come to an end, my years of employment about to commence. A garden boy I was to be, working in the kitchen gardens of the Earl of Chichester on his country estate at Stanmer Park, 4 miles north of Loder Road School".*

Owen Williams must have been one of Mr Weeks' successes and he did go on to have a long career at Stanmer Park and then with the Sussex University when it acquired some of the grounds of the estate. He retired with an honorary MA degree from the University in gratitude for the service he had given. That was some achievement for a 'Blockhead'.

Now, we return to the earlier question about providing a canvas awning in the playground which re-appeared on the agenda at the next meeting.
A letter from Miss Mills on the subject dated June 8th 1910 was submitted.
It was resolved to recommend to the Sites and Works Sub-Committee that a wooden shed with a corrugated roof be erected in the playground for use in connection with open-air work, and in order to provide shelter for the scholars when they assemble in bad weather.

The October meeting was very interesting indeed.
The seemingly never-ending question of toilets re-emerged yet again alongside an even earlier question about developing an access to the School from Osborne Road by constructing a flight of steps. Miss Mills could say that she had first raised the issue in 1905.

(a)   A letter from Miss Mills dated September 21st 1910 re: provision of lavatory accommodation for female Staff was considered.

It was agreed that the Surveyor should be asked to furnish an estimate of cost.

(b)   A letter from Mr Weeks dated October 7th 1910 re: the provision of a path from Osborne Road to Balfour Road was submitted and considered.

Resolved:-
That the Clerk be requested to write to the Town Clerk pointing out that, in the opinion of the Managers of Loder Road School, it is highly desirable that a path should be formed between Osborne Road and Balfour Road before the land is completely built over, and requesting him to bring the matter before the proper Committee of the Town Council. Also, attention should be drawn to the fact that two paths already exist between the two roads.

In November, Miss Mills tried to improve on the shed that had been built in the playground.
It was agreed that the Surveyors should be asked to arrange for a seat to be erected in the shed that has recently been erected in the playground

Now, would Miss Mills' quest to win the battle of the lavatory accommodation be successful?

A letter from the Surveyors dated November 1st 1910 re cost of lavatory accommodation for female Staff was submitted and considered.

It was to be "considered" but nothing resolved apparently. So Miss Mills would have to wait a bit longer for the toilet break.

However, the following Applications from Secondary School Governors were considered.
(a) For the use of a room as a dressing room for purposes of football, etc
(b) For the use of the storeroom to store apparatus for games, and
(c) For the services of the Caretaker to act as groundsman in his spare time
It was agreed that the requests should be granted

Remember in 1909, the Caretaker was directed by the Managers to look after children in the Hall during lunch-time. Now, as suggested in line (c) above, the Caretaker could spend his 'spare' time as groundsman on the playing fields over the road, which the children at his school were not allowed to use. He might have been a bit 'miffed' at this instruction especially if spare time was synonymous with 'own' time

Also, Miss Mills had a reason for being a bit annoyed at this decision having been sent the following letter from the Education Committee on the same issue related to the use of the playing fields earlier in the year. She wrote the following note in the Log Book:

> *Information has been received from the Clerk to the Education Committee – that the children of this school may not use the Loder Place Field, as the ground has been allotted to the use of the Municipal Secondary School.*

In Miss Mills' opinion, *the use of this field (owned by the Education Committee) proved invaluable to the children of this school – by reason of the rough surface of the Playground – the effects will be keenly felt.*

The decision to allocate the playing field had been made possible following the acquisition of the land north of Loder Road in 1909. Given the very large area involved, it is unfortunate that some arrangement couldn't have been found to share part of it with the Loder Road School. Alternatively, perhaps the Education Committee could have paid a bit more attention to the large number of requests made by Miss Mills to produce a useable Playground. Also, a point that was made earlier about the education committee not being sufficiently responsive to children's physical welfare, could properly be repeated here.

Now the Managers were providing a changing-room and storage space in a school that hasn't been provided with sufficient classroom space for the children that have been enrolled and that hasn't been provided with a playground suitable for being played in. And to cap it all, the Managers offered the caretaker's 'spare time' in order to maintain the playing fields that were clearly not part of his responsibility. Salt and Wounds come to mind.

Believe it or not, it wasn't until 1931, 21 years later, when a letter was received from the Government's Board of Education, which gave formal permission for the elementary aged children to use the playing fields on their doorstep (although there had been some sort of tacit local agreement to allow access to the playfields by 1924).

Again, no answer at the next meeting to the lavatory question, but a playground problem re-appeared instead.

It was reported that the Sites and Works Sub-Committee had agreed that the Managers should be informed that the Committee regret that they are unable to accede to the request that the playgrounds should be coated with tar.

After which, at the next meeting, the MoH becomes involved with the saga of the sanitary accommodation.

Thus, a letter from the Medical Officer of Health (Dr. Forbes) dated November 21st 1910 with reference to the provision of lavatory accommodation for female teachers, was submitted. It was agreed to take no action in the matter.

So, no further comment is needed here then.

> **In 1911** - The Caretaker was in line for yet another 'odd' job and there was evidence of a more streamlined approach to appointing new staff. The subject of Gardening and the use of the playing fields across the road returned to the agenda.

In the days before the NHS a question of the payment of an account for medical attendance on a scholar had to be considered.

It was resolved:- That the sum of 3/6d be paid without prejudice to Dr Simpson for payment on account for medical assistance to Harry Harmer, a scholar attending the Mixed Department, who accidently cut his head in the School lavatory.

Footnote

Dr. G. H. Simpson, who came from Scotland, was the local family GP who bought a flagging practice housed in a surgery at 138 Beaconsfield Villas (at the corner with Preston Drove and opposite to the end of Balfour Road). The property is now houses a children's nursery.

In his time, he built up a successful group practice there before moving on to develop another practice in Withdean.

People in Brighton as a whole, may well have been more familiar with Dr. Simpson's son, Keith born in 1907, who went to a preparatory school near Preston Park and later, to Brighton and Hove Grammar School. After qualifying as a pathologist at Guy's Hospital, he became a teacher in the pathology department at the age of 25 yrs. By the 1950s, now as Professor Keith Simpson, he held a number of posts as a forensic pathologist including the one at the Home Office that was to bring him into contact, as an expert witness, with most of the infamous murder trials over four decades. To name few heading-grabbing cases; John Christie of Rillington Place, Haigh, Hanratty, the Kray brothers and Lord Lucan (which, he said in his autobiography, was unfinished business).

Letters from Mr Weeks and Miss Mills followed, drawing attention to the leakage of water through the roof. These were duly considered. It is not revealed how much consideration was given by resolving to buy a new ladder *for the Caretaker in order that he may be able to reach the roof of the building.*

Reaching the roof and then repairing the damage was something that the Managers may have assumed would happen. The same problem reappeared later, so their simple solution was abandoned and the Sites and Works Sub-Committee were called in.

The next item provides clear evidence that gardening report, which Mr Weeks tabled for the Managers' consideration last year, did prove to be successful.

A letter from Mr Pine dated July 31st 1911, was submitted. It stated that he had been successful in passing the School Teachers' Examination in Cottage and Allotment Gardening of the Royal Horticulture Society, and asking that his Examination expenses (amounting to the sum of £2.14.0) might be refunded to him by the Committee.
Resolved:-
That the Education Committee be requested to refund the Mr Pine an Assistant in the Mixed Department who has recently passed the School Examination of the Royal Horticulture Society, the sum of 23/- being the amount expended by him in payment of the cost of text books and tuition and examination fees; the text books in consideration of the payment of this sum to become the property of the school.

(This left him £1.11.0d short of his claim; no explanations seemed to have been given. From other records, it is known that Mr Pine joined the Mixed Department from Warren Farm Industrial School, which was linked to the Brighton Workhouse. The teaching experience he gained there may well have paid dividends in helping to develop Mr Weeks' initiative of a gardening course as part of the school curriculum)

We are still on the gardening theme for the next item.
A letter from Mr. Weeks dated July 19th 1911, applying for water to be laid onto the Garden was submitted, but the decision was deferred to the next meeting. The Clerk was requested to ascertain the cost of laying on the water and the rental of the meter.

Six years after taking on responsibility for Loder Road School, the next item demonstrates a more streamlined approach to dealing with the resignation and appointment of teachers, which had been a fairly long-winded process in the past. The following Minute appears to record the outcomes of the process that has taken place, and not the process itself.

(a) *It was reported that Miss English U.A in Infants' Department has been appointed at Finsbury Road Infants' School.*
   Resolved:-
   That the resignation of Miss English to take effect from September 30th 1911 be accepted.

(b) *Appointment of a successor was considered and the Misses Bayliss, Hollands, Hurst and Maides were interviewed by the Managers. A letter from Miss Mills dated 6th October 1911 with regard to the matter was submitted.*

It was resolved that Miss. A. Hurst of the Municipal Day Training College be appointed a JTCA in the Infants' Department in place of Miss English at a rate of salary of £65 per annum to take effect from 16th October 1911, subject to one month's notice to expire at the end of any calendar month.

The appointment of Miss G Hollands "on supply" in Infants' Department was considered. And it was resolved that Miss Hollands be appointed "on supply" in place of Miss English at a salary at the rate of 25/- per week to date from 2nd to 13th October 1911.

The earlier letter from Mr Weeks about water for the garden was considered again, alongside a letter from the Waterworks Engineer. Again, the matter was deferred but the Clerk was requested enquire about the cost of water per thousand gallons and also the cost of extending the present service pipe as had been suggested.

Having been successful in his efforts to introduce gardening, Mr Weeks now sought to succeed where Miss Mills failed last year in gaining use of the playing fields over the road from the garden.

A letter from Mr Weeks about the use of ground for football practice was considered.
It was agreed that Mr Weeks should be informed that the Managers feel that they cannot with any hope of success make any recommendation with regard to the use of York Place School Field.
The Managers then tried to find a sweetener to balance this negative decision, perhaps understanding that it would be seen that, with a huge expanse of playfields 100 metres away, commonsense would have determined that some form of sharing should be possible. Thus:
The Clerk was requested to ask the Surveyor whether he could offer any suggestion for the improvement of the surface of the playground.

So, it seems that Mr Weeks was doomed to failure as well. Just what the Surveyor was expected to suggest in order to improve a playground that had been a problem from the day the school opened, would have been anybody's guess. The Managers were simply passing the buck!

Question of laying on water to the garden was considered again and it was resolved that the water would be laid on to a stand-pipe in the garden from the service in the School Buildings at an estimated cost of £4.10s

Also, surprise, surprise, a letter from the Surveyors dated 23rd October 1911 as to improvement of surface of playground, saying it had been agreed not to take any action in this matter at present. The buck had been well and truly passed.

Now the Elementary Schools Committee got into the discussion about the supply of water to the garden by *enquiring what action the Managers proposed to take to restrict the use of water on garden.*
Their solution was that a *stop-cock should be provided inside the school premises and placed under lock and key, and that the Caretaker* would be responsible for it.

In 1912 – There was an immediate return to the state of the playground, gardening, and yet again, the playing fields over the road.

Now, not for the first time, and definitely not the last time, the Managers turn their attention to the fact that Loder Road School is a temporary Balfour Road School.

Letters from Miss Mills and Mr Weeks dated February 1st 1912 re: transfer of scholars were submitted and considered.

Resolved that the letters should be forwarded to the School Accommodation and Attendance Sub-Committee for their information and to inform them that, in the opinion of the Managers, the time has arrived when the question of the provision of permanent school accommodation in the District should be considered. (My underlining)

Since the School's opening, Head teachers had been writing to the Managers with concerns about the state of the playground but, in the last year, Mr Weeks has managed to over-shadow the focus on the playground with frequent missives related to the garden.
Thus:
A letter from Mr Weeks dated February 5th 1912 with reference to the balance sheet of gardening a/c was considered and it was resolved that the balance sheet of the gardening a/c be approved, and that the Headmaster be authorised to spend the balance viz. 9/8d on the purchase of fruit and rose trees.

(In 2005, 9/8d would have been equivalent to about £21.50, so not many trees and roses would be bought today for that amount.)

A letter from Miss Haffenden TCA in Infants' Department dated 18th February 1912, *with reference to her position was submitted and considered'*
Resolved:-
That the letter from Miss Haffenden, applying for recognition as First Assistant in the Infants' Department should be forwarded to the Elementary Schools Sub-Committee, and that they be informed that Managers desire to heartily support her request.

Miss Haffenden was seeking to be the Deputy Head in today's terminology and according to the School Log Book, she certainly had already deputised for Miss Mills on a number of occasions.

The Managers agreed to increase the salary of the Infants' Dept's Monitoress from 1/- to 2/- from 1st May 1912.

And more gardening news as the *question of payment to Caretaker for services in the garden was considered and the action of the Secretary in paying the sum of 6/s to the Caretaker for attending to the garden during the August holidays, was approved.*

And yet more gardening news with an *application from the Evening Schools Sub-Committee for the use of tools in connection with the instruction on gardening was received and it was agreed to allow the Sub-Committee to make use of the tools on the understanding that any damage done will be made good at their expense.*

It was reported that the use of the Hall been granted to Mr Weeks for the purpose of an entertainment on Friday 11th October 1912 on behalf of the Benevolent and Orphan Fund and that the sum of 3/- had been charged on the account.

Mr Weeks was soon back with a short shopping list *applying (1) for the approaches to the school to be tarred and (2) for a further grant in respect of books for the library.*
It was agreed thus:
That the Sites and Works Sub-Committee would be requested to arrange for the tarring of the

playgrounds in the early spring and that in the meantime footpaths should be formed either of cinders or another material.
That the Requisition Branch Sub-Committee be asked to consider favourably the request of the headmaster for a grant to enable the school library to be extended.

Another year, another attempt was made to allow the Loder Road School children to gain access to the playing fields over the road. The Managers framed their response this time as follows:

The question of the application for permission to use the Secondary Boys School Playing Field was considered and *it was resolved that the letter from the headmaster be forwarded to the Governors of the Municipal Secondary Schools with a request that the permission asked for, be granted.*

Well, at least this time, the Managers indicated their support for the request. That is some sort of progress.

Perhaps Miss Mills could make similar progress on an even harder-to-solve problem.

A letter from Miss Mills dated November 26th 1912 with regard to conditions of work in this school was received and it was resolved:
That the letter from Miss Mills should be forwarded to the Elementary Schools Sub-Committee and that they be informed that the managers strongly endorse the remarks contained therein.

Again, the Managers have been a bit more supportive but she wasn't pressing the case of the new school. The request related to improving the current conditions of work, which could involve buying a new boiler – much cheaper than the promised new school building.

A letter from Mr Weeks applying for the use of the hall on Monday, December 16th 1912 for the purpose of a concert in aid of the recreation fund was received. It was agreed that the gratuitous use of the hall should be granted.

In 1913 –There was a question of how long it would take to refund the bus fare paid by a young monitoress and how much to pay the Caretaker to look after the garden. There was a more serious issue of criticisms made by the HMI in their school inspection report. In the end, the problems of the earlier leaking roof, HMI conclusions and the time it took to pay the monitoress, were all resolved – more-or-less reasonably.

More extracurricular activities from Mr Weeks
A letter from Mr Weeks dated January 8th 1913, asking that the sum of 1/3d paid for the use of lantern slides in connection with a lecture on Canada given to the elder scholars during school hours, may be refunded. It was duly agreed that it would be paid by the Education Committee.

A letter from Miss Mills dated January 10th 1913 asking that the lower step at the entrance to the Infants' Department might be raised, was received and unsurprisingly, was forwarded to the Elementary Schools Sub-Committee.

There was no explanation was given for the next item, which was a decision by the Education Committee which it appears, did not apply at this time to the caretakers at the Loder and Ditchling Road Schools

It was reported that the Committee had decided that Caretakers should be required to submit to the Managers for their approval particulars as to the persons they employ or propose in future to employ to assist them in their work.

Letters were received from the Caretakers of Ditchling Road and Loder Road Schools stating that they did not employ anyone to assist them in their work, which was noted.

Question: How long does it take to agree to pay the tram fares of a young monitoress, which she paid from her weekly wage of two shillings per week?

A letter from Miss Mills dated January 9th 1913, applying for payment of trams fares of monitoress was received, but was deferred until the next meeting.

A further letter from Miss Mills dated March 7th, applying for payment of tram fares of monitoress was received.

It was agreed to defer decision on the matter until the Secretary had reported with regard to the question.

The Answer is that it took two letters and two months and she is still waiting. However, additional payments to the Caretaker are being arranged here ahead of the work being completed.

Question of payment to the Caretaker for services in garden, was considered.
It was resolved that the sum of 9/- should be paid to the Caretaker for attending to the garden during the six weeks ending September 5th 1913.

Major Bloomfield arranged to see the Borough Surveyor to inquire whether, in view of the fact that the road outside the school is about to be repaired, a coating of tar might be placed on the surface with the object of reducing the external noises which seriously disturb the school work, and to which special reference is made in the recent report of HMI.
It was agreed that a letter should be sent to the Works Committee of the Town Council with regard to the matter.

A letter from Mr Weeks (2.10.1913) with reference to the school sports and the recreation fund was considered.
It was agreed that the portion of the Mr Weeks' letter referring to the open-air swimming pool at the new school should be referred to the Sites and Works Sub-Committee for their favourable consideration.

[**Note:** Whether it proved to be favourable or not, the eventual outcome in 1924 was that there was to be no open-air pool at the new Balfour building but there was a pond provided which served the school well as a focus for Nature Studies. The pond may have disappeared in later years when the school building was extended to provide additional classrooms.]

Letters from Miss Mills in September and October about the epidemic of scarlet fever, and to the leakage of the roof of the school were received.

It was agreed that the letter from Miss Mills with regard to leakages in the roof should be referred to the Sites and Works Sub-Committee with a request that the necessary repairs may

be carried out. The Secretary was instructed to request the Surveyor to take some immediate action in the matter.

The portion of the letter from Miss Mills with reference to certain school stock which had been burnt under the order of the M.O.H. was referred to the Requisition Branch Sub-Committee.

No mention of what the Sites and Works Sub-Committee did about the leakages was recorded in the Minutes. As we saw earlier, one of the previous solutions was to provide the Caretaker a ladder but perhaps this time the appropriate repair work was undertaken by a builder.

What followed this item was a much more serious issue.

Report of H.M.I. was considered, and Mr Weeks had an interview with the Managers thereon. Mr Weeks was, by permission of the Managers, permitted to withdraw the letter sent in by him at the previous meeting.
Resolved:- That the following observations be forwarded to the Elementary Schools Sub-Committee.

Mixed Department:- The Managers have gone very fully into every detail of the Inspectors' Report, and after their interview with Mr Weeks, they do not consider it necessary to make any alteration in the staff, the curriculum, or the timetable. They feel sure the points referred to by the Inspectors will receive the careful attention of the teachers.

If the letter that Mr Weeks was allowed to withdraw was one of resignation, then the Managers unqualified support for Mr Weeks and the work of the school was a robust rejection of much of the HMI Report. Through the pages of the Minutes we have seen so far, Mr Weeks comes across as a very energetic, innovative teacher who appears to be doing an excellent job in difficult circumstances.

The Managers had no special comments to make on the Report which they considered is of a very satisfactory character.

BRIGHTON, LODER ROAD TEMPORARY COUNCIL SCHOOL (No. 14)

Copy of Report by H.M.I. Mr. E. M. Field, after visits of the 26th and 30th June, and 4th and 7th July, 1913

<u>MIXED</u>

The disadvantages under which the school is conducted in these temporary premises have already been reported to the Board and need not be further specified, except as far as regards their bearing on classification and physical training. Four classrooms are clearly insufficient for 240 children, properly distributed in six different grades; but the 277 children on the books are, in fact, organised in five classes, one of which occupies, in the winter, a section of the hall, divided by a mere curtain from infants' quarters, and, in the summer and autumn, a shed in the playground. Even this organisation would not be possible if the four lower classes were not disproportionally swelled by the inclusion of numerous older children; the sixth and seventh standards are together fewer in number than any of the lower classes singly, and they are taught together in all subjects

---

except Arithmetic. It is to be noted also that 15 children who might have been promoted to the Mixed School have been detained in the Infants' Department since April 1st for reasons of accommodation, though some of them are less advanced than others

There is no doubt about the deficiencies noticed in physical training are due to some extent, though not altogether, to the condition of the playground, the surface of which is rough and dusty in summer and, and very wet in damp weather.

The following criticisms relate to points which deserve the consideration of the Head teacher, and are independent of special circumstances.

(I) The general aim of the teaching of Arithmetic seems to be good, but the children are, nevertheless, not quick and resourceful enough in their work.

(II) The progress of composition would be assisted if more original work was done in most of the classes; and there is much weak spelling.

(III) History and Geography, in which both interest and some knowledge are shown, only need rather broader treatment.

(IV) The training of speech needs attention. Indistinct enunciation is conspicuous in several classes, and, for the most part, recitation is ineffective. Reading is fairly good in some classes, but less satisfactory in others.

(V) It should be possible to bring the work of the classes to a rather more even level of merit. The first class and Standard II, show plenty of active interest in their work. Standards III and V are much less alert, and the teacher of Standard IV, seems to do too much for his scholars.

(VI) The needlework scheme requires reconsideration. Three successive classes, Standards IV, V and VI, are cutting out and making the same garments. In Standards V and VI, the girls cut out on a line marked by the teacher, even in Standard VII, the teacher lays the pattern on the material. Yet, in Standard IV, the girls cut out the pattern and fix it for themselves; Standard III cut out in paper, but not in material; Standard II do not cut out at all. There are no trestle tables for cutting out.

The children are thoroughly well behaved, and the teachers have worked dutifully and to much good purpose under many disadvantages. The temporary shed used by the playground class is by no means conveniently planned.

INFANTS

The infants are, in all classes, well behaved and happy; they are encouraged by their teachers to take an active part in their lessons, and to depend upon their own efforts. Hence they are spontaneous and natural in their ways, play their games well, and respond readily. Their drawing is good, their clay-work, for some reason, less successful. A few points of detail have been discussed with teachers, who deserve all credit for pleasant and effective management of the school

Note by the Board of Education:- The Board should be informed about what steps will be taken to improve the condition of the playground at this school

A letter from Miss Mills (11/11/1913) applying for full salary to be paid to Miss Taylor during her absence on account of scarlet fever was received.
Consideration of the matter was deferred until Miss Taylor has returned to duty. It was agreed that the M.O.H. should be asked for his opinion as to whether Miss Taylor's illness was contracted in school.

At last, we have now we have found the answer to the question, 'How long does it take to get a tram fare paid to a monitoress?"
The answer – nearly 11 months. It should be noted that Miss Mills had to write a third letter (below) in November to repeat her first two requests made in January and in March.

A letter (18/11/1913) from Miss Mills with regard to the payment of tram fares of monitoress was received.
Resolved:- That the Secretary be authorised to arrange for a small allowance to be made to the school for the delivery of letters and small parcels by the Tramway Authorities.
It was agreed that larger parcels, books for the managers' meetings etc should be delivered by the caretaker.

Presumably, this meant that the monitoress could now be given the bus fare and the Caretaker seems to have been appointed the postman in addition to being the lunch-time supervisor, the roof repairer and the playing field groundsman in his spare time.

Application from Miss Mills (11/11/1913) for full salary to be paid to Miss Taylor during her recent absence on account of scarlet fever was considered. A report (12/12/1913) from the M.O.H. was received
Resolved:- That, as the M.O.H. is of the opinion that Miss Taylor, an assistant in the Infants' Department, probably contracted scarlet fever in school, she be paid full salary during the whole of her recent absence on this account.

Obviously, there was no sick pay legislation in place but it is extremely difficult to see how on Earth any M.O.H could determine for certainty, when or where anybody became infected with a disease. Surely it was the right decision to make, but one based on commonsense, not evidence. Given the previous decade of serious illnesses that had occurred on epidemic-proportions at times, this was a very strange issue to raise now.

In 1914 – the year of the outbreak of WW1, there was only a limited number of items that were considered, they were reminders really. The steps down from Osborne Road, state of the school building were mentioned as was the more sombre news that the first teacher had been called up for war service,

---

An application (4.2.1914) from Mr Weeks for the sum of 5/2d to be refunded to Mr Pine, one of his assistants, being the amount expended in connection with a lantern lecture on Ireland to the scholars in the upper standard, was received.
Resolved:- That the sum of 5/2d incurred in connection with a lantern lecture on Ireland should be paid by the Education Committee.

The annual reports of the Head teachers (of Ditchling Road and Loder Road) were submitted, but consideration was deferred until the next meeting.

Major Bloomfield explained that the reports, which were ordered to be circulated to the managers, had not reached him and he was given the opportunity of considering the reports between this and the next meeting.

It was reported that the screen in the Infants' department had not yet been repaired in accordance with the resolution passed at the last meeting and it was agreed that certain inquiries should be made with regard to the matter.

Two more significant resolutions were made at this meeting:

Resolved:- That the Sites and Works Sub-Committee be requested again to bring before the appropriate Committee of the Town Council the urgent necessity of the provision of a right of way between Osborne Road and Balfour Road and that they be informed that the managers of this school will be glad to hear as to the present position of the negotiations in regard to the matter.

Resolved:- That the managers beg to request that the matter of the erection of the new school will be expedited as fast as possible, as the school work under present conditions is most seriously hampered.

After 11 years of being in office, managers appear to be resigned to the fact that certain key requests – especially involving repairs and new buildings – have to be repeated and sometimes, repeated many times. The condition of the Tin Hut and the building the Osborne Road to Balfour Road steps were prime examples.

A letter (12.3.1914) from the Surveyors reporting that the screen in the Infants' Department is too bad to repair and suggesting the provision of a curtain in its place was received.

However, the Managers seemed unimpressed by the suggestion that the screen should be replaced by a curtain. Thus, it was resolved that *the Requisition Branch Sub-Committee be recommended to supply a new screen for the Infants' Department in place of one which is quite worn out.*

In regard to the Managers' resolution passed at the last meeting with reference to the right of way between Osborne Road and Balfour Road, it was reported that the Committee had forwarded a resolution to the Improvements Committee of the Town Council drawing attention to the urgent necessity for such a provision being made.

The Managers also drew attention to another 'distance-travelled' issue by expressing concern at the great distance of the Canteen from this school and resolved to call on the *Canteen Branch Sub-Committee to recognise the desirability of making arrangements, if possible, whereby the necessity for the Loder Road scholars to travel such a great distance to the feeding centre, may be obviated.*

The next entry was made in the Minute Book four months after the start of World War One and this is the first time the war has been mentioned.

It was reported that Mr Pine, T.C.A Mixed Department, had gone on service. A letter (7.12.1914) from Mr Weeks, as to the appointment of a "supply" teacher was submitted.

Resolved:- That an advertisement be issued for a master in place of Mr Pine, absent on service, at a salary of £110 per annum, and that the Board of Education be requested to give permission in the very exceptional circumstances, in order that steps may be taken, if necessary, to secure the services of suitable private tutors and ex-university men who would be willing to act on supply in the schools.

Section IV

World War One as it affected life at Loder Road School from Log Book, Minutes and other sources

The Great War, which started on 28th July 1914 and ended on 11th November 1918 when the Armistice was signed with Germany at Le Francfort, nr Compiègne in northern France. The significance of timing of the signature to end hostilities; at the 11th hour on the 11th day of the 11th month was to remain the permanent moment at every Remembrance Day in November to begin the two-minute silence

Many books and articles have been written about the effects that the Great War had on Brighton and its population. Extracts from three publications have been included in this section because they relate quite specifically to the Loder Road School and its environs. The first of these is one we have already seen, which is Owen Williams' oral history about his time at Loder Road. Part of what he wrote includes several paragraphs about his First World War experiences. He describes an interestingly short journey from excitement, even bravado at the outbreak of war to a sober understanding that it wasn't really about a game of toy soldiers.

"For many of us, boys especially, war was exciting; the attendant horrors and tragedies not fully understood.

When troops of soldiers paraded through the town, led by bands playing stirring marches, with crowds of people looking on, cheering and waving flags, we rushed to watch. Army camps were set up on the Downs on the outskirts of Brighton. There were army manoeuvres with mock battles and soldiers firing blank ammunition. My brothers and I with various schoolmates, spent most of our spare time hanging round these camps, eager to see all that was going on. Some folk said, "The war would be over by Christmas." We sincerely hoped not, our ambitions were to be soldiers too and march off to fight for our country.

But gradually the harsh realities of war became more apparent, the picture changed. Food became scarce; children appeared at school wearing black arm bands or with diamond shaped patches sewn onto sleeves of coats, mourning fathers and brothers killed fighting in the trenches in France. Most of the able bodied young men disappeared, my older brother among them, swallowed up by the hungry maw of the war machines.

Teachers were now mainly women, lessons were mornings only. Another school took over in the afternoons, their premises requisitioned for war purposes. Maps showing the progress of the war were chalked on to blackboards as various battles were fought. Dire consequences awaiting us if Kaiser Bill and Little Willie won the war; this filled our hearts with dread. We set-to with a will, sewing coarse material into sandbags, one of the tasks we were given in place of some of our lessons. This probably encouraged us to think we were doing our bit, but did little for our education".

Extracts from the Loder Road School's Log Book during WW1 while Owen Williams was at the school

1914

- *'Paper Pillows' are being made by the children in each class in the school and at home, to send to the local Military Hospital. Magazines and material for bandages have also been bought by the children.*

1915

Notes from Ditchling Road School's Log Book [1907 – 1915], which relate to the Loder Road School

April

- *School reopened. In order to accommodate the draft from, the Infants' department, an additional class (Standard IVb) will be worked at Loder Road School in the central Hall.*

May

- *Mr Greysmith, Drawing Superintendent, visited Loder Road School section for drawing. The girls in Lower Standard attending Loder Road were granted free rides on trams from St Saviour's Church and Preston Circus to Balfour Road. Similar privilege was granted to Standard I girls attending Preston Road, from the top of Ditchling Road.*

Now back to the Loder Road Log Book:

- A full "Plan of Action" re school and Air Raids, etc., has been formed and a statement of the same is now hung on the school Notice Board.
- Visit paid by Rev. J. E. Page and tomorrow, being French Flag Day, various forms of celebrating the occasion will be adopted. Small tricolour flags will be sold in school at 1d each, the proceeds to be sent to the National Fund, (to relieve suffering in the Provinces, which have been under the subjection of the Germans). Simple lessons bring to the minds of the children the reasons for the day's celebration:-
- o An assembly in the Playground
- o The Tricolour saluted with the accompaniment of the Marseillaise
- o A few words from the Head teacher, a 'March Past' and the singing of the National Anthem
- o The announcement of a half-holiday in the afternoon followed by dismissal
- Owing to the withdrawal from the staff of Miss Guildford (now appointed First-Assistant in the Finsbury Road School) and no further appointments being made (by reason of the "War" conditions), the classes in the school have been re-organised.

Two local schools, which had over-lapping wartime experiences with Loder Road, were York Place Higher Grade and Ditchling Road School (now Downs Primary School). The following extracts from their published histories, describe the occasions when their historic paths crossed.

1. An extract from "The York Place/Varndean Story", (1884 – 1984)

Without warning, Miss Ellis was summoned to the Education Office to be told that the school premises were required for an Indian Military Hospital and must be vacated within 24 hours. The Boys Brigade was engaged to remove all the furniture. This exercise was linked to the conversion of the Royal Pavilion, Dome and Corn Exchange for use as the Hospital. These premises needed clearing, so other buildings needed to be made available to take all the fixtures and fittings. It was said that the Boy Scouts were enlisted to help but the local paper, The Gazette reported, probably more accurately, that "40 sturdy energetic young fellows of the Boys Brigade were responsible".

Miss Ellis rescued the pictures and took them home for safe keeping.

The girls carried their possessions to their new school in rooms scattered through the nearby Technical College and, for the very youngest, a room in the Police Institute. Surplus desks and equipment were stored in the emptied North Road Baths, some of it not to appear again until the War was over. **The biology department's skeleton did not re-emerge until 1926!**

Eleanor Horsley*, who was in the Sixth Form at the time, writes sympathetically of the problems facing Miss Ellis and her staff as they spent the next week in a heroic struggle to re-arrange classes, time-tables and accommodation.

Yet work was scarcely interrupted and although, in Miss Strange's words, "some things – parties, form prizes, inter-school matches and tournaments had to be given up," the girls involved themselves with equal enthusiasm in war activities. They knitted socks, rolled bandages, made jam, "adopted" a prisoner-of-war and sent him a weekly food-parcel and tried – for an unspecified period, but certainly useful purpose – to collect a million tram tickets. They dug and worked the allotments beside the newly-acquired flat hockey pitch where the Balfour Schools now stand and won an Honourable Mention at the Allotments Holders' Show.

* See the reference to Eleanor Horsley in the section describing Varndean Girls School experiences in WW2 (Chapter Two, Section II)

2. An extract from "The history of Ditchling Road School", (1890 – 1954)

During its sixty-four years, the School has seen three wars. The earliest, the Boer War, seems to have made little more impact than the celebration by holidays of the successful reliefs of Ladysmith and Mafeking in 1900, and the final signing of peace at Pretoria in 1902.

The First War made more serious demands. The Girls School was compelled to evacuate the lower rooms, the bulk going to Preston Road, the remainder to Loder Road, and the vacant classrooms were occupied by the York Place Secondary Boys School. A school working "double sessions" in buildings as far apart as the two schools mentioned inevitably suffered in efficiency despite the heroic efforts of the Head teacher, Miss Comley, and her staff, while the "emergency war" education schemes and frequent exchange of teachers put a further strain upon personnel.

After nearly five years of constantly interrupted effort and a shadowy existence, the Girls School returned to their original home on November 17th 1919 and a week later everyone commenced full time working.

Finally, the Managers' record of their meetings, which spanned the Great War

In the four war years – the Managers met spasmodically and were clearly constrained by the difficult situation with which they were faced and which meant that there was little scope for decision-making of any significance. All that they seemed able to do was to increase the number of issues that they referred to the appropriate Sub-Committee for their consideration. The items covered were all familiar such as gardening (replacing Mr Pine called up for Service), the poor state of the buildings, illnesses to the Caretaker and Miss Mills and reminding the Committee about the need for steps from Osborne Road.

This is the first reference to the War and the first indication that emergency procedures would replace normal employment practice wherever necessary. Managers also moved to discover what was happening to the scholars who were being affected by the war-related changes that were made to look after the injured soldiers from France. One such change involved 'double sessions' whereby groups of children would have lessons for half-days in the schools or in alternative accommodation such as church halls near to their normal school. Thus, the Managers discussed:

The annual reports of Ditchling Road and Loder Road schools were submitted and noted. It was agreed that, at the end of six months experience of the schools in 'double sessions', reports as to the working of the arrangement should be submitted to the managers.

Note: 'Double sessions' were introduced in response to the loss of school accommodation through the requisition of a number of schools that were then adapted for use as hospitals as part of a network of medical facilities. The Royal Pavilion was, for example, used as a hospital for Indian soldiers injured in Europe. This situation has been well documented in the publication, "Dr. Brighton's Indian Patients" by Joyce Collins. The publication also identified other institutions and buildings in Brighton and Hove that were part of the network of local 'field hospitals'.

In the summer of 2014, an exhibition entitled Dr Brighton's War commemorating the 100th anniversary of WW1, which was arranged by the Royal Pavilion & Museums, Brighton & Hove and which provided additional information on the extent of the network of hospitals. Specifically, in relation to the schools that were involved, the hub to which the 14 auxiliary hospitals were attached was the main 2nd Eastern General Hospital housed at the Brighton and Hove Grammar School, now the Brighton Hove and Sussex Sixth Form College (BHASVIC). Six more schools were involved; those at York Place, St Luke's, Stanford Road, St Mark's, Portland and Holland Road Schools.

In all, nearly 2,000 beds were provided by the school sector and it understandable that the managers should seek to investigate the effects on the school community of the working the system of 'double sessions'.

A footnote attached to Brighton Museum's Exhibition display drew attention to the importance of the role played by the network of hospitals by describing the soldiers' journey from the battleground. *"This was a weary journey, jolted 350 miles across France, shipped to Southampton and brought by train to Brighton. The suffering of our injured soldiers cannot be realised."*

Also at the meeting, two resolutions were made:

Resolved:- That the Requisition Branch Sub-Committee be recommended to make a special additional allowance on account of the recent epidemic at the school

Resolved:- That the Elementary Schools Sub-Committee be informed that the managers are of the opinion that a permanent Roll of Honour to include teachers and old scholars on service should be provided at every boys' and girls' departments in the town.

The Managers seemed to be having second thoughts about appointing a replacement for Mr Pine by turning to employees already in the service of the Town Council.

The question of the appointment of a master for the gardening class in place of Mr Pine was considered. And it was resolved that, until Mr Pine returns to duty, or until the new school is opened, whichever occurs first, arrangements if possible should be made with the Parks and Gardens Committee for one of the Corporation gardeners to attend at the school for the purpose of giving the necessary instruction in gardening to the scholars.

At the next meeting, the Managers learnt that a 'supply' teacher gardener would be needed until Mr Pine returns. The option that the new school building might be open before Mr Pine's return disappeared, as indicated by the next Education Committee's communication below:

The decision of the Education Committee of February 23rd 1915 to postpone the erection of the new school was reported to the Managers.

This report couldn't really have come as much of a surprise to the Managers and, to be fair, the Country was at War.

Having resolved to seek a replacement for Mr Pine while he was on war service, Mr Weeks came back with an alternative suggestion.

It was reported that the Committee had confirmed the managers' recommendation with regard to the Gardening Class but, on the Head Master being approached for details as to the class, he had stated that he was of opinion that it was desirable that action in the matter should be deferred and that the Secretary thereupon decided against bringing the matter before the managers proceeding further therein.

This was a very long paragraph to say that 'we will wait and see'.

The Committee did not have too long to wait because, as usual another letter was soon received from Mr Weeks

A letter (9.3.1915) from Mr Weeks was submitted.
Resolved:- That the proposal of the Head Master to arrange for a gardening class to be conducted out of school hours be adopted in lieu of that as set out in the recommendation of the managers passed at the meeting, and that application be made to the Board of Education for a grant to be paid on account of the class, in view of the exceptional circumstances occasioned by the war.
Also, it was resolved that a sufficient quantity of stable and patent manure be supplied at once for this class.

Mr Weeks, who might have felt that he was on a winning streak having kept control of his gardening class, now seeks to have the interior of the school up-graded.

A letter (13.5.1915) from Mr Weeks applying for the school to be redecorated internally was received.
Resolved:- That the Sites and Works Sub-Committee be requested to consider the question of improving the interior of this school, especially in regard to the lighting as affected by the colour of the woodwork and ceiling and the insanitary condition of the woodwork, which are in need of very urgent attention.
Also it was resolved that arrangements be made for the refuse at the school to be removed more frequently if necessary during the coming summer months.

At this point the Managers decided to develop a process whereby a précis of items on each meeting's agenda that were common to all four schools would be made, and only those items that related to a single school would dealt with in more detail. So, the next meeting the Managers received a note on common items and concentrated on reports from each school which contained the individual concerns.

<u>Common to all Reports</u> – Difficulty of cupboard accommodation and utilisation of stock
(It is not clear from the Minutes whether the common items were recorded and filed separately. This record of the Minutes will continue to highlight all items that were specifically relevant to Loder Road School.)

An individual report from Loder Road School was discussed at this meeting, which was a report from Mixed Department on the arrangements that had been put in operation for schools across Brighton to cope with the difficulties caused by a shortage of classrooms that was created by need to requisition some school buildings to support the war effort.

> *"The arrangement is the best that could be conceived and worked, but I find that the work must eventually suffer in quality". Necessary to work at a tension. Boys suffer in the afternoon session through outside work in the morning. Gardening imposes additional work, and particular strain on the Head Master. More homework is thrown on teachers; difficult to find time to correct homework. "The shorter time at our disposal necessitates good organisation, and a regard for the minutes that might possibly be employed profitably. The lessons in some instances have been shortened, and this helps to avoid undue weariness, and keeps the children to a certain extent from flagging".*

At the next meeting, a more familiar concern for Loder Road School, the state of the property, was aired for umpteenth time.

Resolved:- That the attention of the Sites and works Sub-Committee be drawn to the condition of the playground, and that they be requested to arrange for it to be cleared of stones, and for paths of tar to be made from the school gates to the entrances of the building and for the playground generally to be improved during the forthcoming Summer Holidays.

The Chairman of the Elementary Schools Sub-Committee undertook to see what could be done in regard to the provision of new pictures of Loder Road and Preston Road Schools.

A letter (1.11.1915) from Mr Charles, resigning his position as caretaker, owing to ill-health, was received.

Resolved:- That the resignation of Mr Charles, caretaker be accepted, such resignation to take effect on November 30th 1915, and that Mr Charles be paid full wages for the period of absence from duty, owing to illness, up to the date on which he will leave the service of the Committee. Question of steps to be taken to appoint a successor to Mr Charles, was considered.

Resolved:- That the Elementary Schools Sub-Committee be asked to sanction the appointment of a successor to Mr Charles, being deferred at the present, and to approve the services of the 'Supply' Caretaker being continued in the meantime.

References from the Elementary Schools Sub-Committee as to wages of a temporary caretaker and as to the suggested tenure of the appointment were considered.

Resolved:- That the Elementary Schools Sub-Committee be informed that the Managers are of the opinion that it would be undesirable during the War to proceed with the appointment of a permanent caretaker.

They therefore desire to postpone the filling of the post and to assure the Committee that when the permanent appointment is made the usual steps will be taken to obtain candidates.

They therefore recommend that the services of Mr Taylor, the temporary caretaker who is carrying out the duties satisfactorily, should be continued. The Managers have interviewed Mr Taylor and explained to him that his appointment is purely a temporary one and will not necessarily entitle him to a claim to the permanent post

1916

An application from the temporary caretaker for an increase of wages was submitted and considered, and Mr Taylor had an interview with the Managers.

Resolved:- That the wages of Mr Taylor be increased from 25s to 27s 6d per week to date from January 1st 1916.

Annual Report of the Headmaster on the School Garden was submitted and noted.

It was resolved that the Annual Report should be received and forwarded to the Elementary Schools Sub-Committee. It was agreed that Mr Weeks should be thanked for the Report and also for the work in connection with the garden which he and his assistants have been doing for the benefit of the scholars.

Illnesses dominate the next two meetings and it was evident in the School Log that Miss Mills did have several absences because of ill-health. It must have been an extremely difficult time;

following a decade of bouts of epidemics, in a building of poor quality, and now with the exigencies of wartime to cope with.

A letter (25.2.16) from Miss Mills applying for leave of absence, and enclosing a medical certificate was submitted and considered.
The Secretary was instructed to write to Miss Mills to the effect that the Managers were sorry to hear of her illness, but trust that the change she is to take will completely restore her to health.
Resolved:- That the leave of absence from March 15th until April 20th next on account of ill health be granted to Miss Mills in order that she may leave Brighton for a change.

Appointment of a temporary Caretaker was considered
It was reported that the M.O.H. had expressed the opinion that in view of the state of Mr Taylor's health, it was not desirable to continue his engagement as a temporary caretaker, and that his services had, therefore, been terminated.
Resolved:- That Mr Thomas be appointed temporary Caretaker at a weekly wage of 27s 6d to date from 10th April 1916.

Mr Weeks continues to draw attention to the state of the dilapidated building. *A letter (6.10.16) was received from Mr Weeks with reference to (a) bad state of the playground (b) worn steps at Boys' entrance , and (c) provision of blinds for certain windows.*
Resolved:- That the letter be forwarded to the Sites and Works Sub-Committee

1917

Another case for Dr. Simpson

A letter (25.4.17) was received from Mr Weeks with reference to an accident to a boy named Smith.
Resolved:- That, as an act of grace and without admitting liability, Dr Simpson's account for the sum of 4/6d for attendance on the boy Smith, who met with an accident whilst at play, be paid by the Education Committee

Mr Weeks drew attention to the problem (below) six months ago but it wasn't included in the Minute at the time, just the Resolution below. I think we can imagine what Mr Weeks said. The clue is in the last two lines.
Resolved:- That the attention of the Sites and Works Sub-Committee be drawn to the unsatisfactory state of the playground in very wet weather and that they be urged to arrange for its being put into fair order as soon as possible.

Just two items relating to Loder Road were discussed in 1917.

Wartime fatigue and shortages of various kinds must have played their part in reducing the frequency of meetings. Also, the complicated system of Double Sessions, which affected classes across the Authority with a limited curriculum on offer and presumably having to make do with the resources that they already had, meant that Managers had little power to intervene positively. The Managers had to settle Dr Simpson's account and they weren't doing much for Mr Weeks in referring to the Sites and Works Sub-Committee. It would have been straight into the in-tray as usual with the Managers' request for action as soon as possible. They were still being asked to fulfil to the request in 1919.

A letter (4.7.18) was received from Miss Mills asking that in the assessing of the coal and other necessary fuel for heating of the school next winter, careful consideration might be given to the defective nature of the building.
It was agreed that the matter should be referred to the Secretary to deal with.

A letter (23.9.18) was received from Mr Weeks with reference to a war honour gained by an old boy.
Resolved:- That the following war honour gained by an old boy be reported to the Committee Sergeant Re-James Maynard, M.M.

A bit of house-keeping that Miss Mills would like attended to; Screen and Curtains

Resolved:- That the Committee be asked to provide a curtain for the external door of the Infants' Department, in order to prevent the sharp draught into the school premises.

Resolved:- That the Committee be asked to arrange for the folding screen in the Infants' Department to be repaired.

The Managers thought a report from Mr Weeks was very interesting and it was a good example of the inevitable damage that was done during the War caused by restricting the curriculum to the basic subjects.

A copy of the report was not attached to the Minutes but some of its contents can be guessed at from the second half of the sentence.

A report was received from Mr Weeks on the school work before the war, together with some specimens of the art work done by the scholars.
It was agreed that Mr Weeks should be thanked for his highly interesting report and that he should be informed that the Managers desire to congratulate him, the members of the staff and the scholars on excellent specimens of art work submitted and that he should also be informed that the Managers hope that the various branches of school work, which have had to be abandoned or curtailed owing to the war, will soon be able to be resumed.

At the end of 1918, with the War over, reminders were again sent to the Sites and Works Committee about the steps to be built from Osborne Road and tar on the playground.

Resolved:- That the Committee be informed that the managers are of opinion that it is very important and most desirable that the steps which are being formed between Osborne Road and Balfour Road should be proceeded with as speedily as possible in order that, for the convenience of the younger children, they may be completed before the coming winter.

Resolved:- That the Committee be asked to arrange for surface of the playground to be sprayed with tar.

Section V

Continuing the final episode of the Loder Road Infants' School story (1918 – 1924)

Continuing the Minutes of the Managers' meetings (1918 – 1924)

The Balfour Road Junior School Visitors' Book

Firstly, the Infants' Department Log Book

1. The School Building and Playground

As the Great War was coming to an end in 1918, there was a distinct change of emphasis in the entries made by Miss Mills in the Log Book. Thoughts seem to have turned back to the view expressed six years earlier in 1912 by Mr E Lethbridge, which were:

E. Lethbridge Esq. (former Headmaster at York Place Senior Boys, School, which became Varndean GS), *visited the school this morning. The very draughty conditions of the building and also the lack of Hall accommodation were commented on by him.* <u>*He expressed the opinion that strong representations should now be made for a permanent building.*</u>

It may not be cause and effect, but Mr Lethbridge's intervention might have been timed in the light of what was then known about the ownership of the land on which the permanent Balfour Road School was destined to be built.

When the temporary building was erected in 1905, the farm land beyond Loder Road to the north was not owned by the Borough of Brighton. It was bought by the Council in1909. So, one can assume that there will have been planning discussions related to potential building developments in the area as a result. Mr Lethbridge may have been putting down a timely reminder about the temporary nature of the Tin Hut

Reminder or not, it is now six years since the issue had been raised by Lethbridge and 13 years since the 'temporary' school opened. Reading through Miss Mills' Log Book entries from this point on, she clearly continued to develop the edge to her comments that had been noticeable just before the War started.

She didn't just record the various difficulties that she identified but also sent chapter and verse direct to the Education Committee and/or the School Managers more often than not. The exchanges included both an emphasis on the adverse effects on the children's education and, significantly, on the damage being done to the school's reputation. In so doing of course, she was drawing attention to the reputation of the local authority by implication.

These are a few of the Log Book entries in the last three years of Miss Mills' time as Head teacher that may have helped to put pressure on the local authority to finally replace corrugated iron with bricks and mortar.

1918

- *The Playground is in a very disgraceful condition, owing to the mud. It is quite unfit for children to move about and the interiors of the building, also the boots of the children and teachers, suffer considerably. The extreme conditions cannot be realised unless one can actually see them. These discouraging factors <u>do much harm to the reputation of this school</u> and a letter is being sent to the <u>Education Committee on this matter.</u>*
- *The furnace has completely broken down (it has been defective for some time), and the school is not heated at all today. The rooms are very cold but the children are being actively employed to meet the emergency. The matter has been placed <u>in the Surveyor's hand.</u> In the meantime, the Time Table work will be modified, if necessary, to keep the children warm and all arranged as advisable, by <u>the advice of Mr Toyne.</u>*
- *The defective state of the floorboards in the Playground shed <u>has been reported to the Surveyor.</u>*
- *A bad leakage has occurred from the roof in Room III. This has been reported.*
- *<u>Councillor Wilkinson visited</u> the school on the 17th October to enquire about the need for the curtains requested on 15th May last. Owing to the dilapidated Exit Door and to the draughty nature of the north end of the school, the need is particularly urgent.*

1919

- *The condition of the Playground, from 23rd January until yesterday, was deplorable. Much <u>harm is done to the well-being of the school</u> during such days, in point of cleanliness and outside reputation.*
- *Constant attention is required towards the condition of the school building. The defective roof, the draughty nature of the walls, windows, doors and floor, and the state of the Playground – all show the <u>need for a well-built and satisfactory environment.</u>*
- *The restrictions in all Physical work still prevail, owing to the Hall being used for a class in the Upper Department. The equipment of the school shows much to be desired, eg. pictures, chairs and tables, nursery apparatus and open-air employments.*

1920

- *The school is without any heat and the atmosphere is very cold and damp, very unhealthy for the children. The celebrations for St George's Day and Empire Day have taken place and the children have been <u>sent home for the rest of the day. (The registers were closed at 9.00 – scholars were dismissed at 11.00 owing to the very low temperature of the classrooms).</u>*
- *<u>A special meeting has been called for the 18th inst at the Education Office – to consider the Plans for the new school.</u> I have been invited to be present. Preliminary to this meeting, Mr Weeks and I are visiting the school in Coombe Road, as the plans for the new building are based on this type of school.*

Note: In the Brighton Education Week Brochure, the photograph below was included to illustrate one of the styles being used for school buildings; this one being the bungalow style at Coombe Road School that Mr Weeks and Miss Mills would have seen on their visit (the one that was chosen for Balfour Road School).

Fig 16
New Balfour building was designed on Coombe Road School's model of the bungalow style.

A Red Letter Day in July

The steps down from Osborne Road have been finished and opened for Public use. The first letter requesting the construction of these steps was <u>sent by myself – fifteen years ago – to the Town Council</u>

Fig 17

So, Miss Mills' wish was granted at last. The flight of steps were in place connecting Osborne Road with Balfour Road providing children living in the proximity of 113 Osborne Road where the steps started, easy access to their school.

In all, there were over 80 steps and about the same number of paces for children to make in order to reach Balfour Road using this short-cut; the alternative route via Osborne Road, Preston Drove and Balfour Road is a little over a half-a-mile. Cutting the distances children had to travel was an important development at a time when many had inadequate footwear which was often made worse in pre-climate change winters. Walking was their only option.

The Sites and Works Committee *have considered the request re paving the ground under the Playground Shed; the result is the following: "It is not desirable that the expense of carrying out this work should be incurred, as the Sub-Committee anticipate that the erection of the new school will not be much longer delayed".*

Just another 3½ years to go at that point!

1921

- *A deputation, consisting of the Architect of the Board of Education, the Chief Inspector of the District, the School Surveyor, and various representatives of the Education Committee and the Town Council, inspected the school building. A short conference was held after the school was examined.*

- *All of the work of the school is restricted owing to the limited space and cramped conditions, the dusty or muddy conditions of the Playground and the numerous defects of such a building as the present one.* **The recent publicity of the true character of the building has increased the prejudice and dislike towards the school in the minds of the parents who are greatly disappointed at the further delay in regard to the new school.**

- *I am attending the Managers' meeting this afternoon as the question of the school accommodation in the northern part of the Town, is to be considered; also the subject of the extra consumption of gas in the school during the past Winter. The urgency of proper provision of blinds to the windows of the classrooms, the serious nature of the present conditions of the school fence and the broken lock of the gate; the need to renovate the boiler for the heating apparatus during the summer months – these points will be submitted by me for early attention.*

This was to be the last time Miss Mills would refer to the state of the building and its surroundings in her Log Book account. She didn't underline the references of course, but these statements may have drawn the 'movers and shakers' attention to the never-ending catalogue of faults.

Confirmation of this would seem to be implicit in the reference of *'recent publicity about true character of the building'* indicating that her messages were being heard more widely but the 'official' talk was still about 'further delay' as it had been in 1920.

2. School Attendance

After the War, there were very few references to attendance; the focus of attention remained on the building and the playground.

1919

- *The weekly attendance is 63.2% (Inclement weather; school district almost impossible with the snow since 28th January, three days ago*
- *The serious nature of the roads in the school district (the snow was lying, usually in a frozen state for nine days, quite uncleared), has prevented the attendance of the younger children.*

This section ends on an entry, which shows, not for the first time that transfers can sometimes go in both directions.

- Three scholars have been admitted recently from a private school; all are 7 years of age, but are unable to do the ordinary work that is possible at that age. (Two of the three have no groundwork in Reading at all.) Cross-classification methods are being adopted for these scholars, for the subjects of Reading, Writing and Arithmetic.

3. Sickness and Injuries

Reports on sicknesses and injuries continued post-War although, apart from an outbreak of measles, there were not so many instances of the epidemics that had been prevalent before the War.

1918

- *A boy fell in the Playground this afternoon and hurt his right leg. The nature of the accident is difficult to ascertain (whether the bone was bruised or broken); the leg was therefore treated with First Aid and the boy was carried home (which is situated opposite the school). The medical opinion, subsequently obtained, was also uncertain as to the harm done, until an examination by X-rays had been taken. The accident has been reported to the Education Committee. The teacher was in the Playground at the time. (The leg has since been found to be fractured.)*

1919

- *A very bad attack of faintness occurred during the morning, but some time elapsed before the attack passed. After a sleep, the boy had a warm drink and was taken home by the Monitoress.*
- *A bad fall occurred in the Playground during Playtime. The boy concerned hurt his forehead. This has been treated and after a good rest, the boy was taken home by the Monitoress.*
- *A Standard 1 scholar collapsed with a severe heart attack. The usual remedies were applied but failed to relieve. Eventually, the mother was sent for and the patient was carried home on a hammock.*

1920

- *An instruction has been received from the Secretary of the Education Committee, "that all Infant Schools are to close after the afternoon session today, until after the Easter holidays, on the advice of the MOH" (by reason of the prevalence of Measles in the Town).*
- *The cases of measles have greatly increased during the weekend; 18 definite or suspicious cases having been reported to me this morning. All of these are now notified to MOH.*

In a section that didn't contain any 'lighter' moments, the last entry is simply a very sad indication that there was little in the way specialist facilities for children with severe learning difficulties.

1921

- *A request of the school Doctor, Dr Cramb – has been complied with. This is to the effect that Eileen G. Fern, aged 9yrs, unable to attend school before, owing to a serious physical deformity, be admitted to this Department in order that a good start can be made. (This girl is unable to read or write, and is unable to work with her hands as other children.) All that is possible will be done and special provision will be made to ensure her wellbeing in every way.*

4. Events

After the War, on 17th July 1919, children assembled in the Playground as Miss Mills instructed:

- *The "Peace" celebrations in this school will be held this afternoon at 2 o'clock. The register will not be marked therefore. School is now dismissed and will not meet again until Monday.*
- *The Chairman of the Managers presided at the above mentioned celebrations, and a programme of a Hymn, Prayer and Speech was taken. Cheers for the King, Chairman, etc. followed by the National Anthem.*

Another July event in the next week and another Sunday school treat:

- *Owing to the large number of scholars wishing to be absent on the 24th for St John's CC treat, the Managers have allowed the school to close throughout the day*

Finally, there was another wartime connection with the visit of Field Marshall Douglas Haig who had been created an Earl in 1919.

1920

- *The school will be closed on the afternoon of the 30 November by reason of the visit to the Town of Earl Haig*

5. Miscellaneous

In this collection of odds and ends, we start with an entry about a message received that Miss Mills didn't relish – a lack of places in the Upper Department of the School.

1918

- *The Headmaster of the Mixed Department has informed me that only 31 children (out of a draft of 61) can be taken into the senior school on April 1st. The reason for the above is the lack of the necessary school places*
- *Regarding the above remark of (lack of school places in the Upper Department for St 1 infants). The Education Committee has decided that 4 girls must be admitted to the Ditchling Road Girls School and 10 boys into the Ditchling Road Boys School.*
- *14 children are to be retained in this school for a further training of six months, (two scholars have left the school and district during the past month).*

1920

And yet another message that Miss Mills could happily have done without:
- *Miss Haffenden has received promotion to Headmistress of Crown Street Infants' School; she will therefore terminate her work in this school on 31st August*

A change to the school leaving age after the War, which raised compulsory secondary education to 14 years in the 1918 Act, led to a new contract being introduced for the employment of Monitoresses at the school. A young girl would be able to carry out the role for a year. The Log Book records one appointment in more detail than others that normally just gave a name and age. So, at the end of April 1920, we learn that:

- *Doris Youell, 157 Waldegrave Road, aged 15years of age (March 29th 1905) has been engaged as the monitoress for this school to commence duties on May 31st next. The present Monitoress will be leaving on May 21st next, by reason of age.*

Unfortunately, this monitoress was later to be hit by part of a window that collapsed. No account of any injury was given but she did eventually leave before her year was completed.

The next question is, will it be flag stones or pots of paint?

1921
- Repainting of the school has commenced today
- The Sites and Works Committee have considered the request about paving the ground under the Playground Shed; the result is the following:

It is not desirable that the expense of carrying out this work should be incurred, as the Sub-Committee anticipate that the erection of the new school will not be much longer delayed.

Ah well, the painting job won the day and the building work was only delayed for another 3 ½ years.

At this point, entries in the 1905 Loder Road (Balfour temporary) School Log Book rather fizzle out.

A new Log Book for the Infants' Department

1922
We do know that on 1st January 1922, Miss Mills began a new Log Book with what she called the "fourth term" by sending the children home for the morning because the building was too damp to be used. Coal and coke were delivered and the boiler fired before the children were allowed to enter in the afternoon. I had not come across a reference to a fourth term before, but I have mentioned several times elsewhere, the start of the year of the academic year as being 1st April (or there about). So, roughly, the four seasons defined the school terms during this period.
She gained Mr Weeks' support to allow a nine-year old girl who had been ill and had not developed well academically, to remain with the Infants.

As the month wore on, Miss Mills had to adopt an 'influenza-watch' as more and more cases were reported and attendance rates fell accordingly. While children were being counted in, the nurse was visiting to inspect their teeth and Miss Crawford was confirmed as the new member of staff.

Finally, time-tables were adjusted to make room for extra sessions on English, writing and reading, generally at the expense of hand crafts as usual.

On 1st February, Miss Mills recorded a surprise (for me at least) by reporting that the Managers of the four north Brighton schools had granted a half-day holiday that afternoon *on the occurrence of the Brighton and Hove v Windsor and Eton football match.* The only local team that I know would have matched that name was Brighton & Hove Albion. Windsor and Eton was a reasonably well known amateur club which joined the Athenian League in 1922.

Without any other information, my initial thoughts were that this might have been a friendly match involving the Albion's Reserve team. Checking my copy of the "Story of Brighton and Hove Albion FC" I discovered that the First XI were playing away against Huddersfield Town in an FA Cup 2nd Round replay on that day, so it was possible for the Reserves to be involved.

However, Tim Carder, who co-authored the book with Roger Harris, came to my rescue by finding a reference to the match in a newspaper, the Sussex Daily News, which was Brighton Boys v Windsor Boys in the English Schools Shield, played at the Goldstone in front of 7,000-8,000 spectators. The Education Committee, via the school Managers, had given the children a half-day off to attend the match, which ended in a 2 – 2 draw. Two north Brighton school boys played; Hammond (Stanford Road) and Matthews (Preston Road). Tim Carder added that Jim Hammond went on the play professional football with Fulham and also played cricket for Sussex. By the way, Brighton and Hove Albion lost 2 – 0 at Huddersfield.

Fig 18
Brighton Boys in action at the Goldstone Ground

This photograph appeared in the 1939 brochure celebrating Education Week in Brighton. It is probably a match from the 1930s rather than the one mentioned above from 1922 when Brighton Boys played Windsor – the venue is the same; the old Goldstone Ground.

Miss Mills was absent for most of the rest of February, probably suffering, as others were, from the affects of the influenza outbreak.

On her return, there was another holiday; on the 27th February when schools were granted a whole day to celebrate the wedding of the Princess Mary, the daughter of the future King George V.

Another holiday was reported at the start of March; the mid-term break on the 6th March. The day after, the attendance level had fallen to 51%. Bad weather and influenza was still taking its toll. On that day, children crossing the playground were in danger of injury from parts of the fence that had fallen and other parts that were about to fall. Half of the chimney stack had fallen and half was hanging over the entrance to the Infants' classes. Storm damage about which Miss Mills immediately contacted the Managers and Surveyor and their response was fast. Fence and chimney were fixed next day. Unfortunately, March hadn't completed its full winter repertoire of weather – ending the month with a very heavy fall of snow; reducing the attendance to 50% again.

The new school year started on the 3rd April but the attendance was still low at 57% because the area was still snow-bound and dangerous under foot. As usual, the playground was largely unusable for long periods.

Also as usual, Miss Mills recorded that the schemes of work had been updated and set out in the Head teacher's Scheme Book. The Infants' staff members were listed as the Misses Puttock, Taylor, Knight and Crawford with Miss Mills providing assistance across all classes as required.

By May, the playing field had been used a few times for physical activities after months when such exercise was restricted to classrooms and the odd occasion when the playground was fit for purpose.

Now, organised walks were planned, as they usually were in late spring, to such places as Blaker's Park, Hollingbury Camp and the Preston Park.

At the end of June, Miss Mills filled two whole pages of the Log Book to record an accident that had happened in the playground when two boys collided. One of the boys had just returned to school following an earlier injury in which he suffered a fractured leg. After Dad was called, he was carried home. His parents reported that the leg had again been fractured but, after being interviewed, declared themselves very satisfied with the care he had received at school, thanked everybody concerned and thought that accidents do just happen.

Finally, and unexpectedly towards the end of the summer term in July, Miss Mills recorded her own absence from school to visit the Lewes Road Primary School ahead of her taking up the Headship there, replacing Miss Baker who was retiring.

Miss Mills then wrote her last paragraph, thus:
My duties as Headmistress of this school are now given up to Miss Seward, who has been appointed in my place, commencing with the new term on 4th September 1922.

Postscript:
The Managers recorded their appreciation for her dedication to the school over the 17 years of her service recognising that she had coped well in very difficult conditions and agreed to send her a copy of this expression of thanks for the work she had done.

The Changing of the Guard was completed at the start of the new term on 4th September 1922 when Miss Hilda Flanders Seward commenced duties as Head teacher. By now, with the new school building just 16 months away, Miss Seward seems to have restricted the range of entries she made to the Log Book to the bare necessities, much as Miss Mills had done earlier in the year. It's only speculation, but once the decision to go ahead with the construction of a new school, Miss Mills may have felt that it would be better for her to seek a move to a well established school and leave the way open for a younger teacher to take the challenge of developing the new Balfour Road School.

So in September, there were references to the number of children on the Roll, attendance percentages, registers checked by managers, nurses' visits, fire drills, staffing matters, illnesses and weather conditions that had plagued the school from the start.

The original plan for the school in 1905 was for the 4 classrooms to hold a maximum of 240 children in the Infants' Department, 60 per classroom but, in 1922, Miss Seward recorded a Roll of 156. Given the level of absence over the years because of illnesses and weather conditions, the class sizes were often in the order of 40 and now, at 156 they would always be below that level. The other limiting factor that caused class sizes to be held down was the unwillingness of many parents to send their children to Loder Road. Miss Mills often recorded examples of parental opposition, which, all other things being equal, should largely evaporate when the new building was ready for occupation.

The term had just started when Miss Puttock was knocked down by a car while riding her bike to school. She was absent recovering from her injuries for nearly six weeks. Miss Seward wasted little time in sending a letter to the Managers requesting bigger desks, something that Miss Mills had asked for years ago. She asked for other items of furniture as well, the first of many such requests that she dispatched to be heard at the Managers' meetings.

One interesting change Miss Seward made in the time-table was to align all classes to take recreational activity at the same time, ensuring that the Hall would be available to be used when conditions outside prevented the playground from being used.

On the 1st November, Miss Seward recorded that another half-day holiday had been granted on the occasion of another football match. No details were added this time but I think that it is safe now to assume that it was another match involving the Brighton Boys' team.

Winter arrived and there was an outbreak of scarlet fever and diphtheria in Grade III, followed by cases of measles and mumps. A few days later, cases of influenza were notified. In fact, just before the Christmas holidays it was announced that the MOH had ordered that all schools should be closed for an extra week because of the high level of illness that was being suffered in the Town. The attendance level at this time was 65%.

1923

Back to school after the Christmas break on 15th January 1923, the attendance level was 62%, lower than it was last term. Clearly the level of illness had not diminished and actually, a week later, it was down to 52% with the explanation that "measles are still rampant".

The measles' epidemic proved difficult to defeat and it was not until the start of the new year in April that attendance levels returned to 80+%.

Miss Seward followed Miss Mills' procedure that she started again when using the new Log Book, in naming the staff in post for the coming year, here unchanged from 1922. She lists them with a little extra detail about pupil numbers in each class.

Standard	I (42)	Miss	H. Taylor
Grade	II (41)	"	E. Puttock
	III (28)	"	M. Knight
	IV (25)	"	E. Crawford
	136		

This year, 39 scholars were promoted to the Upper Department and the effect of this transfer is easily seen in the low class numbers in Grades III and IV. The total on the Roll was 20 children fewer than last year's total of 156.

At the end of April, Miss Seward lost no opportunity in getting various classes out of school and across Loder Road to the playing fields for physical activities whenever the weather was set fair.

On Thursday, 26th April, there was a day's holiday for the marriage of the Duke of York to Elizabeth Bowes-Lyon. He became King George VI in 1936 on the abdication of his brother, Edward VIII. On the eve of the wedding, there was a whole school assembly, 3.45 – 4.00pm, *"to arouse loyal enthusiasm and extend kindly wishes to the Bride and Bridegroom."*

In May, Miss Seward adjusted time-tables again slightly to maximise the time that the children could spend on the playing field. Miss Mills had spent a decade trying to persuade the Education Committee, through the Managers, to allow her school access to the playing fields. We will see later in the Managers' Minutes that the Government's Board of Education had authorised that access to the fields should include elementary schools. The letter was sent to the Education Committee in 1931. In making the position clear, the letter quoted a section of the legislation dating from 1921 to support the Board's decision. So, I think that the Authority had quietly decided to turn a blind eye and was now minded to permit access to the Playing Fields to children at Balfour Road School. I have found no written evidence that the policy had been changed by 1922 but, given that the Head teachers had been campaigning for more than 10 years to overturn the frankly absurd restriction, perhaps Mr Toyne did have a quiet word or two to the schools involved. Something like, 'use your good judgement and let's not make it a news item, eh.'

The only situation that I can think of that would cause the Government to send the confirming letter to the Education Committee in 1931, was the emergence of the second of two secondary schools on to the Balfour campus: the Varndean Girls School opened in 1926 and now, more significantly, Varndean Boys School in 1931/32. Let's guess that there might have been some discussions about who controls which bits of the territory now there were three schools in situ, not just one. If this was the reason, then from my personal knowledge, it wasn't the last time such 'discussions' took place in regard to the use of the fields.

So, as Miss Seward was now taking over with an enthusiasm for outdoor activities, she clearly intended to take full advantage of her good fortune.

Little has been recorded in the Log Book recently about the poor working conditions in the school. Perhaps, it was because of the imminent move to the new school plus evidence of past experience, which showed that complaints normally fell on 'deaf ears'. However, after writing many entries during the rest of May and through June about out-of-doors activities - walks, nature studies, open-air classes and physical exercise – suddenly, the past re-appeared in July when the classroom temperature rose to 94°F.

The term ended with another problem from past re-surfacing when several cases of scarlet fever were reported. Consequently, several family summer holidays were starting badly.

In September, the new term started where the last one ended with more cases of scarlet fever being reported and the playing fields were out of bounds until 11am because of heavy dew. The better news was that the classroom walls had been cleaned, and the floors scrubbed. The first fire drill came in on time, as usual at 1½ minutes. (The very first drill carried out after the school was opened in 1905, was reported as taking 38 seconds. I wonder if this should have been 1 min 38 sec)

However, by early October, after 5 weeks of persistent inclement weather, more gravel had to be spread on the playground. 150 pairs of muddy footwear will, by then, have removed the shine of the summer makeover where the floors were concerned. The bad weather continued throughout October causing more problems with the playground and was probably responsible for low attendance figures.

The half-term break of two days at the start of November allowed time for the floors to be scrubbed afresh.

After which, Miss Seward started to record activities she was involved with in relation to the new school. On the 5th November, she visited it and had an interview with the Borough Surveyor. In the following week, she wrote to the Surveyor and to the Sites and Works Sub-Committee with a set of suggestions, which were also considered at a meeting of the Managers.

An election meeting was held on 19th November ahead of the General Election on the 6th December, the second election of three that were held between 1922 and 1924.

The school was not closed on Election Day because the Council had determined to use the Hall, which had to be cleared to make room for the voting booths and other furniture. Miss Seward was not best pleased with this decision and wrote at length in the Log Book about the inconvenience of having all the classroom furniture piled up around the walls of the Hall. It was used, of course, as a classroom and even two classrooms with a screen at times. The Council's response was simply that other schools were closed. Aiming to have the last word, Miss Seward's counter-response was that other schools were divided into Departments with sufficient space to keep the Hall for assemblies and the like. All the familiar arguments went into her 'missive', which she then rounded off with her signature, in her own Log Book. So there.

This was the first time she had performed such a discourse but it wasn't the first time that a Loder Road School Log Book had been used in this way. Miss Mills used the approach repeatedly to draw attention to the bad working conditions, shortages, poor access to the building without the Osborne Road steps and a few more things as well. She wasn't writing the material to herself, letting off steam or for any other reason. She was putting it down in a book that would be read by a Manager, or Managers who came on a regular basis to inspect aspects of the School such as checking registers. It was a way of adding pressure on the authorities to understand better the needs of the School.

When the children returned to the Hall on 7th December, the country was waking up to an election result that had seen Stanley Baldwin (Cons) defeated by Ramsey MacDonald (Lab). Labour however hadn't won enough seats to form a government. The Liberal leader, H. H. Asquith had a choice in what was a hung Parliament but didn't fancy a coalition with Labour, thinking that MacDonald wouldn't survive very long by governing as the largest Party. He was proved right and the Liberals went on to win the third election in 1924.

In the next week, the Sites and Works Sub-Committee met to discuss the suggestions made by the Head teachers about the new school and also the furniture that would be needed. One of the managers visited later to discuss the same thing. With Miss Seward's attention increasingly turning to next year's move, she soon had to return to a familiar present as the school year ended with an outbreak of mumps.

1924

With two months to go before the day arrived when the doors at the Tin Hut would be closed to children for good, 1924 began where 1923 ended – more cases of mumps, to which chicken pox and whooping cough were added. Attendance figures remained low, being made worse by snow which prevented some children from reaching school. The time-tables had to be adapted to provide opportunities for children to get some physical exercise in-doors while the inclement weather persisted.

Miss Seward reported that she would have no time for class teaching in the mornings and, for the rest of January, she continued to juggle teaching sessions with meetings with the Requisition Committee, Mr Toyne the Secretary to the Education Committee, stock-taking and visiting the new school to consider the suggestion made for the lay-out of the grounds.

In fact, in February 1924, Miss Seward wrote very little in the Log Book for the first three weeks apart from regular health reports listing the usual illnesses, attendance figures and visitors calling to check registers. Until that is, the final week when she recorded the transfer from the old school to the new one across Loder Road about 100 metres away.

This is her week's Log Book entry in full starting on Monday, 25th February.

> *This week, the school has continued to the best of each teacher's ability owing to the week being the Universal Education Week for the Town. The Head teacher has been extremely busy preparing both the old and the new schools for Visitors. Tuesday was Open Day and the evening was devoted to the Exhibition of Work. The school was thronged with parents and friends from 2.30pm – 4.15pm and from 5.30pm – 7.00pm. The parents expressed great appreciation for the opportunity afforded to them.*
>
> *Wednesday afternoon (27th) the new Balfour Road School was opened by Morgan Jones Esq. M.P. Again, numbers of parents visited.*
>
> *Thursday afternoon was given up to a Display of Dancing Rhythmics, Dramatization, Singing and Recitation in the new Hall, which was again over-crowded with appreciative parents.*
>
> *The School has been well visited.*

Before the new school opened, the Education Committee's Secretary, Herbert Toyne, informed the Head teachers that the Committee had resolved that the New School would be organised as Senior Mixed and Junior Mixed Departments and that age for promotion from lower to the upper department be fixed at 10 years.

As the Minutes of the Managers' meeting recorded, ***the new school would be publically opened by Mr Morgan Jones*, M.P., and Parliamentary Secretary to the Board of Education on Wednesday, February 27th, next.*** (What wasn't recorded at this meeting was the cost of building the new school, which was reported to be £14,872)

*Morgan Jones (Labour) MP for Caerphilly; a teacher, trained at Reading University and Baptist lay-preacher, who was imprisoned as a conscientious objector and became the first MP to be elected as a conscientious objector after WW1

Now from the Minutes of the Managers' meetings (1919 – 1924)

> **By 1919** – there was a sense of 'changes afoot' and just one meeting of the Managers with just two conclusions drawn, which could be simply described as 'no' and 'wait'. Perhaps the Managers were still ffected by a slow recovery after the end of the War and equally likely, they were beginning to mark time ahead of what must have been known about anticipated new school building.

The reminders sent to the Committee at the end of last year were responded to in terms that the Managers would not have welcomed. They were told off!

It was reported:-
That the Committee were of opinion that it would be useless to spray the playground with tar, and that the managers should be informed that they undertook, when the pathways were made, not to ask for anything further to be done; and that in these circumstances the Committee regret that they are unable to accede to the managers request.

Also it was reported;
That the Committee had decided that the managers should be informed that the Borough Surveyor had stated that in view of the high cost of building, the matter of the erection of the steps between Osborne Road and Balfour Road had been deferred for six months.

It would appear that this was the only meeting in 1919 that Loder Road School was mentioned in the Minutes. One plausible explanation about this lack of activity would be that by 1919, there was evidence in the public domain that the new school was gradually becoming a reality. If so, then it must have been tempting to continue to mark time on any requests to improve the facilities at Loder Road School. There was also the hangover from the war efforts that were suggested in 1917 to explain the lack of meetings of Managers then (two).

> **In 1920** – there was no doubt about the imminence of new school with both Heads submitting suggestions for its development. Miss Mills will have been pleased to see the building of the steps down from Osborne Road even though it took 15 years to come about after her first letter was sent.

The Managers received a report about the effects of the War on the work done in the classroom

The school has been working 'double sessions' during the war:
Arithmetic: The work is of fair quality but the subject is taught on somewhat mechanical lines and is probably based too exclusively on the example books in use. There is a very poor supply of rulers.
Composition: The books do not contain as much written composition as they ought to do and the work does not rise above average. The imaginative subjects are set. A quality mark is given and in Standard 4 there is some attempt to mark for ideas.

This rather confirms the problems that were apparent in the earlier report that Mr Weeks wrote about the loss of art work. The above suggests that even the basic subjects suffered. Perhaps the best way to understand the difficulties of maintaining the education system during a world war is in the words of the scholar, Owen Williams who was at Loder Road School at the time. This is a paragraph from his description of days spent at this time.

> *"Teachers were now mainly women, lessons, morning only. Another school took over in the afternoons, their premises requisitioned for war purposes. Maps showing the progress of the war were chalked on to blackboards as various battles were fought. Dire consequences awaiting us if Kaiser Bill and Little Willie won the war filled our hearts with dread. We set-to with a will, sewing coarse material into sandbags, one of the tasks we were given in place of some of our lessons. This probably encouraged us to think we were doing our bit, but did little for our education".*

The next Minute confirms that, by 1920, there was no doubt that the new school was on the horizon.

A letter (2.6.20) was received from Miss Mills making certain suggestions as to the new school, and Miss Mills and Mr Weeks were in attendance and conferred with the Managers on the matter.

Resolved:- That the letter from Miss Mills suggesting certain features in the construction of the new school be forwarded to the Sites and Works Sub-Committee for their favourable consideration and that the Sub-Committee be informed that the Managers have carefully considered these suggestions in consultation with Miss Mills and Mr Weeks and that they approve the suggestions generally and specifically recommend that the following suggestions be adopted and included in the plans under preparation.

1. *A separate Hall for the use of the infants*
2. *An extra room to the ordinary classrooms to be used for various purposes (Handiwork, Play, Rest, Dining or Relief Room), such a room to be fitted with folding tables from the walls and provided with 2 long trestle tables, also a sand corner, and later to be provided with hammock, mats, toys, etc.*
3. *A Teachers' Common Room, Head Teacher's Room and adequate Lavatory accommodation for the staff.*
4. *All rooms to be fitted with ample cupboard room for teachers and low cupboards and lockers for the children's use. Shelves can be formed by the tops of the small cupboards. Window-sills should be wide and hanging book shelves fitted for use of the school.*

Suggestion by the Headmaster:-
That, in addition to a staff room, an extra room fitted for practical work should be provided in each of the Boys' and Girls' departments.

> **Note:** Miss Mills' suggestion about a separate Hall and an additional room for general use for her department, which didn't happen, would have prevented so many arguments and improved the conditions in which the children were able to work in class. The Senior School didn't get the extra rooms for practical work for the Boys' and Girls' departments and, as we will see, the two departments didn't survive the reorganisation of education in Brighton in 1928, when it became the Senior Girls School.

It was reported that the Committee had decided:-

1. That consideration of the question of the provision of new desks for the Mixed Department should be deferred until the general question of the supply of desks is under consideration.
2. That the question of the provision of new blinds for the Infants' Department should be deferred pending decision on the question of repair and re-decoration of the blinds.
3. To inform Miss Mills that they regret that the new Scale will not permit exceptional treatment being applied in her case.

Note: the new "Scale" was the first indication that the Burnham Committee had started its work in setting national salary rates for schoolteachers, a system that was to remain in force for much of the 20th Century.

At last, they have arrived!

In July 1920, the long-awaited steps between Osborne Road and Balfour Road that had been further delayed at the end of last year were finally built. Miss Mills first wrote about the need for them in 1905.

> **In 1921** – the two Heads may have had their sights set on the new building but spent much of this year in their never-ending battle to improve the old one. Never-ending and they were rarely successful. The phrase that had popped up on a number occasions in the past, "it is only a temporary building", must have still been in the minds of the Managers. The name of Miss Young re-appeared in this year and would do so on many occasions later on.

The first letter of the year is a reminder that needlework was still a permanent feature on the girls' curriculum.

A letter (15.3.21 from Mr Weeks requesting the provision of a Sewing Machine, was received. Resolved:- That the letter from Mr Weeks be forwarded to the Requisition Branch Sub-Committee, with a strong recommendation that the request be granted.

Was the next item the start in the development of a system of school catchment areas; a system with which we are familiar today?

An extract from the Annual Report of the Headmistress of the Infants' Department, which suggested a partial remedy for the congestion in the northern part of the town, was submitted. *It was agreed that the matter should be further considered at the next meeting, and that particulars should be obtained as to names, ages, classes in which they were taught and the addresses of all scholars in attendance at Ditchling Road Infants' and Preston Road Infants' Schools, who reside in the neighbourhood of Loder Road School.*

The next item was first raised by Miss Mills early in 1918.

A reference from the Finance Sub-Committee as to increased consumption of gas during the *March, 1921 quarter, as compared with the same quarter last year, were submitted and Miss Mills and Mr Weeks, who were present, and reported in regard to the matter.*

Resolved:- That the Finance Sub-Committee be informed that the Managers have conferred with the Head teachers in this matter and that the following considerations are put forward in explanation of the increased consumption of gas:-

1. *It is understood that leakages have been frequently reported which were left unrepaired for several weeks. (The attention of the Sites and Works Sub-Committee is being called to this matter.)*

2. *That more gas had undoubtedly been used owing to the darkness of the rooms which must be in a more dirty condition than a year ago, whilst there are but a few pictures to relieve the depression.*

3. *The mantles are defective and there is no stock kept at the school from which broken ones could be replaced.*

Resolved :- That the Sites and Works Sub-Committee be informed that it is stated that leakages of gas at this school have been frequently reported which were left unrepaired for several weeks.

What follows are yet more requests for improvements to be made to the old building in the build-up to the new school being opened. Information from other sources like the local press, which indicated that parents were vocal in their frustration at the length of time it had taken to replace the Tin Hut.

It was agreed that the Surveyor should be requested to arrange for a hole in the fence close to the children's offices (lavatories) to be repaired immediately, and also for the locks on the outer doors of the school to be repaired to prevent the school being over-run in out of school hours.

Resolved:- That the Sites and Works Sub-Committee be informed that it is understood that the boiler needs attention before next winter, and that the new blinds, which were requested in February last, are urgently needed for the classrooms at the school in view of the present hot weather.

1. A letter (19.7.1921) was received from Mr Weeks requesting that the roof of the school might be whitewashed during the forthcoming summer holidays.

   It was agreed that Mr Weeks should be informed that the request could not be entertained as no funds are available for this work.

2. A letter (19.7.1921) from Miss Mills requesting the provision of a disused Army hut for an extension of the open air classes was received,

   Resolved:-That the letter from Miss Mills be referred to the Sites and Works Sub-Committee for consideration.

This next item was more significant than most staff changes as outlined below.

Resignation of Miss W Mitchell, TCA in the Mixed Department, was submitted
It was resolved that the resignation be accepted and to take effect on 21st December 1921.

An appointment of a successor to Miss Mitchell was considered, a letter (9.12.1921) was received from Mr Weeks in regard to the candidates. And Mr Weeks attended the meeting on the matter.

Miss E.A. Young then had an interview with the Managers and, on her giving the Managers an undertaking that she would endeavour to qualify herself to teach the needlework at the school, it was:

Resolved:- That Miss E A Young at present a temporary Assistant at Coombe Road Boys School, be appointed as a TCA in the Mixed Department for a period of six months on trial, in place of Miss Mitchell at a rate of £222.10s, according to the Scale of the Committee, to date from January 1st 1922, to be subject to one month's notice to expire at the end of any calendar month and is made in accordance with the terms of Art 15 (a), Clause (1) of the Code of Regulations for Public Elementary Schools.

It was agreed that Miss Young's permanent appointment should be considered in June next.

Miss Young became a good friend of Miss Seward who was soon to become the Head of the Infants' Department of Loder Road School. She went on to deputise for Miss Seward as Acting Head of Balfour Road School, once at the time of Miss Seward's death in October 1945 and a second time to deputise for Miss Seward's replacement when she became seriously ill. Finally, in 1947, she was appointed as the Head teacher of Hertford Road School.

In 1922 – there were a limited number of meetings but the issues dealt with during them, were very important ones. First, there was a concern about the gardening lessons, then an awkward HMI report that needed some diplomacy and finally, the resignation of Miss Mills followed swiftly by the appointment of a new Head teacher, Miss Seward.

Seemingly as regular as the changing of the Seasons, gardening questions start the New Year.

Question of further use of ground at Loder Road School for gardening instruction was considered and Mr Weeks who was present, reported on the matter.

Resolved:- That the Elementary Schools Sub-Committee be informed that the Managers have carefully considered the question referred to them as to whether more use could be made of the ground at Loder Road for gardening instruction and they have ascertained that in the nineteen plots which are cultivated by the boys, there is twice as much ground as is required by the Board of Education, that a large part of the ground is not fit for cultivation as the soil is poisoned by water which drains into it from the surrounding district and that the Managers are of opinion that there is no further ground which can be economically used and also that any change would not be worthwhile in view of the contemplated erection of the new building.

Resolved:- That the Committee be informed that the Headmaster has brought to the notice of the Managers that the fence at the School which was recently repaired is not high enough to prevent persons in the neighbourhood from making a short cut across the school gardens.

The Chairman submitted a letter he had received from the Rev. G E Page in regard to the Report on the Loder Road School.

EDUCATION COMMITTEE FOR THE COUNTY BOROUGH OF BRIGHTON

LODER ROAD SCHOOL   No. 14

Copy of Report by H.M.I. Mr. E. F. Davidson, after visit of the 16th April, 1922

MIXED

After every allowance has been made for the prolonged "double-session" period and for the difficulties of temporary premises, it cannot be said that this school is in a satisfactory state. The teachers are diligent, but except in the First Class, do not secure the attention and co-operation of the children. The work does not reach a high standard, though some of that in the First Class is creditable.

The Head teacher has not made any periodical reports on the various classes, and there is very little evidence of that vigorous supervision on his part which the circumstances demand.

The following additional points were mentioned to him:-

The possibility of his relieving the teacher of the First Class by making himself responsible for a small group of the most advanced children.

The number of old and backward children who have failed to reach the First Class, and for whom some special provision is desirable.

The further extension of sectional work, especially in Arithmetic and Reading.

Various points in the Schemes of Work, such as the provision of Science lessons for the upper classes, and the widening of the English syllabus so as to include Literature lessons for all the children; and the intensive study of short passages for the older ones.

INFANTS':

The work is thoroughly planned and supervised, and the teachers carry it out diligently and conscientiously. The children are happy and industrious, and reach a very creditable level of attainments at the top of the School.

Individual work in the elementary subjects has been well developed, and much useful apparatus in connection with it has been devised.

Nature walks and the cultivation of small garden plots are good features, but it is doubtful that enough time is given to Nature and Observation lessons and to other forms of Language Training, or to Handwork

Resolved:- That the Elementary School Sub-Committee be informed that the Managers consider the Report of the H.M. Inspector on Loder Road Infants' School to be generally very satisfactory

and that they are satisfied with the explanation of Miss Mills as to the concluding paragraph of the Report.

Resolved:- That the Elementary Schools Sub-Committee be informed that the Managers have carefully considered the Report of the H.M. Inspector on the Mixed Department and regret that in respect of the given written reports, the criticism of the H.M. Inspector appears to be justified.

The Managers feel that the Headmaster should have made periodical reports on the various classes as is usual and have arranged for this to be done in the future. They have received Mr Weeks' explanation as to the absence of such reports and have ascertained that reports of the children's progress are made half yearly and that verbal reports have been made by Mr Weeks to the teachers but that these have not been recorded. Mr Weeks has made himself acquainted with the progress of the various children in the School.

With regard to the question of the Headmaster's supervision, they have obtained from Mr Weeks' particulars of his work as regards supervision covering a period of some months and are satisfied that has given as much supervision to the various classes as is necessary or possible in the circumstances in which he is placed.

Unfortunately, Mr Weeks did not communicate these particulars to the Inspector before the latter made his report. Mr Weeks attributes his some of his difficulties to an inexperienced staff and, as he considers, an insufficient staff.

The Managers feel that they have, in Mr Weeks a capable and conscientious Headmaster.

So, not for the first time, the Managers stood by their Head teacher in the face of HMI criticisms although they did acknowledge that some of his actions might have been done differently.

In May 1922, Managers agreed that *staff must be reduced by one teacher (Mr Creswell, Supernumerary) who shall be required to seek a transfer within a reasonable time to departments where vacancies occur. Mr Creswell to be available for service at other schools as required in the meantime.*

In the way that the Managers approached this situation it appears that they may have held some form of register of teachers who were available for work – perhaps a very early version of 'supply' staff, though this one was organised by the local authority.

And now there was a very significant staffing development in the Infants Department.

It was reported that Miss Mills, Head Mistress of the Infants' Department had been appointed Head Mistress of Lewes Road Infants' School. A letter (17.7.1922) of resignation from Miss Mills was submitted.

Resolved:- That the resignation of Miss E. Mills, to take effect on August 31st 1922, be accepted.

Resolved:- That the Managers place on record an expression of their thanks and appreciation of the excellent service rendered by Miss E Mills during the 27½ years she has been connected to this Board of Management. After 10 years as a Assistant at Ditchling Road Infants' School, Miss Mills became the first Head Mistress of the Infants' Department of Loder Road Temporary School, where in spite of great difficulties and

---

discouraging conditions, the results have been such as to evoke satisfactory reports from H.M. Inspectors. Whilst parting with her services with much regret, the Managers congratulate Miss Mills on her appointment as Head Mistress of Lewes Road Infants' School, where with the larger number of scholars and more convenient premises, the Managers feel she will have wider scope for her undoubted abilities.

Having read all of the 17 years worth of diary entries made by Miss Mills, one can fully appreciate the Managers' assessment of a job well done despite the incredibly difficult circumstances.

The next meeting received the following letter from Miss Seward who had been appointed as Head Mistress of the Infants' Department in place of Miss Mills.

A letter (19.9.1922) was received from Miss Seward as to the obsolete and unsuitable desks in the Infants' Department and applying for a zinc-lined tray and an additional cupboard. Resolved:- That the letter from Miss Seward be forwarded to the Sites and Works Sub-Committee with a request that the matters may receive their favourable consideration.

However, the reply to this request was rather swift: *That the Committee are unable to supply new desks and tables and chairs for the Infants' Department at present, but are dealing with requests in order of urgency, and they regret that have no funds available to supply an additional cupboard or a zinc-lined tray, but that the Requisition Branch Sub-Committee had been asked to make provision in next year's Estimate for the supply of the cupboard.*

In 1923 - the penultimate year of the Loder Road School's existence, there was a very limited number of items to be dealt with (just two). This situation has frequently prevailed since the start of WW1. Here, Miss Young's temporary appointment was converted to a permanent one and the Heads of the two schools submitted more suggestions relating to the plans for the new building, which were duly passed to the appropriate sub-committee.

Question of permanent appointment of Miss E. A. Young TCA, Mixed Department, was considered, and a letter (20.2.23) from Mr Weeks recommending her permanent appointment was submitted
Resolved:- That Miss Young who has been working on trial in the school for a period of 12 months be now permanently appointed at a salary rate of £202.10s per annum. This appointment will date from 1st March 1923, will be subject to one months notice, such notice to expire at the end of any calendar month and made in accordance with the terms of Art18 (a), Clause (1) of the Code of Regulations for Public Elementary Schools.

In July 1923, letters from the Headmaster and Headmistress were received requesting modifications in the plans for the new school.

Resolved:- Letters from the two Heads of Loder Road School as to the planning of the new school are referred to the Sites and Works Sub-Committee for consideration.
It was agreed that Mr Weeks and Miss Seward should be informed that the Managers have taken the only course open to them and have sent the letters on for consideration by the Sites and Works Sub-Committee, which is the Committee responsible for carrying out the plans.

> **At last, 1924 has arrived** – and now we get to the long-awaited moment when the new building for Balfour Road School would be opened and the Tin Hut consigned to the scrap heap, probably literally so, given its dilapidated condition.

As can been seen from the very limited number of Loder Road items that appeared in the Minutes recently, the Managers had little day-to-day involvement in the building of the new school. This would have been undertaken by an appropriate committee of the Education Committee.

That said, we will see that the first few meetings in January represented the calm before the storm.

On 14th January 1924 the *question of the appointment of Caretaker was considered and a letter from Mr Weeks as to the desirability of the Caretaker living near to the school was submitted*
It was agreed that the question should be further considered at the next meeting and that the present temporary Caretaker (Mr Jupp) should then appear before the Managers for interview.

Two days later on the 16th January 1924, a very significant entry in the Minute Journal for Loder Road School was made, which confirmed the names of the Head teachers who would take charge of the new school – the Balfour Road Junior Mixed and Senior Mixed Departments.

It was reported that the Education Committee had appointed Mr W Weeks and Miss H F Seward as Head Teachers of the Senior Mixed and Junior Mixed Departments respectively of the new Loder Road School.

But, a week before the new school was due to open, the Managers may have been rather surprised to receive Mr Weeks' letter of resignation as Headmaster of the Mixed Department.

They resolved that the resignation should be accepted with regret, to take effect on 31st March 1924.

Mr Weeks was appointed a Headmaster of the Loder Road Temporary School in November 1908, after service as an assistant at Lewes Road School from June 1883 to January 1894 and afterwards as Headmaster of Circus Street School from February 1894 until November 1908. Mr Weeks has, therefore rendered 30 years service as a Headmaster in schools of a somewhat difficult character, in the first in the type of scholar and in the second in the matter of the premises. (However) he has always performed efficient and conscientious service and the Managers have had complete confidence in his work, which they warmly appreciate and for which they desire to thank him.
Mr Weeks will retire on the date mentioned under the Teachers Superannuation Act and the Managers tender him every good wish for many years of health and happiness in his well earned retirement.

A very Sad Note: A year after the new school opened, Miss Seward wrote in the Log Book about an issue involving the current Head teacher of the Senior School and the late Head teacher, implying that Mr Weeks must have died not long after leaving on 31st March 1924. Any reference to his death would presumably have been recorded in the Senior School's Log Book (which has not been found) and his death probably explains why he was forced to retire in the days before the new school opened.

At the same meeting it was *reported that the new school would be publically opened by Mr Morgan Jones*, M.P., and Parliamentary Secretary to the Board of Education on Wednesday, February 27th, next.*

*Morgan Jones (Labour) MP for Caerphilly; a teacher, trained at Reading University and Baptist lay-preacher, who was imprisoned as a conscientious objector and became the first MP to be elected having been a conscientious objector after WW1

However, before we finally leave the story of Loder Road (temporary) Balfour Junior School, there is one outstanding piece of its history that is contained in the Visitors' Book.

Finally from the Balfour Road Junior School Visitors' Book

The Visitors' Book was opened in 1907 and ran alongside the School Log Book, which had already been recording visits from day one in 1905. The emergence of the Visitors' Book two years later may partly explain why the number of entries in the Log Book suddenly declined. Visitors not only signed their names but, as might otherwise have been recorded in the Log Book, often described the outcome or impressions of their visit.

Like the very first entry. "Visited all classes, children all busily and happily at work. School as usual bright and cheerful. Attendance, in spite of inclement weather, very good."

Emily A Miller

For the next 81 years until the last entry in 1988, this leather-bound book held the recorded snippets of such information. Actually, the substance of the entries went through various, quite distinct phases almost as though, if one person decided to alter the format, all subsequent scribes followed suit. Emily Miller set the first phase on its way, which contains some stereotypical phrases reminiscent of school reports of yesteryear; eg 'a good terms work' or 'satisfactory progress made'.

So, visitors noted:

> *Much improved with order and efficiency*
> *Everything in good order*
> *Found everything satisfactory*
> *All going on quietly and well*
> *Children were very tidy and under good discipline*

In June 1905, Major Bloomfield popped in the give out the prizes, an event that, as later entries indicated, became an established occasion with a different local dignitary doing the honours each year. Perhaps not surprisingly, in view of the emphasis given in the visitors' comments quoted above, the prizes in these early years were for good conduct rather than academic progress made.

Major Bloomfield dominated the signature signing in the first five years, so frequent that he developed the habit of using just his initials, JAB. Once the journals holding the Minutes of the Managers' meetings were discovered, it was evident that he held a position of authority as Chair of the Managers' Committee. When he did note his purpose, which was not very often, he indicated that he was there to check the registers.

Another frequent visitor was Rev. G Corfield who always signed himself as MA (Oxon), Principal of Brighton Training College. The main purpose of his visits was to see the pupil-teachers who were in training at the college while they were working at the school.

By 1910, the pages of the Visitors' Book simply held signatures of a relatively small number of individuals who visited the school. Checking registers was probably the main purpose.

Between 1914 and 1918, there is no mention made of the First World War nor are there many signatures, just a handful each year made by two or three regulars.

After the War was over, the number of visitors to the school remained very low and it was not until 1921 that the picture changed significantly and class registers were again being checked and a few inspection reports (one-liners) were recorded. Now, for the first time, a stream of councillors visited the school and added their names to the book. The trigger for such interest was undoubtedly the imminent construction of the new primary school in Balfour Road.

On 4 September 1922, the Visitors Book read: *School taken over by Miss Seward.*

From then on, inspections and register checking were commonplace and on 11 December 1923, there was a sign of things to come with a meeting of the Sites and Works Sub-Committee led by Mr. Councillor Teasdale to *"consider suggestions sent by the Headmistress".*

On 8 February 1924, Mr Brooks visited the new school "re: *Programme of arrangements for the Opening Day.*

The "Opening Day" of the new Balfour is recorded elsewhere as 27 February 1924. But not, apparently, in its Visitors' Book. Perhaps everybody was too busy with the "Programme of arrangements".

Or, perhaps people were reflecting on the past 19 years in a more melancholy frame of mind, much as Owen Williams seemed to be doing in "Turn Back the Years" when he reflected on his life at the Tin Hut:

"And there it remained for the next 19 years or so, despite promises and assurances made from time to time. "Yes the school is shortly to be pulled down and you will be taught in a fine new one." But years went by, so did our school-days, our ugly old school remained, nothing materialised. In 1924, with my school days long passed the old school finally closed and the pupils were transferred to a brand new building".

So, Balfour Road School recommenced its life in that "brand new building" across the road.

Before resuming our journey through the records that were made by the Head teachers and Managers in Chapter Two, there are some photographs taken at the time, which will illustrate the transition from corrugated iron to bricks and mortar quite starkly.

Firstly, the object of the whole exercise – a photograph of the new school, which shows clearly the divisions of the playground with metal fences surrounding areas reserved for senior, junior and infant children, (older children would have been in the area closest to the camera).

While still at the Loder Road School, the next two photographs are of teachers outside the old building, presumably posing for the camera on the last day, before crossing the Loder Road to sit in the grounds of the new school beside the wooden fence that enclosed the site of the pond at the west end. The single photo of Miss Seward is undated but, if it wasn't taken on that day, the smile that lights up her face would I think, have been seen many times during it.

The aerial photograph of the surrounding area was printed in the Brighton Education Handbook, 1939, which also carried the one of Varndean School. It was opened in 1926, so was there on the campus but out-of-shot. Perhaps the aircraft involved wasn't high enough. Varndean Boys School, now the Sixth-form College, was opened in 1932

The barn, shown separately, can be seen at the far end of the group of buildings to the right of the woods, which have been reduced significantly to make room for the Dorothy Stringer Secondary School opened in 1955. The barn was used by a blacksmith in the time I was at Balfour at the end of the War. Many a lunch-time trip across the field was made to see him at work.

The postcard image is not dated but I have included it to show the tram shelter in the middle of the road opposite the end of Balfour Road. The tram rails can be seen in the road and the power lines above it. Trams began to be phased out during the 1930s as car use increased. Two vehicles can be seen parked below the shelter but the absence of any others suggest this picture was much earlier, closer to 1924. The fence at the left-hand side of the picture is where Dr Simpson's surgery was located and from where he would have travelled to Loder Road to patch up injured children as was reported several times in Miss Mills' Log Book.

Fig 19

Fig 20

Fig 21

Fig 22

Fig 23

VARNDEAN AND BALFOUR ROAD SCHOOLS—FROM THE AIR

Fig 24

VARNDEAN GIRLS' SCHOOL

Fig 25

Fig 26

Fig 27

Chapter Two

Section I

Entries made in the Junior School's Log Book (1924 – 1937)
Minutes of the Managers' meetings (1924 – 1937)
Log Book entries now that the School has been reorganised as a Junior and Infants' School

In the first full week after the opening, Miss Seward was still engaged in stocktaking while children were gradually returning after the epidemic levels of some of the illnesses. Many more returned in the following week and may have seen Miss Seward stocktaking the needlework stock and carrying out an examination of children's reading levels throughout the department.

By mid-March, the stresses and strains of managing the transfer were taking their toll. Miss Seward was absent with a severe chill and nervous exhaustion and Miss Puttock was absent for a month suffering from influenza, "leaving Miss Taylor to supervise the heavy duties of changing from Old to New". She was assisted in this by Miss Young who had been transferred from the Senior Dept. on 1st April and by a supply teacher from the Richmond Street School.

April was still regarded as the start of a new school and Miss Seward was back in time to publish the Organisation chart for 1924 – 1925.

Standard II	Miss E. Young	40
I	" E. Puttock	44
Grade 1	" H. C. Taylor	34
2	" E. Crawford	31
Nursery	" M. Knight	27
		176

H. F. Seward

Like the organisation chart in 1923, the biggest change in the Roll this year is again an increase in numbers of children admitted and the numbers in each class heading towards the class sizes that were still evident in the 1950s.

On the day before the start of the Easter holiday (17th April), a presentation was made to Mr Weeks who had announced his resignation as the Head of the Mixed Department a week before the new school opened. The Managers recorded in their Minutes an appreciation of his work at Loder Road School and in his career as a whole. They and other visitors attended the presentation to the man whose master stroke was to make the best use of a playground that didn't have proper surface, by turning part of it into allotments.

After the holiday, Miss Seward returned to stocktaking and furniture. More visitors visited and student teachers from the Diocesan College arrived to undertake teaching practice. Already, the new school was attracting attention of educationalists elsewhere interested in a new development and keen to learn any lessons from it. It is also understandable that the teacher training college wasn't too keen to approach the Loder Road School very often given the very difficult working conditions. Students would not have got an experience that could have matched that which they would encounter in other schools in Brighton.

So, we can expect to see more visitors and students arriving in the months ahead and, in the summer they will notice one of Miss Seward's distinctive approaches to learning – lessons and physical exercise out-of-doors whenever possible and wherever suitable; the lawns, playing field and the countryside around.

That said, the next entry recorded that a letter had been sent, presumably to the Sites and Works Committee about the need to cut the grass on the lawns and playing field, but that nothing had happened. Perhaps a more direct approach by phone had taken place shortly afterwards as Miss Seward observed the next day that two men were engaged in cutting the grass using scythes. She also agreed to "lend back" Miss Young to the Senior Department for Friday afternoons so that she could conduct swimming lessons.

There was more co-operation between the Heads when they agreed to co-ordinate the timing of play times to keep the age-groups apart.

What followed was an entry that might strike a chord with television viewers in 2015 but not in 1924 when Miss Seward welcomed a visitor from the Waterloo Road School in London.

Still in May, some teachers were engaged in building a rockery at the back of the school while their classes were being taken by another group of student teachers from the Diocesan College. While that was going on, Miss Seward was discussing with members of the Committee about the potential use of the space underneath the nursery classroom at the west end of the building, which she thought could be turned into a useful storeroom.

June must have been a good month for weather in 1924 because most of the entries in the Log Book record the many instances of outside activities of all (educational) kinds. The downside was the frequency of interruptions for the Hall class which were caused by continuous movement of children and teachers in and out of the room. *The Class Work is not speeding on as it might and the teacher is getting very nervously exhausted".* (The use of the Hall at Loder Road School had been a constant source of friction and Miss Seward had other occasions to express her concerns about the new Hall, which she did later on during one of the HMI inspections in the 1930s.)

At the end of June there was more work being done out-of-doors and one rather special event. "The whole school has been taken out to watch the haymaking going on in the surrounding fields. In organised games the children have played in the hay." Others went on observational walks in the Hollingbury area.

In July, one of the building adaptations that was needed in the light of experience after the first few months, was carried out when hand rails were fixed to the children's steps down from the verandah to the playground . However, the "Protection" fixed to the nursery window was, according to Miss Seward, *"useless. Such a rail enables the children to climb still higher, giving a firmer hold to the climber."*

The last week in July was occupied with examinations and marking across the school. The four-week summer holiday started at the end of the week.

New term started on 1st September and Miss Seward was able to report that many of the requested repairs had been carried out but there were still more to do. Something else she needed was a grant for a set of reading books for Standard II, the *"transferred stock was too poor, dilapidated and insufficient"*.

Like last September, the weather was inclement to the point where the classrooms had to be used for physical exercise.

By October, Miss Seward was still engaged with stock but took a moment to report (for the third time) the unsafe condition of the wash bowl in the first cloakroom. It is now propped up with a clay bin and slates.

Next week she reported that some things do get fixed – the Sun dial in the drive.

On 22nd October Miss Seward attended the ceremony of the Laying of the Foundation Stone for the new Secondary School (which was Varndean Girls School).

A week later, the third General Election in three years was held and this time, Balfour Road School was closed, unsurprisingly given the angry response the Loder Road School made last year over the use of the Hall which, like Balfour currently, was a classroom. (Stanley Baldwin's Conservative Party won power.)

Armistice Day was celebrated in a ceremony in the playground. A Poppy and Lily of the Valley wreath was subsequently placed on the Brighton War Memorial by Monitors of the School in the charge of teachers.

At the end of November, 250 bulbs were planted in the lawn.

The Christmas holiday started after a week of low attendance caused by the usual range of illnesses.

1925

The new term started on 12th January with a Roll of 191, the highest noted so far. On Friday, the school closed early so that children could attend the Dome Mission Tea at 4.00pm

Later in January, the two Heads met to discuss the April promotions from Junior to Senior Departments. The problem that was presenting itself was the effect that the War had had on birth rates in its wake. Junior schools had been experiencing the drop in Rolls for some years and now the problem had arrived at the senior schools. It was no surprise that there were no solutions on offer to solve this problem.

In the first week of February Miss Seward was engaged in examining the monthly test papers and in the second week took the St II class for mathematics.
Two HMI inspectors visited in the third week and Mr Davidson eventually wrote the Report, which was considered by the Managers.
In the last week, the Handwork lessons were limited to allow more time for teaching Arithmetic and Reading "to the lower division of each class". This was ninety years ago when Miss Seward devised a scheme to help all children in a class keep up to a common standard. A rather different approach to that taken by Mr Weeks ten years earlier when he developed the gardening curriculum for boys of below average ability.

In March, Miss Seward looked again at the issue of imbalance in class sizes due to the drop in birth rate. The Roll of the Junior School was rising steadily and was the highest it had been for three years. She wrote: *"The classes are small at the top of the school, but are filling up at the bottom. The average age of the Draft for the Senior School is about 9.6 yrs. Good work had been done in the top class. The one regret is that they cannot be retained until the actual Scholarship age. There are some very promising bright children".*

Mr Davidson's HMI Report was received in March and Miss Seward had her say about it in a letter to the Managers.
Back to the earlier issue of pupil movement from Junior to Senior classes.
Miss Seward repeated a note written in March 1924 by Mr Cole who signed that the register for St III was found to be correct. The Resolution sent by the Education Committee (copied into the Log Book in February 1924) confirmed that the age for transfer to Senior School was fixed at 10 yrs. Therefore, Miss Seward concluded that *"it was obvious that St III is part of the Junior, not the Senior School".*

At the beginning of April, Miss Seward seems to have continued to display her assertive manner when required. In her words:
A dispute has arisen in respect of the Junior class that needs to be accommodated in the Hall. The Headmaster does not admit that the South side is already the portion allocated to the Junior School. The late Headmaster and present Headmistress had decided the question at stake twelve months ago, before the present Headmaster commenced duties here. The Hall has been vacated each Assembly morning, but the Headmaster refuses to use it until the dispute is settled. He maintains that if the South side is used by the Juniors, he should have it for four periods per week. As there is no space to accommodate these young children, it is not justifiable to turn them out.

April is also the start of the new academic year and Miss Seward completed all the necessary form- filling and schemes of work and before setting down the staff organisation list, she made the point that no supply teacher had been provided for the extra St III class. This was being taken by Miss Knight, who transferred earlier from the Seniors but Miss Seward was still a teacher short.

After Easter, Miss Puttock was again absent and Miss Seward had to re-organise classes and was no doubt pleased to welcome another batch of student teachers who could help to bridge the gaps. This may have given her a useful respite to collect her thoughts for the Managers' meeting at the end of April.
Both Headteachers were called to the meeting to discuss which school should occupy the South side of the Hall. A Sub-Committee had been appointed to come to inspect the Hall. Two (Mrs. Reid and Mr. Long) suggest that it is possible to turn the babies out of the Nursery in order to use their room for Rhythmics. This, the Headmistress refuses to do. It is not justifiable to turn them out and seat them in desks where children from 6 – 10 years of age sit. "They do in many schools" was the argument and "they did ten years back". The result of the meeting was to be reported to the Managers. The Junior children cannot vacate the Hall for six periods a week to allow the Senior curriculum to be carried on. There is no where to put them unless they are congregated in another classroom. <u>It is impossible to accommodate two Handworks and four other lessons each week</u>

Miss Seward underlined her own message for all to read.

The next day, she was absent with a bad throat. (Maybe, her blood pressure was a bit high as well.)

She was back at work on Monday12th May, and in time to read the Managers' conclusion to the dispute. They decided that the Senior School should occupy the South Side and furniture was transferred on the Friday. (Miss Mills had anticipated this situation in 1920 when arguing for two Halls.)

A few days later, it was reported that class V had been "swept" with measles and whooping cough, not something one might expect as summer approaches.
In the same week, the young children have now been accommodated at the North end of the Hall where they cannot get in and out. The door is unmanageable. (This was a bit before the Health and Safety Act was introduced.)
By the next week, the measles and whooping cough outbreak had spread throughout the School and the Medical Officer, Dr. Forbes ordered that the Whitsun Holiday should be increased by a further week.

By the time the school reassembled after the holiday, there were still 59 children absent and whooping cough was still affecting children into July.
The Annual School Outing had been held on the previous Saturday when a char-a-banc took 39 children on a trip to Beachy Head and Eastbourne and back through Lewes. Enjoyment all round was the verdict and two more weekday summer trips were made to the Booth Museum in Dyke Road. Lots of lessons were held outside as might have been expected and may have been witnessed by five visiting mayors from Japan.
However, the term ended on a damp note with illnesses still prevailing, wind and rain, and low attendance caused partly by children going on holiday early with parents.

The new term started on 31st August with "everywhere nicely cleaned" but the grasses were out of control again. Miss Seward's main concern was the continued failure to provide the additional teacher she had requested. Still taking the young children's class, which she said was "completely unacceptable" as she needed to be free to supervise the whole school. She wanted to teach in every class and take games to get a good impression of progress that was being made. She still took the needlework class when the younger children had to be dispersed across all classes.
Therefore, yet another letter was posted to the Managers. Whether or not coincidental, Mr Shearer soon visited followed by another manager, Mr. Coun Aldrich who saw that the grass was so overgrown that games were impossible.

On 5th October there was an Open Day to celebrate the Harvest Festival. (A description of the Festival that was held in 1932, which was the subject of an article in the local Press, can be found at the end of the Section II following the 1930s oral histories.)
The format of the festival changed little over the years.

No change in the saga of the 'missing' extra teacher, so the school examinations were cancelled as a result. Later, the weather turned rough and the children's clothes were getting wet because the exit doors couldn't be shut.

Another letter was duly sent to the Managers.

Miss Puttuck was sick again in the last week of October, so Miss Seward had to look after two classes, this time with the help of a 'supply' teacher. She will have been pleased to have reached half-term at the end of the week

After half-term, the Roll had risen to 225. Very unhelpfully, the Committee had again refused to sanction an extra teacher to compensate for the class that was transferred to the Infants. There were now 45 more children in the Infants than in the Senior School with one teacher less so it was of little compensation that a groundsman then arrived to start to tidy the grounds.

With bad weather signalling the advent of winter, the MOH excluded two children until Christmas because of whooping cough and noted a suspicion of measles in the nursery class.

In mid-November, the simmering tension between the two Heads surfaced when Mr.Toyne called them for a meeting at the Education Office on 12th November at the request of the Managers to settle the dispute about promotions to the Senior School. As had become her approach in such matters, Miss Seward resorted to using the Log Book to record her side of the story for all to see.

She wrote *"that there was "really no dispute". A conference of the two Heads was held in the last week of September and informed that there <u>were no children ready</u>. From the course of the conversation, Mr Hughes mistrusted the Head Mistress and apparently applied for permission to examine as well as the Head Mistress, thus impinging on her prerogative.*
This is the first year that the Std. III has been attached to the Junior School. The children in this class were those backward children of Std. II in 1924 – 1925 plus children promoted from Std. I. It stands to reason that there cannot be any promotions as they have already missed the course of Std. II. The brighter section of Std. II of 1924 – 1925 were promoted to the Senior School <u>but Mr Hughes said</u> they could not go to the Std. IV proper because they could not write. They were kept down until October (Std. IV Lower) working with children of below average ability, who were being taught by the teacher who had Std. III last year, she being allowed to be retained in the Department instead of coming down to take Std. III in the Junior School".

(That does appear to have been a pretty persuasive argument. And Miss Seward continued her practice of underlining key points for emphasis.)

Armistice Day was celebrated in the same way as last year and a further example of the way in which Miss Seward was organising activities to her own educational prescription – maximum use of lessons out-of-doors, an annual outing, a Harvest Festival and teaching across the School to keep in touch with progress.

During 1925, a series of post-card photographs were taken of outside activities, which Miss Seward clearly encouraged, breaking free from the confines of the Loder Road School. We have already seen photographs of her with some of the teachers as they left the old school last year, so perhaps these were seen as part of a pictorial record of the transformation that was taking place in Balfour Road. Most had been kept stored at the school and, 90 years on, they still provide recognisable glimpses of the past while presenting pictures of openness that one would expect to see in the first few years at the school.

Fig 28

Fig 29

By 1924, the steps built in 1920 had been flanked by new properties. Not identifiable in the left-hand photograph above, are two house, Nos.140 and 140A that were built behind what was the last house in Balfour Road, No.138 in 1920. On the other side of the steps are No.142, the Cole's Laundry, and 144, 146 & 148, which are still in place today. By the end of this history, in 1955 the Laundry had become the Four-square Gospel Church and today it has been replaced by semi-detached houses 142A and 142B. The recent photograph on the right-hand side above was taken at the end of the flight of steps and Nos. 140 and 140A can now be seen behind the fence on the right.

Fig 30

Another picture of the entrance drive showing the wide open spaces that lay beyond the school and the last houses in Balfour Road. They were soon to be filled by the new school, Varndean Girls, built two years later and the rest of Balfour Road's houses by 1931. Below, are pictures of out-door activities on the lawn of the infants/juniors' end of the school – with one escapee. Going home or to spend a penny, perhaps.

Fig 31   Fig 32

Below is another early picture; definitely one of the infants at play on the lawn

Fig 33

With a backdrop of Loder Road, a more formal outside activity with rows of boys and girls which looks a bit like the earlier photograph of the Drill lesson at the turn of the century – but I don't think that is what is happening here.

Fig 34

Is this an Armistice Day ceremony by the flagstaff? The coats could point to an autumnal day

Fig 35

The last four weeks leading up to the Christmas Holiday was full of all the seasonal activities one would expect, which were interspersed with class examinations, marking, classroom decorations and a carol concert in the Hall to which parents were invited. This must have been quite a tight squeeze for, as we will see later, Miss Seward did complain to the HMIs about the inadequate size of the Hall. I can confirm that it was small and it remained so, unaltered to and beyond my time there.

Apparently, Miss Seward used the Carol Concert to address the parents attending with a reading of the School Fund balance sheet and a short discourse on school social life. Her Log Book entry then reports that "many contributions were received". One can assume that the 'reading' and the 'contributions' was an example of cause and effect.

The final piece written that year in the Log Book was clearly another one for 'public' consumption in her battle to get the extra teacher so that she would be being treated fairly by comparison with the staffing level of the Senior School.
"The classes have been re-organised to free the Head Mistress from the responsibility of a class so that she may assist at each class and thoroughly know the school. It is impossible to carry on successfully any other way. No new teacher having been granted for the new class, the Head Mistress finds duties to pressing and difficult to carry on with the class of six year olds, thus the class is dispersed for the remaining three months".
(She didn't underline the piece this time but I guess the page on which it was written will have been in full view whenever a Manager visited in the New Year)

1926.
The School re-opened on 13 January 1926 with Miss Seward enacting the re-organisation she outlined before Christmas by dispersing Class IV, the more advanced children to Class III and the lower division to Class V. This freed her to look after the lower division of Std. I and gave her the time to cope with the immense amount of clerical duties this term.
Winter weather ruled out the use of the playing field for much of January

In February, Miss Seward reported on a Staff Meeting that had been called to discuss many points for improvement in the tone of the School.

Standards III and II were taken to the Dome on Thursday afternoon (4th Feb) to see the "Livingstone" film. The party was conducted by the Head Mistress and two class teachers. (68 children were taken). It was a silent film biography of the life of the African missionary, David Livingstone, made in 1925.

Later in February, the children were allowed to spend some time tidying-up and digging the garden at the back of the school. (So, the gardening initiative started by Mr Weeks at the Loder Road site, was maintained at the new School).

When the children returned after the half-term break the weather was warm enough for more outside activities – recreation and reconstructing the Rockery ready for re-planting.

Into March and on the first Saturday, a Ramble was held. Twenty children, who had worked well during the term, were taken on a ramble with the staff. In fact, it involved a walk to Ditchling Beacon and a return home from Hassocks by train. At a rough guess, this would have been an eight mile walk from School to the Beacon and down to Underhill Lane and exiting from there, taking the footpath alongside the rail track to the Hassocks platform.

The new academic year started on 13th April with the lower part of the School full with largely very young children and Miss Seward recognised that Miss Knight's Class V would be a difficult one with such a wide range of ages. As usual, the start of the year meant the completion of much paperwork including the Annual Report, which was sent to the Education Office by the end of the month.

At the same time, an application was made for a new teacher to replace Miss Crawford who had submitted a letter of resignation. The hope was for a teacher to be in place by the Whitsun break to avoid the need for a supply teacher. Things seemed to have moved quickly because Miss Seward was given the opportunity to assess the strengths of the candidates for the post and Miss English was appointed on 19th May.

However, when the School returned after the Whitsun Break, it was discovered that Miss English would not be joining the staff until 1st July so the supply teacher Miss Reeve was required after all.

Into June and there was an invitation to all teachers (12th June) to visit the new secondary school (Varndean Girls) on the Balfour campus.
Back to an old issue – Miss Seward sent the Managers another letter still seeking that illusive extra teacher now that even more four year olds had been admitted.

Two school closures on the 17th and 23rd for treats at St Matthias and Gordon Road respectively followed, on Saturday 26th June by the School Outing to Arundel via the coast and Worthing. Two Char-a-Bancs carried the children and visitors on the trip starting at 9.30am and ended back at school at 7.30pm.
Yet more treats on 29th June when the School was closed so that children could attend them at the churches of St. John's and St. Augustine.

On the 1st of July, the girls from Std. III were taken on a visit to the Booth Museum of Natural History in Dyke Road by two members of staff; a trip that was repeated for the boys on the next Thursday, also accompanied by two members of staff.

As expected, Miss English joined the staff this month but, unexpectedly, was unable to teach and was signed off for six weeks being seriously ill and said to be near to breakdown.

This left Miss Seward two teachers short again. As usual, she made noises towards the Managers to get the replacement and the extra teacher. She was successful in getting Miss Reeve on supply but the cover for her fell on deaf ears.
Instead, she was involved in selecting the School's gramophone records for use next term.
The term ended with the children being photographed in their classes.

The School reassembled on 30th August with 17 new entrants including one girl from a private school who was discovered to be "very backward and extremely delicate and hardly fit for Std. II".

Miss Seward now had 44 children in the nursery class and still no teacher.
Miss M. Wilson had arrived to replace Miss English who presumably must have resigned due to ill health.
Miss Seward carried out a re-organisation of classes II, II and IV because of the extra numbers of children and also because several rooms were not designed to hold them. She also made yet another request for an extra teacher and used to the Log Book to stress the point by setting out the statistics.

In 1924 the Roll was 176 with accommodation for 280. Now in 1926, the Roll is 263 (nearly a 50% increase) and the two smaller classrooms were accommodating more than the maximum of 40. Or, as Miss Seward wrote; *"Although the numbers show an increase of 87 the staff remains the same"*.

The autumn half-term ends today, 24th September and tomorrow, Friday, a half-day holiday was granted so that teachers could attend the Class Teachers' Conference and Miss Seward as granted leave to visit the Kennington Road L.C.C. Infants' School.
Miss Reeve was sent on Supply in the next week for temporary duties until the additional teacher is appointed.
(That last sentence needed a second reading – was this really the teacher that Miss Seward has been requesting for months?)
Perhaps it really was, as Miss Seward was sent correspondence a few days later seeking her observations. Presumably the correspondence contained the application forms.

It clearly was, as the managers met and filled both posts. The first teacher appointed was for the Infant's School as Miss Seward wanted but, unfortunately, her advice on the second one was ignored. A senior teacher for Needlework and Music was required as these subjects could be interchanged and worked between two senior mistresses. It is extremely difficult to arrange a good working timetable under existing circumstances, Miss Seward said, and in her view the second appointment was unsatisfactory.

Very quickly (25th October), Miss Boxall arrived to teach in the Infants' School just at the time when another outbreak of chicken pox was reported.

On 5th November, Miss Seward was summoned to the Office of Mr Toyne, the Secretary to the Education Committee to discuss the disputed 'second appointment'.

In the next week, the children watched a Children's Welfare Cinema show in the Hall. The subject of the film was "The Harvest of the Sea" and, at the end of the week, the annual Armistice Day celebration was held and this year, it was Miss Seward who escorted the small group of children to lay the wreath at the War Memorial at the Old Steine.

Christmas celebrations were slightly different this year because Miss Seward introduced something of an innovation by arranging three social evenings for groups of older children in addition to the Carol Concert to which parents were invited.

Just before the Christmas holidays, Miss Boxall was absent because of her mother's ill-health. The 23rd December was the last day of term and it was necessary to call for quantities of sand to be spread on the playground and surrounds because the icy conditions.

1927

The School reopened on the 10th January 1927 and on the 12th there was a visit from the HMI inspector. Welcome to the New Year.

Life soon returned to normal with an outbreak of mumps in the nursery class
Later in the month the attendance was down to 75% because influenza had arrived and was affecting staff as well. Miss Puttock was absent and so was Miss Boxall following the death of her mother. Shortly after this, the MOH closed the School until the first week of February when the attendance had fallen to 47%.

When it reopened in February, influenza was still prevalent and supply teachers were standing in for Misses Puttock and Boxall who now had influenza as well. By the middle of February the attendance level was creeping up and Miss Seward would have been content to welcome four student teachers who could provide some relief by filling some of the gaps in staffing. Two helped in Std. II and two in Std. III.

Half-term was Monday, 7th March and by then, the effects of winter illnesses had subsided.
Highlights recorded in March included a record number on the Roll of 278 (School accommodation was set at 280), a Welfare Lantern Lecture in the Hall and 3 Overalls and 2 Cakes entered in the Handicrafts and Hobbies Exhibition. One child's cake was 'Highly Commended'. Finally, an afternoon holiday was granted at the end of March on the occasion of a visit to Brighton by the Prince of Wales.

Apart from regular attendance figures, not much else of note was entered into the Log Book until just before the Easter holiday that started on 14th April when whooping cough cases were reported along with mumps. The MOH again stepped in and excluded two classes affected until 9th May.

After Easter, a letter was sent to Mr Toyne about the dangerous condition of the temporary wall in classroom 1. (I think that the wall in question was part of the development of two additional rooms.)
Miss Boxall was absent having been seen by a surgeon, which resulted in her being given leave for two months concerning a heart condition.
Later in the month, children and staff set about constructing a rockery in the pond. Empire Day was celebrated as usual and a half-day holiday followed in the afternoon. (The Empire Day

ceased to be recognised in 1958, and was replaced by the Commonwealth Day which is formally celebrated on the second Monday in March by a multi-faith Service held at Westminster Abbey.)

When the School re-opened after the Whitsun holiday on 14th June, Miss H. C. Taylor was absent having suffered a breakdown and, sadly she died on the 21st June after what was a short illness. On that day, the School was closed for Sunday school 'treats''. On 22nd June, the School was closed early when the sad news came through.

This year, the Annual School Outing took place on 2nd July and was a tour of the four Forests of Sussex, which lasted from 9am to 7.45pm. Fifty children arrived back, and very tired one would have thought.

In the middle of July, ten student teachers from the Diocesan College completed their practice and Miss Seward's assessment was "that they all did fairly well, except Miss W". Oh dear, damned by feint praise or no praise at all.

Later, after a load of sandstone had been delivered, the children and staff finished their work in constructing the rockery. Miss Seward's assessment of work completed this time was that *"it is now a thing of beauty and will be beneficial in the study of animal and plant life".* And that was praise indeed.

Before the School closed for the summer holiday on 28th July, there was an afternoon off for the annual School Sports event and a letter was sent to the Managers concerning the staff vacancy.

On return on 29th August, Miss Seward did an initial round-up of news. Fourteen new entrants took the Roll to 285, now 5 above the theoretical accommodation limit. Miss Boxall returned to work and Miss Sloan has been sent on supply and is apparently the tenth teacher to have taken this group of children since 1924.

By the second week, Miss Wilson was absent with mumps and Miss Reeve was back yet again on supply. A letter is sent to the Managers concerning the new supply teacher advising that she might be offered the vacancy following Miss Taylor's death. The Managers appointed Miss Purchase instead, so she became the eleventh teacher in charge the group of children in question.

By the first week of October, the illness count had reached three – mumps, scarlet fever and measles. Miss Wilson resumed her work in the next week while HMI Mr Davidson was carrying out a fairly long inspection. The rest of the month was taken up with examinations, medical inspections and an inspection of the Drill lessons.

After the half-term break at the start of November, the examination reports for classes I and II were sent to parents. Class III took their examinations in the next week, which also included the Armistice Day celebration. After which, more classes were involved in taking examinations, bulbs were planted and epidemics of mumps, chicken pox and measles were still prevalent.

It was a sombre December as reflected in the entries that were made in the Log Book – all were updates of the state of children's health following on from the last line of the November entries. Perhaps to emphasise just how downbeat December must have been, there was no record of any Christmas celebration having taken place. Of course, this may have been a sensible approach in order to limit the further spread of the diseases.

1928
The School reopened on 9th January 1928 and the first entry was about chicken pox affecting Class IV and also about Miss Wilson not returning from illness because she now had chicken pox. The ever familiar Miss Reeve is back on supply.

By the end of January, Miss Wilson had returned but Miss Puttock had been given leave to visit a specialist in London. She did not return having been admitted to a nursing home suffering from nervous exhaustion.
Miss Puttock is still absent and Miss Boxall has been told that she must not take Physical Culture for the next twelve months (as per Dr Eves' report to the Education Office.)

After half-term, the class examinations started and were still taking place when the School closed for a day (23rd March) because of an Election, which required a polling station to be sited in the Hall. At the end of March, school reports and class lists were prepared for the new term after Easter. At that time, 39 children were to be transferred to the Senior School in the new academic year and the Roll of the Infants stood at 312, which would then be lowered by the transfer.

After Easter, the School re-opened ahead of what was to be an important year of re-organisation in Brighton. However, it started with a return to cases of chicken pox, this time in classes V and VI. Still no return of Miss Puttock after four months, so Miss Evans continued on supply.
There was a meeting of all Head teachers to consider the arrangements for the September reorganisation plans at the Education Offices on Wednesday, 18th April at 3.30pm.

In fact, a lot of the summer months were taken up in preparing for the re-organisation. However, to begin with, there was another meeting at the Education Offices, this time to discuss the Beating-the-Bounds* programme which was to be part of the Greater Brighton Celebrations. The boundary of Brighton was expanding, something that those living in the north of the town near Balfour would certainly have recognised.

> **Note:** *There is a Wikipedia reference that explains the ancient custom of Beating-the-Bounds that can be traced back to the Norman Conquest and the times when maps were rare. It is apparently a ceremony that is still observed in a few villages but the original purpose was for parishioners to walk the boundaries of the parish to check on any encroachment from neighbours or missing boundary posts. There was a religious connection to this at the time.

Still in May, there was the Empire Day holiday followed by the Whitsun break. On return after this holiday, the School hosted the *"Greater Brighton Tea-Party at 4pm. The Mayor, Mayoress and daughter, Mr Bernard Baron, Mr. Ald. Carden, Mr. Coun Hone and Mr. Coun. Wardell were the visitors, who stayed for an hour and became our guests for tea in the Hall, which was charmingly decorated in the blue and gold School colours. The children partook of tea on the lawn, seated at small tables. The Head girl read the address after being presented to the visitors."*

Early in June there was a meeting for Head teachers of Junior Schools at the Education Offices on 13th June, presumably concern the impending re-organisation and the next day was Open Day at Balfour at which Mrs Toyne and Mr Dunn, HMI for schools in West Africa, were the visitors. This was followed by a half-day's holiday for the School Sports.

There was another holiday on 19th June when children could attend the two Sunday school treats. Next day there was another meeting for Head teachers, still on the question of re-organisation, and a third one, this time held at Circus Street on the 26th. The children had another day off for more 'treats' on the 29th.

Yet more re-organisation meetings; the Junior Heads on 3rd July and all Head teachers on 9th July, which was the last one recorded. After these meetings, preparations switched to the schools as they were closed to children on 20th July to provide time (2 weeks) for teachers to make the necessary changes at school ready for the new term in September. The school finally closed on 2nd August for the summer vacation.

The school re-opened on 3rd September officially as Balfour Junior School (the name the Education Committee gave the Loder Road School in 1905). It was to be organised as seven classes: Thus

| Classes | I to IV | Juniors |
| " | A, B, C | Infants and Preparatory |

The school was now using the new wing (two classrooms) attached to the corner of the west end of the building.
Miss Puttock still had not returned so Miss Evans came back on supply. The Roll rose to 337.

Holes were being dug in the lawn and playground to try to find a leakage in the water system.

Workers putting the finishing touches to the New Wing caused noisy conditions that hampered school work, which was also interrupted in the playground by barriers set up to protect the holes being made in the search for the leakage.

Miss Evans was recalled to cover Miss Puttock's class as she was feeling sick from a chill. She had been away for nearly eleven months before returning recently. However, in the following week, Miss Seward learned that Miss Puttock had begun an application for a breakdown pension and wrote to the managers to seek a replacement. It had been ten months without a teacher and a permanent member of staff was required.

By the end of October, the work to complete the west wing still hadn't been finished and water was trickling down the outside wall and making everything damp and musty. The noise hadn't died down either and Miss Knight was having difficulty in making herself heard.

Miss Seward failed to get new reading books for Class IV and must make do with ones from Class III readers, one between two children.

Miss Seward was away sick in November and Miss Young wrote the Log Book entries as she would eventually do more often. Several members of staff were also absent, so supply teachers were called for.

When Miss Seward returned, clearly rested and ready to post the Managers another sharp letter about the failure to appoint a permanent replacement for Miss Puttock who had been absent for eleven months. There had been 16 changes of staff in the last two years. She went on to add an extra paragraph about the disruption caused by the building work to her general expressions of frustration. After which, it was Christmas and, for a second year running, no mention made of Christmas celebrations.

The School closed on 21st December but Miss Seward did get an unexpected present after all. The Education Committee determined that her school should now be Grade III based on the larger Roll and there would be two new assistant teachers starting at the School in January. So, Miss Seward had extra money and extra teachers, Misses Bishopp & Tidy. Perhaps this was a kind of prize for persistence.

1929
The new term started on 7th January 1929 and with it, Miss Bishopp and Miss Tidy commenced their duties. As the building of the New Wing still hadn't been completed, all classes had to continue with their old classification, using the entire Hall and with Miss Bishopp helping out with various classes.
However, Miss Tidy was recalled to the Central School in Church St. as her successor could not be appointed until February. So, a supply teacher (oh yes, Miss Evans again) was called back until February.

In the next week, the School was closed to the children for two days while all the furniture was moved into place for the new class structure, using the New Wing that was ready at last. An extra class, IIIa had to be made for backward children and to be located in the Hall.

A request for trestle tables was made so that more handwork may be done and tables can be easily moved to provide space for Folk-dancing and Rhythmics. The extra class couldn't be fitted in yet to avoid collisions with other classes.
A plan of the School including accommodation and Rolls was sent to the Managers' meeting on 23rd January. At the time the Roll was 350. The New Wing will have increased the capacity significantly above the old 280 figure that was set in 1924.

In February, the class of backward children had been accommodated in the Hall with all sorts and conditions of desks that were collected from different rooms. Several managers visited to enquire about opening the space under the New Wing.
Later in February, seven students started their teaching practice and while they did this, class teachers took the opportunity to repair and make good apparatus, though they did go back into the classrooms to allow the students to have a break.

Visits were made by HMI Mr. Theobold to inspect the students in their classes. He would have encountered very low temperatures in the three westerly classrooms and difficulties caused by ice in the lavatories. The children's lavatories that is, as they were outside.
Monday, 18th February was mid-term holiday and, on the 20th, there was another one because the lavatories were completely frozen – and "insanitary".

March seems to have continued with the presence of very cold weather; Drills were arranged to be done in classrooms; Infants' work was reviewed and not examined because this term had been truncated; the Juniors were not so lucky, there was time to fit in both activities.

An interesting school visit was made to Seaford and Bishopstone to see a Saxon porch in a church. No more information was recorded.

The last week in the month was given over to marking before the School broke up for the Easter holiday.

The new academic year started on 9th April and in Miss Seward's Annual Report it was pointed out that there was an accommodation problem with the Roll now at 366. The New Wing has been more of a magnet rather than a solution to the old problem.

Miss Knight was absent (influenza) at the end of the month, which meant that all teachers had to take their own class for Drawing.

Into May, and swimming lessons started with Miss Young taking twenty girls to St Luke's School Baths and Mr Privett took twenty boys to the North Road Baths.

The next significant entry was the notice of the Whitsun holiday, which was to be 17th May to 26th May, except it wasn't because the MOH directed the school to remain closed until 2nd June. Very little information was recorded in May

In June, there were the usual holidays, and several new ones this year.

The first holiday was on the 12th for the visit of Prince George who performed the ceremony of opening the Aquarium. (In fact, he opened the reconstructed building; the Aquarium was opened in1872 and acquired by the Brighton Council in 1901and it was the municipal corporation that re-developed the building. Prince George became the Duke of Kent in 1934 and was killed in 1942 while on active service in WW2).

The next day was a holiday for the Sunday school 'treats' (St John's and St Matthias) and the following day, the School welcomed a visit from The Hon. Arthur Henderson M. P. who was the Foreign Secretary in the Labour minority government (1929 – 1931). He was accompanied by Mrs. Henderson, Mr. Ald. Carden and Mr Coun. Denney.

There was an afternoon holiday a week later for the School Sports.

Another week later, on Friday 28th June, there was a half day holiday for the Sussex Schools Sports.

Finally, in a very busy June, the Annual School Outing took place on the next day. Miss Seward noted in her Log Book – "See Guide for details. Well, I found that Guide* in a box in a cupboard almost exactly 70 years later in 1999. From it, I knew the Outing took place on 29th June but there was no year mentioned (you would hardly need to know which year it was when reading it in1929). Eventually, finding this Log Book solved the question. It was 29th June 1929. You will see that this year's Outing matched the others that were described earlier, in the producing an itinerary involving a substantial journey through the Sussex countryside.

(*Note: A copy of the Guide can be found at the end of this Section on p167)

Below are four photographs of children preparing to go on an outing, or being on one, but no details were attached of date or place. So they could all have been about taken on the 1929 excursion around Sussex or up to four separate events. We may never know. We do know that Miss Seward's records showed that she saw great value in taking opportunities to get children out-of-doors as much as possible for both educational and recreational activities.

Fig 36
Sight-seeing with Miss Seward?

Fig 37
Stopping for refreshments

Gathering at school before leaving?

Fig 38

Was this the char-a-banc that is being loaded the one that took the school party on the tour of Sussex in 1929? It is definitely after 1926 because the Varndean Girls School, built in 1926 can be seen at the top of the road.

Fig 39

The rest of the term came to an end with mentions being made of the Open Day, of the School swimmers who could swim 10yds being taken to the Hove Baths and of the School reports that were sent home to parents.

The new term started on 2nd September and, with the increasing numbers on the Roll, there were now eight full classes. Miss Seward's next move would be to request more accommodation.
Miss Tidy, who had been appointed to the headship of the new Moulsecoomb School, was at Balfour as a supernumerary teacher until the School opens.

Having said that, Miss Seward then wrote to report that Miss Tidy had been called to Moulsecoomb and ended her time role at this School.

By the second week, Miss Seward noted that the Roll was now above the accommodation 'limit' by one child. A large class of 45 was now in the Hall using old dilapidated tables sent from Loder Road and not the Art desks and trestles that were requested but not sent. They cannot be stored when not in use so there was no space for Rhythmics.

This year the Chairman of the Education Committee, Mr. Coun. Hone, addressed the parents and children at the Open Day and Harvest Festival in early October. Later Miss Seward reported that Class IIIb had insufficient seating and that a request had been sent to the Requisition Committee. The request was turned down. The Roll is now 382.

At the end of October, the last swimming lesson was held. Three children swam 50yds, six their 25yds and fifteen their 10yds in the lesson.

The next day, 22nd October, Miss Seward attended the opening of Moulsecoomb School.

The School was closed on 31st October for an Election and again on Friday 1st November until Tuesday 5th November for the mid-term break.

A Short Peace Service was held on Armistice Day and a wreath taken down to the War Memorial.

The first two weeks of December were taken up with examinations throughout the School and at the end of the third week, 20th December, the children had a games afternoon before breaking up for the Christmas holidays. Apart from colds in the nursery class, this year seemed to be free of the illnesses that had dogged the children at this time last year.

1930

A new decade started at school on 6th January 1930 and Miss Seward lost no time in writing to the Managers again regarding the need for more accommodation.
Almost all of the entries made in the Log Book during first five weeks of term were related to staff illnesses with supply teachers coming and going. Not one outbreak of children's illnesses was recorded.

The first substantial issue mentioned was the visit of the Education Committee to decide on what steps could be taken to provide more accommodation for the Junior School.
The South side of the Hall, it was decided, should be used. The desks that are already there, which accommodate big Senior Girls, are to be used by the small children. The S side is to be given up to the Seniors one hour (the last) in every morning. This means that the class needs to be turned out for ten morning sessions for Senior Singing and every afternoon after 3.00pm for Singing of eight Junior classes. This will be met, but must cause considerable disturbance and restlessness in the whole of the Junior School.

We have learnt from experience, that when Miss Seward is less than satisfied with a decision she gets out her ruler and underlines key words. She must have thought that a quart was being squeezed into a pint pot (in old measurements)
Miss Seward set about re-organising classes to accommodate a new additional class. As the clean bill of children's health before Christmas had given way to coughs, whooping cough and mumps in February, she used the resulting low attendance to leave the Infants' classes B and C to work with new children as attendance was very low.
School was closed for an Educational Conference on 21st February and again on the 28th for the mid-term break.
Students started a month's practice after the break and Miss Wilson was away for an interview in Swindon.
Shortly afterwards, Miss Wilson submitted her letter of resignation after being offered an appointment in Swindon and Miss Seward immediately sent a letter seeking two supply teachers until August when two College students might be appointed.

The students' month of practice was over at the end of March and they just missed the outbreak of Mumps (45 cases) in April and by the last day of the term on 17th April, the number of cases had risen to 67. This was the last day for Miss Wilson who left for her new post in Swindon

The School reopened on 29th April with 403 on the Books and a welcome for Miss Reeves (yet again) who returned on supply. Mrs Dickisson was the second supply teacher that Miss Seward had requested who started on 19th May and the School closed at the end of that week for the Empire Day holiday. The additional class has been put in the Hall and the Education Office confirmed that Mrs Dickisson can remain until the summer.

In the week before Whitsun, a class of 5 year olds were entered for the Musical Festival Singing Games and gained 86% and 4th place.

After Whitsun it was announced that Howard Smith had been declared the Top Boy in the Brighton Scholarship Examinations and Mabel Notcutt won a Hedgcock Scholarship. (More information about Howard Smith, who went on to have an outstanding career, can be found in the reflections of Margaret Johnson (see page 160) who was one of his contemporaries and who wrote about her past school memories in1984 on the 60th anniversary of the school building).

For the rest of June and July, the entries recorded little else than the various holidays that were normally taken in this period.
Specifically, holidays for the School Sports, the Sunday school treats, a School visit to a Zoo, for the Top Boy of Brighton event. There was also an event called the Swimmers' Tea Party which involved a visit to the St Luke's baths. In between all this activity went the school examinations, marking and reports for parents.

The last entry made before the summer holiday confirmed that the School was now organised in 9 classes, 6 Junior and 3 Infants. Just two years ago, it was based on seven classes.

The School reassembled on 1st September. Mrs Dickisson returned as a supply teacher and Miss W. B. Quigley commenced duties as a permanent member of staff.

In the second week there was a Tea Party for 50yds swimmers and an excursion to Hove Baths.

The Harvest festival was held on 29th September and 455lbs plus collected for the Queen's Nurses' cupboard. Mr. Coun. Hone and the Rev Taylor-Mills addressed the parents and children.

150 children were taken to the "Safety First" Lecture.

Games were held on the Secondary playing field making good use of the permission that had been granted by the Education Committee.

Seven days were spent in the second and third weeks on October carrying out medical inspections, much longer than usual but in keeping with the size of the School now over 400 compared with less than 200 when it opened.

Half-term was on 31st October to the 3rd November and, when the school opened again, the children listened to a recital by an internationally famous Estonian violinist Eduard Soermus and the youngest child presented a bouquet to Mrs Soermus. She was Virginia Soermus, a British pianist who accompanied him in some of his performances.

The months of November and December heralded the examination season throughout the school followed by marking and report writing. This year Miss Seward reverted to her normal practice of reporting on Christmas activities. All rooms were decorated and handwork (presents for parents) made. Each evening in the last full week was given over to Socials. All staff stayed on for them.

A Carol Concert was held on the 22nd and the School closed on the 23rd December.

1931
The School re-opened on 12th January 1931 with 425 on the Roll and with Mrs Dickisson still on supply but Miss Seward was very poorly during the week and was absent for a day. She was well enough to repeat her concern about the difficulty in running a school where the Hall was a large classroom. Activities that should be done in the Hall were being dropped. She didn't

underline the text this time; the Managers were well aware that their 'compromise' was not a solution.

The College staff met with Miss Seward to arrange future teaching practice sessions, which included a Demonstration lesson in Handwork to be watched by 17 students. This took place in early February and a second was held later in the month.

The Log Book entries then became fragmented and infrequent. The reason was to be found in the recordings made in April. Miss Seward left school on 14th February and didn't return until 14th April have had multiple operations to correct a nose fracture that was caused by an earlier accident at school.

Miss Young took over making the entries, fewer in number as she also had a full teaching commitment to carry out.

In the two months of Miss Seward's absence, the Log Book's record listed staff absences, the arrival and departure of the student teachers and the visit of the HMI who came to assess their progress.

One event that was reported, will read as very much of its time. On 27th February, Doris Emmett, the monitoress had a tumble in the street and was brought back to school in a Police Ambulance. She wasn't injured but shocked, so she was taken home by ambulance, accompanied by a teacher. A monitoress would invariably be a young girl between 14 or 15 years of age.

Another event that wouldn't happen in normal circumstances today was mentioned, almost in passing, that, *"The Hertford Road transfers have been filled in and sent to the Education Office (10.3.31)"*. Exactly what this information meant became clear on the day Miss Seward returned to school on 14th April. On that day, she wrote that 61 children had been transferred to Hertford Road School, which had just opened in order to ease the over-crowding at Ditchling Road School. Coincidentally, it was about to do the same thing for Balfour Junior School.
Miss Seward lost no time in setting out what she was doing now back and fit.

Her first tasks involved unpacking, checking and placing stock. Arrangements were made for swimming, and then teaching Handwork and Needlework.
Mrs Dickisson finally completed her time at the School as a supply teacher, having been employed for more than a year.

Then Miss Seward turned her attention to using the Log Book as a means to present Managers who arrive as visitors, with information she wants them to read and inwardly digest.
She wrote that: "Miss A. E. Young has acted as Deputy Head during my absence. She has proved to be most capable. She has carried out every duty thoroughly and promptly, including the very difficult task of reorganising after the transfer of 61 children to the new school, when many details had to be carried through requiring much attention and time."

She then started to take charge of three classes when the swimmers were out with their class teachers. These lessons began at the beginning of May and went the summer months.

The Whitsun break at the end of May was followed by the visit of the HMI to watch the student teachers finish their practice period.

June arrived with its programme of various holiday days, which this year included the 'treats', School Sports and a trip to Hampton Court as the final treat. It appears that the Annual Outing in the char-a-banc ride across Sussex had been replaced by trips farther afield.

July as usual, meant examinations, marking and writing reports to be distributed to parents on 30th July when the four-week summer vacation started.

The school reopened on 31st August, which was now organised into eight classes but because of the number of infant children, one class must be housed in the Hall.
The School has been redecorated throughout and everywhere is looking bright and clean.

The field is now "at our service" Miss Seward notes and "affords, weather permitting, splendid space for Recreation and Physical Culture".
Mr Weller, the Caretaker was absent on holiday in the middle of September but supply caretaker wasn't measuring up to the job as far as cleaning was concerned.

As happened last year, all proficient swimmers had a tea party on 15th September and then taken to the Hove Baths.

In October, the student teachers were taking a History course with classes 1, II, III and timetables had been modified to enable this to take place. There was a two-day holiday on 26th and 27th October to allow the Hall to be used as a Polling Station, which was followed by the half-term break.
This holiday had to be extended for some children because of an outbreak of whooping cough.

A slight change to the way the Armistice Day Service was organised this year with children listening in the Hall to the BBC broadcast from the Cenotaph, after which the School wreath was taken down to the War Memorial as usual.

Medical Inspections were held in December alongside school examinations and reports. No mention was made of any Christmas festivities this year before the school closed on 23rd December for the holiday.

1932

The School reopened again on 11th January 1932 and the first entry was about three cases of mumps and by the end of January, there was an epidemic of influenza.

In the first week of February, seven students were watching Demonstrations being given by staff from the training college. The Demonstrations continued into the next week when the attendance was down to 72 % because of the influenza infection. Snow was preventing any outdoor Physical Culture so one hour of sports in the snow was allowed. A School Snowman* was modelled on the lawn. The use of the Gramophone was a great inconvenience to class B using the Hall – the problem Miss Seward has been railing against for months.

Note: Four photographs of snow scenes were discovered amongst the archives, three of which were pictures of a snowman that was clearly a centre of attention. Unfortunately, they were without dates. The first is clearly pre-1928 as the building extension was still on the drawing board at this time. The other three do seem to fit the description that Miss Seward gave to a 'snowman modelling' event, which involved Mr Privett and two colleagues capturing a few moments of one of their lost childhood pursuits.

Fig 40

A pre-1928 bleak mid-winter with a snowman surrounded by a small group of teachers and children.

Fig 41

Now, a post-1928 snowman with three teacher-builders including one assumes, Mr Privett

Fig 42

The same snowman with children enjoying a break from lessons to admire the handiwork

Fig 43

The group of admirers has just got bigger still.

Later in February both Miss Seward and Miss Boxall were taken ill and missed several days. On return, Miss Seward found an erasure in Class II Boys' register. Evidently, a blot has been erased. Enquiry will be made when the Class Teacher (Miss Boxall) returns from illness.

In March there were a number of visitors to the School. Three HMIs observing students, and teachers from Bognor and other Brighton schools came to observe classes.

After Easter, in each week of the Log Book, there was just one line of information.
- The HMIs returned to see the students again.
- Visit made to the Aquarium
- German measles very prevalent
- Dental Inspection

In May, swimming lessons began.

Note: It is clear that Miss Seward had altered the way in which she maintained a weekly log in the weeks that have followed her health problems last year. What seems clear from the huge increase in the numbers of children on the Roll and the difficulties of accommodating them, her work load must have been considerable. Her dedication to teaching and the school was transparent but it must have come at a cost. Filling in a Log Book that wasn't likely to change the decisions being made by the Authorities, no matter how many times she underlined the most important sections, wasn't going to be the best use of her time when other more pressing jobs needed to be done first.

After Whitsun, the School was opened to the parents on the occasion of the 'Breaking of the Flag', when Mr Bartlett presented the flag to the School. There were displays of Physical Training, Maypole dancing and Singing on the lawns. The Education Committee and Managers were entertained to tea. Mr Coun. Hone, Chairman of the Education Committee presided over the ceremony.

Early in June, four children under the age of 5 years have been admitted by consent of the Education Committee.

Thereafter, the Log Book simply mentioned treats, exams and a visit made to Windsor by 95 staff and children travelling in three coaches.

What Miss Seward did write about in more than single words, were the results of children successes in getting Scholarships that enabled them to get to Secondary Schools. Nine won Scholarships and eight passed the Entrance Exams for Varndean Boys (4) and Varndean Girls (4).
The school won the Swimming Shield and then examinations and reports became the Order of the Log Book entries. One additional one was the resignation of Miss Knight to take up a post at St. Bartholomew's Infants' School

The term ended on 28th July.

The school reopened on 29th August with Mr Coun. Hone, now the Chairman of the Education Committee visiting to greet the new teacher, Miss Chaffer.
There were 22 admissions and a draft of 56 who are passing into Secondary, Intermediate and Senior Schools. Still in the first week, there was a party of visitors from Bishop Otter School.

Two more sets of visitors in the next week, one from Kennington Road Infants in London and lecturers from the Diocesan College making arrangements for 10 students to attend to observe teaching methods, etc., which they started to do during the next week.

The Harvest Festival celebration was held on 10th October and attracted a large number of parents and friends; better even than last year, said Miss Seward. The produce was dispatched in three private cars to the Queens' Nurses. (This was the first time a reference to a 'private car' was made.)
Later in October, a letter was dispatched to the Managers regarding the borders, wood and fencing and in the next week, there was a visit by Mr Bartlett, Mr Simpson and Mr McLaren concerning this complaint.

Armistice Day Service in the Hall and wreath to the Memorial.

In the first week of December, there were extensive medical inspections and the three infants' classes were excluded from school for two weeks because of the level of their illnesses. When they returned later the attendance levels were still very low.
The School was due to close for Christmas on 23rd December and would open a week later than planned because of measles.
Plum puddings were made in the top two classes. This was the only reference Miss Seward made to Christmas and no reference at all was made to the examinations that no doubt were taken as usual.
Miss Seward has maintained a minimalist approach to making Log Book entries, which she began to use after returning from her health problems in May.

1933
The School reopened on 16th January 1933; the longer holiday granted to help children to recover from the illnesses they suffered at the end of last year. Unfortunately, the attendance was still very low, this time on account of the prevalence of 'Flu'.

In the last week of January the sickness outbreak became more serious. All children with colds or sore throats were excluded as advised by the Education Committee as of the 24th and all infants' classes were excluded on the 25th and the all classes in the School were excluded on the 26th until 6th February by Order of MOH. However, all the Junior Classes did go on an afternoon Ramble on the 26th January.

The school did reassemble on 6th February but the attendance was still very low from the continuing effects of colds, influenza and measles.
By 15th February, the attendance had improved as Mr Hone discovered on a visit and he saw students observing and preparing for School Practice.

A Bird Bath donated by a parent was fixed on the lawn.

In March, the students returned to start their teaching practice and by arrangements made between the college and Miss Seward, all students got the opportunity to teach all subjects in their three weeks' stay.
At the end of the month, the students ended their practice having been inspected throughout the last week by HMIs and staff from the College.

After Easter, admissions pushed the Roll up to 380, quickly recovering from the loss of the 61 children who transferred to Hertford Road School.

On the 23rd May, there was a half-day holiday for School Sports but it wasn't such a good day for Sylvia House who dislocated her elbow and was taken to hospital by ambulance. Miss Seward records that she is progressing satisfactorily.

June passed by with its usual largesse in the form of holidays for treats and more sports events; rounded off at the beginning of July with the Annual Outing, this year to Hindhead and Frencham Ponds.

July's events also followed the usual form of examinations and their results being transferred to school reports. The variations to the normal form this year were an inspection by HMI and a Garden Party just before the School broke up for summer holidays.

The School reopened on 31st August and was organised into eight classes. The timetable had been reorganised so that Miss Young could teach English to classes IVa and IVb and Mr Privett taught them Mathematics and Science.

In the last two weeks of September, another group of students arrived for teaching practice and in the first week of October, 150 children were taken to the Regent to see the film, "Safety First". *(The Regent Cinema was at the top of North Street on the site now occupied by Boots Chemist)*

Harvest Festival and Open Day attended this year by many Queens' Nurses and their Superintendant visited along with the Managers and Mr Coun. Hone. All goods collected were sent to the Nurses but no indication given this year about the mode of transport used.

Later in October, Miss Seward attended a meeting of Managers when Miss Bone was recommended for appointment to the School.
The new Manageress, Mrs Watkins visited the school and was shown around.

Miss Bone commenced her duties on 1st November.

Miss Seward stuck a copy of the HMI Report in the Log Book. A copy of it has been placed in Appendix 2 on HMI reports and Miss Seward's response to it, has been placed alongside it. The big talking point in the Report was the comment made about the use of the Hall as a classroom. This was a topic about which Miss Seward had very strong views. She did make a note in the Log Book that she had sent a copy of her response to the Education Committee.

Ironically, the HMI report appeared when there were medical inspections that required the re-timetabling of Class C – the one in the Hall.

Moving into December, and as we move towards Christmas, the season of illnesses was triggered this year by an outbreak of mumps in Class II. This was quickly followed by chicken pox, tonsillitis, sickness and sore throats. Again, as last year, there was no mention of any Christmas activities. This might have been because of the extent of illnesses and low attendance levels, or perhaps it was in line with Miss Seward's recent approach in keeping the recording to very basic essentials. Or, perhaps it was a bit of both.
Anyway, the School closed on 22 December with chicken pox and mumps still prevalent, and would open again on Monday, 8th January 1934.

1934
The School did reopen on 8th January 1934 and was in the same situation as it had been in when last year ended. Now, there were two cases of diphtheria and two of scarlet fever, with many cases of mumps and chicken pox still being reported.

On a happier note, Miss Seward took 44 children to the Theatre Royal to see "Goody Two Shoes".
By the end of January, mumps and chicken pox were still prevalent in the three Infants' classes. At the end of the week (2nd February), the day was so cold that, instead of Drill lessons, the whole school ran all round the field for 25 minutes with Miss Seward and the Staff.

Things in February were turning out to be worse, if anything, than January. The attendance was even lower as the epidemics continued. Miss Bone contracted mumps, so Mrs Dickisson made a return visit on supply and the situation got worse with more cases of mumps, scarlet fever, which was most prevalent in Class I, and chicken pox.
After half term, more students arrived to start their practice. Miss Bone was given more time to recover from the after-effects of mumps.

In the first week of March, a pupil Fred Calway crushed his finger in a door, which was reported to the Education Office. He had to attend hospital each morning during the next week.
Miss Bone returned as intended on 9th March and Mrs Dickisson finished her stay then.
At the end of the month, HMIs visited to see the students at work and the term ended with the Easter holiday, which couldn't come soon enough after a very difficult period.

After Easter, the entries had a familiar content. Miss Seward and Miss Purchase had days off because of illness and Miss Dickisson came back again to do another stint.
With the Roll up to 393, three under 5's had to be turned away because all the classes were full.

At the beginning of June, the evergreen Mrs Dickisson was back again, this time as a replacement for Miss Seward had to return to hospital for another operation. Miss Young was again standing in as her deputy.

The students returned for their final examination and the School held its own Sports Day on the Intermediate Boys' playing field that, in the past, had not been available for Balfour's use. In fact, not only did they use it, but the Intermediate School lent them the equipment for hurdle races and all children took part in at least one race.

The rest of June was taken up with Medical inspections until the 22nd June when the School closed for the Inter-Schools Sports Day (in Preston Park)

The examinations started at the beginning of July. The money collected at the School's own sports day has been put to buying hanging baskets for the veranda. There was 15/9d left over and Miss Young thought it should be spent on a pedestal for the pond, which could help frogs, toads and newts climb out.

The Annual Outing this year was to London Zoo and Croydon Aerodrome. Four coaches took 121 children and eight members of staff including Mrs Dickisson who seemed to have become a permanent supply teacher, if that is not a contradiction in terms.

The downside of the month arrived with yet another outbreak of illness in the infant classes – whooping cough. As it was summer, Miss Young kept the classes outside as far as possible and tried to isolate them in school as well.

Swimming practices were held at St Luke's baths in preparation for the inter-school competition on 23rd July when the School performed well in Division I and had three winners.

A whole school and class photographs were taken but the normal Open Day was cancelled in an effort to minimise the spread of whooping cough.

The school closed for the summer holidays on 2nd August.

Miss Seward had been away for the whole term and Miss Young stamped her own approach to recording events in the Log Book by taking 6 pages alone to cover July by writing an essay in the space that Miss Seward might have used to cover quite a few months. It was very descriptive.

The new term started on 3rd September 1934 with Miss Seward restored to health. She noted 32 new entrants and paid tribute to her Deputy, Miss Young who had "carried on wonderfully well" during her absence.

Inevitably, Mrs Dickisson was back on supply.

Almost as regular, a party of student teachers arrived to start a month's teaching practice in October. Continuous bad weather in the middle of the month led to Drill being adapted to be taken in classrooms.

The Open Day and Harvest Festival took place with doctors and nurses invited to join with parents and friends.

At the end of the month, Miss Quigley took over Drill lessons because of Miss Boxall's heart condition.

Holiday granted on 29th November to celebrate the wedding of King George V's son who married Princess Marina of Greece and Denmark.

The day after, the first case of measles was reported.

The school examinations began on 3rd December and on the 5th, Miss Seward and staff took 115 children to the Cinema to see "Wings over Everest" *(which was a 1934 British documentary about Lord Clydesdale, who piloted a single-engine biplane on 3 April 1933, just clearing Everest's southern peak by a few feet, having been caught in a powerful downdraught).*

School parties were held on Thursday and reports sent to parents on Friday 21st December when the School closed for the Christmas vacation, having just heard that scarlet fever had broken out in the Infants' Class A.

1935

The School reopened on 11 January 1935 and immediately, Mrs Dickisson was back to cover for Miss Boxall who had been ordered to take a long rest by her medical adviser. As illnesses never seem to be far away, the latest reported outbreak was scarlet fever in classes C and IVb.

Miss Seward had to contact the Education Office having received complaints about the "offensive" lavatories from parents, managers and the Senior Head Mistress.
Later, there was an increase in the number of cases of scarlet fever, plus whooping cough and a mixture of colds and sore throats.

In February, all the entries referred to the new batch of students who started their practice on 1st Feb and finished with the HMI inspection on the 15th March.

The next entry listed the dates of the Easter Holiday with a note that indefatigable Mrs Dickisson had ended her latest spell of supply, covering the absent Miss Boxall.
After the holiday was over on 30th April, the Roll stood at 399 and Miss Seward determined to create another Infants' class as one existed with 60 children in it. No classroom had been designed to hold more than 50. Ironically, all the classrooms at Loder Road were built to hold 60 children but rarely held more than 40 at any one time because of illnesses, adverse weather conditions and parental opposition to sending their children there.

On the 6th May, there was a one-day holiday to celebrate the Silver Jubilee of King George V and the day after, 250 children went to the Duke of Yorks Cinema, but there is no record in the Log Book as the what the children actually saw while there.
Back to Earth, Miss Seward contacted Mr Toyne for an additional teacher. "No", was his answer.

A week later, and another teacher was absent and Mrs Dickisson returned, but swimming lessons had to be cancelled because there was no teacher available to take them. Later still, the swimming lessons were again cancelled when two more teachers were absent. Miss Seward wrote, possibly for the eyes of a Manager, that she couldn't teach two classes at the same time because she couldn't be in two places at once.
She could be a bit more positive in praising the 'Supply' Caretaker for, despite being painstaking, thorough and rather slow, making the School look "clean and bright".

She may have stirred up the Managers following her several letters about the difficulties she was facing because Councillors Hone and Dunne met her to discuss the extra class in the Hall on 3rd June.

Miss Seward followed up her requests for teachers, for extra floor space and now for more furniture because young children had to sit at teachers' tables that were far too large.

After the Whitsun break, Class C still has 60 on Roll; the application for an extra class was granted but there was no furniture. Single entries recorded in the next two weeks up to the 5th July were simply, "no teachers and no furniture".

Her campaign had some success in the next week with the arrival of furniture and, unremarkably, the return of Mrs Dickisson to be an extra teacher in Class C of 60 children. Actually, in an emergency, this wasn't a bad compromise with an experienced additional teacher in to provide support, but not ideal.

This year's Annual Outing was to Westminster, Kew Gardens and Hampton Court.

Finally, it was nearly the end of term with no references made to the many annual happenings that normally filled Log Book in July. I am sure that they all happened, anyway. What did happen, when everybody was heading for the door, was a Staff Meeting at which Miss Seward referred to apparatus; specifically, apparatus that is left around after the class has finished and needs to be put away. Even more specifically, please keep the School tidy.

Then one usual entry was made. "Exams ended on 25th July" followed by "reports signed and sent to parents. Vacation: 1st August – Monday, 2nd September".

New term started on 2nd Sept. The School was organised into eight classes as below:

	IVa	Mr. Privett
	IV	Miss. Young
JUNIOR	III	Miss. Purchase
	II	Miss. Quigley
	I	Miss. Boxall
	A	Miss. Bone
INFANTS	B	Miss. Chaffer
	C	Miss. Bishopp

Miss Boxall was absent from Friday 6th September. Mrs Dickisson returned immediately.

In the next week, there were visits from teacher trainers from Chichester Training College and from one in Australia and in the week after, visits from student teachers from the Diocesan College who were preparing for their period of practice.

There was a reference made in the Log Book as to the progress that students were making and we also learn that 150 children were taken by Southdown Coaches to and from the Academy Cinema to see the 'Safety First' film.

The Harvest Festival was on 14th October and the teaching practice finished at the half-term break.

After the break, there was another holiday three days later to celebrate the wedding of Prince Henry, son of King George V, to Alice Montague-Douglas-Scott.

There were holidays again, 2 days on 13/14th November, for Parliamentary Elections (Polling Station needed at Balfour).

On 22nd November, it was reported that Miss Boxall would not be able to return this term.

A sadly familiar end-of-year report from Miss Seward's Log; exams, marking and parents' reports plus the MOH's order to exclude all Infants' classes and two from the Juniors, classes I and II from 19th December until 13th January on grounds of epidemic illnesses.

1936

The new term started on 6th January 1936 with three classes able to return after last year's MOH order to exclude the other classes until 13th January. This meant that Miss Quigley could cover for Miss Purchase who was ill without resorting to requesting a supply teacher. (Mrs Dickisson though, didn't have long to wait.) The School closed again on the next two days because it was being used as a Polling Station.

On 13th January, all the classes returned but Miss Purchase was still ill, so Mrs Dickisson was back. Miss Boxall returned having been away for most of the last term.

In the next week, the whole School was assembled on Tuesday, 21st January for prayers to be said for King George V who died in the evening of 20th January. There then, was another assembly for the Proclamation of King Edward VIII,

In the next week, there was another holiday on the occasion of the Funeral of King George V on 28th January.

In the first week of February, there was a serious outbreak of measles, tonsillitis and scarlet fever, and in the next week, the cases of measles increased with Class C, normally 60, had only 9 children present.

After half-term, there were 45 cases of measles and an attendance of 63% and two weeks later at the end of February, still measles prevailed leaving the attendance rate almost unaltered at 64%. The new batch of student teachers began their practice in this week.

In the first week of March, another 16 cases of measles were reported along with some with whooping cough.

By the first week of April, the epidemic of measles was abating but there were still some more cases of whooping cough. Miss Seward was absent from 1st April to 9th April in order to undergo a further three nasal operations. The Easter holiday started from 9th to the 20th April

After Easter, on 29th April, 120 children were taken to the cinema to see a film of "Midsummer Night's Dream"

The Log Book for May contained a list of entirely routine entries until, after Whitsun, the School closed on the afternoon of 15th June for Sports Day with a gathering of parents and friends. This was followed on the 19th by the Inter-Schools Jubilee Sports. This was followed by another sporting holiday when B.J.Saunders Esq. J.P. entertained all competitors to tea in the Dome and Corn Exchange.

On 3rd July, there was a rehearsal of Folk Dancing* of groups of Girls from several schools on Balfour Road Junior School's lawn. On Friday, 10th July, there was a school holiday for the Annual Outing, normally held on a Saturday. This year, the destination was the Isle of Wight. After this event, the Log Book entries only related to the examinations and school reports. Summer holidays started on 30th July.

Note: The reference above to 'Folk Dancing' might be the event that was the subject of a photograph that subsequently appeared in the Brighton Education 1939 Brochure and is included in the Postscripts under the heading "Sports and PE activities at Balfour"

In September 1936, Miss Seward didn't date the start of term but she did record that eight children have transferred to the new Junior and Senior School at Patcham. Also, several had moved away from Brighton.

The Hall floor has been planed and polished and a Drinking Fountain fixed to the wall outside. Four classrooms have new cupboards. The School is organised as last year but the Infants' teachers have changed as below.

Class	A	Miss Chaffer	(from B)
"	B	Miss Bishopp	(from C)
"	C	Miss Bone	(from A)

At the end of September, students arrived to start their period of practice.

In October, the Open Day and Harvest Festival was well attended. In the next week, the first case of diphtheria was reported and in the last week, Miss Boxall applied for more leave after long periods of absence only broken by short periods of attendance. Miss Seward referred her request to Mr Toyne.

The first week of November was all about illnesses. Colds and sore throats, Miss Bishopp included, and Miss Boxall left one afternoon "on permission". Presumably, Mr Toyne had given his approval.
Life can be full of ironies as the last afternoon this week was a holiday for good attendance. The last three weeks simply recorded the absences of Miss Purchase and Miss Boxall.

The first week in December was true to form with the first cases of whooping cough, chicken pox and mumps, which were reported to the MOH but at least, Miss Purchase was fit enough to return. The next week contained a day's holiday for the Swimming Trophy and an update on the many colds in the school and the last week before Christmas, exams were being completed and reports written. No mention of the word Christmas was made.

1937

On the last two pages of the Log Book, we learn that the School reopened on 11th January 1937, that only staff absences (and returns) were recorded and that a group of student teachers arrived at the end of February and the **very last entry of all was one you couldn't make up because the words that were written were to report that the 'permanent supply' teacher Mrs Dickisson, had returned on supply.**

We know now, from the records of the Committee of Managers' meetings, that the system of having groups of schools across the town managed by such Committees, was abolished on 31st March 1937, the same weekend that Miss Seward stopped maintaining her Log Book records. With advantage of hindsight, it seems very likely that the day of abolition was well known in advance and Miss Seward's noticeable change of style towards recording mainly staff absence, numbers on Roll and illnesses can be explained. The basic information that she was recording would have been that required by the Education Committee and her frequent references made direct to Mr Toyne, as Secretary to the Education Committee, also suggest that some of day-to-day decisions were already being made there.

Now for the last time, a selection of the Minutes from meetings of Managers' during 1924 – 1937 which conclude with an explanation of the decision made by the Education Committee to abolish this system of managing schools in Brighton

We pick up the thread again after the new school building had been opened on 27th February 1924. It is just possible that the experience of handling the start-up arrangements necessary for equipping the school and its surroundings with everything that was needed for good working conditions, led the Managers to question their own procedures. They had to deal with as many agenda items in the next 3 years as they had coped with over the first 18 years. Ahead of them lay the opening of Hertford Road School (1931) and of Patcham (1937).

Hertford was included in the north Brighton Managers' group but Patcham was opened coincidentally at the same time as the group management system was abolished.

Conjecture maybe, but the system was unlikely to have been jettisoned on a whim. The labyrinthine journey from a Head teacher's letter to the Managers, referred to a sub-committee, which was then authorised (or not) by the parent Committee before making the return journey for the next meeting, perhaps didn't seem to be a very efficient system. And that's probably an understatement.

In March 1924 – The Managers met a veritable plethora of requests for all and sundry requirements that were needed for use in the new school building. Amongst this random collection, there were a few items to be dealt with that didn't fall into the 'requests' category. There was a new Caretaker who would go on to serve at the school for many years; Miss Young finally gets the post in the Junior School; Mr Hughes becomes the Head of the Senior School and Mr Privett's name was seen for the first time and would still be teaching into the Second World War.

It was now too late for the opening ceremony, but *Mr. Councillor Aldwich reported that Miss Seward had requested the provision of a sundial, a flagstaff and a weathervane for the new school, and he submitted that a sundial could be obtained for the sum of 30/-. He also stated that the Superintendant of the Parks and Gardens (Mr Maclaren) had undertaken to provide a pedestal free of cost to the Committee and that he was making enquiries in regard to the flagstaff, which might be obtained from the Aquarium.*

Resolved: To purchase a sundial from Mr T Goddard, 79 and 80, North Road, Brighton for the sum of 30/-.

It also agreed that the matter of the flagstaff should be left with Councillor Aldwich.

It was further agreed that the request for a weathervane could not be entertained.

Into March, *the appointment of Caretaker was considered, and the following candidates selected by the Sub-Committee appointed by the last meeting were interviewed by the Managers:- Mr & Mrs L C Davey, Mr J Evans, Mr & Mrs A C Weller and Mr & Mrs T J Wooller.*

On a vote being taken, there appeared:

For Mr & Mrs Weller	6
" " " " Wooller	3
" " " " Davey	1

Resolved:- That Mr A C Weller and wife be appointed Caretakers and Cleaners at the school at a weekly wage of 35/- plus bonus at the current rate, such a weekly wage to be reduced if and when a house is provided by the Committee for the Caretaker of this School, the appointment to date from 31st March 1924 and to be subject to one month's notice at any time.

A second staffing matter was also considered at this meeting.

Question of appointment of Assistant Staff was considered and the proposals of the Committee in regard to the matter were submitted.

A request from Miss Seward contained in a letter dated 18.3.24 for the appointment of a progressive Infants' teacher for the top class in her class was submitted and considered.

Motion Made: That the proposals of the Committee, involving the transfer of Miss E. A. Young from the Upper to the Lower Department be approved.

Amendment Moved: That a Special Meeting of the Managers be held at which Miss Seward may be present to submit her views in the matter.

For the Amendment	3	Against	4

The amendment was declared lost and, on the motion being put, it was resolved accordingly.

This is the most formal procedure that the Managers had followed in 21 years and the process remains in use today, in Parliament and elsewhere. I think it is fair to say that, in many types of management committees nowadays, there is an expectation that most decisions can be agreed by consensus.

There is an interesting aspect of this meeting, which is hidden from view here, involving the date of Miss Seward's letter - 18.3.24. The meeting actually took place on 19.3.24, the next day. The postal service in Brighton at this time, involved collections from letter boxes being made two or three times a day and deliveries being made within the town, more than once a day. A card posted in the morning could be delivered locally in the afternoon. Clearly, Miss Seward was relying on this service to get her important message put in front of the Managers in time.

More activity in March 1924 of the kind that one might anticipate would be taking place in a new building.

It was agreed that the attention of the Surveyor should be drawn to the fact that the mats supplied are unsuitable in regard to size and that it is understood that two small mats would be preferable to each of the large mats which have been supplied.

Another letter that was dated 18.3.24 from Miss Seward contained more requests related to the new building, which the Managers dealt with as follows:

Resolved: That the School be closed for 3 days to enable the apparatus and stationery to be transferred to the new buildings and that the Elementary Schools Sub-Committee be informed accordingly.
Resolved: That references in the letter as to the following items be referred to the Sites and Works Sub-Committee for considerations and recommendations as under.
Formation of a communicating gateway and steps from Junior playground to the Nature Study Pond and Playing Field and provision of Nursery window protection.
Laying on gas at the back of the building and provision of ring for heating water, etc.
Resolved: That some means of heating water, etc., be provided
That two "Towel Jacks" be fitted to each cloakroom.
Resolved: That this request be granted.

And yet more requests:

Provision of a picture rail and spring bells for the entrance doors

Direct communication by telephone to be established with the Office
Resolved: That the new school be connected by telephone to the Education Office by the same arrangement as exists at present via Ditchling Road School.

Resolved: That the references as to the following items be referred to the Requisition Sub-Committee for consideration, with recommendation as under.

Provision of portable wash bowl for the temporary nursery cloakroom
Resolved: That this request be granted

Provision of mackintosh sheets in lieu of hammocks for nursery classes
Resolved: That no action be taken on the request for the removal of the platform.

It would appear that the volume of requests that had been listed at this meeting may have left the Clerk to the Committee somewhat confused at the end where 'requested provision' and 'resolution' were about different items. We will find out later what happened to the mackintosh sheets, picture rails, spring bells and platforms.

We do now know who would be replacing the Mr Weeks as the new Head Master of the Mixed Junior Department.

It was reported that the Committee had appointed Mr C. Hughes of Halling Council Mixed School, Rochester as Head Master of the Senior Mixed Department once Mr Weeks, who is retiring and who was continuing to take charge of the School until Mr Hughes begins duty on the 28th instant.

In April, *letters were submitted by the Headmistress of the Junior Mixed department in regard to the height of the fence; the provision of a letter box; the making of the Sun Dial and the provision of green sun shades.*

It was agreed that the remarks of Miss Seward in regard to the fence and provision of the letter box should be referred to the Surveyor to the Committee for his attention and that he be informed, in the case of the fence that the Managers are of the opinion it should be at least 4ft 6ins high and that they recommend the letter box should be funded.

It was also agreed that the request in regard to the making of a Sun Dial together with a rough sketch made by Miss Seward and now submitted to Mr. Councillor Aldrich, should be referred to the Special Branch Sub-Committee appointed for the purpose.

Also, it was resolved *that the Managers recommend that green sun shades be provided for the South and South West windows of the School Hall.*

Resolved:- That the managers are strongly of the opinion that the platforms in this school be removed as it is understood that, in the opinion of the Head teachers and Inspectors, they are inconvenient and occupy much needed space.

Resolved:- That a new school bell be provided for this School

Moving on to May, still involved with the residue of issues related to the Loder Road site and the question of the platforms pops up again.

It was reported that:
  (a)   *That the bell from the Loder Road School had now been transferred to Balfour School.*
  (b)   *That the Committee had deferred, sine die, the question of the removal of the platform from the school*

A letter was received from Mr Hughes, requesting the provision of a hose pipe for use in the offices (lavatories) and playgrounds and drawing attention to the fact that no provision has been made for removal of refuse from the dustbins.
Resolved:- That the remarks of the Headmaster in regard to the provision of 450ft of hose be referred to the Requisition Branch Sub-Committee for consideration.
It was reported that the matter of the removal of refuse was receiving attention of several members who had recently visited the school.

Another letter was received from Miss Seward, requesting the provision of handrails for the steps leading down to the playgrounds. It was recommended that this request should be granted

More requests
Resolved: That requests from Miss Seward for the provision of rush mats for the mackintosh sheets that have been provided in lieu of hammocks, and for a stool, bowl, jug, mall pail and soap dish in lieu of a portable bowl for the temporary nursery cloakroom.

However, Miss Seward didn't get the spring bells for the entrance doors – they were deemed to be unnecessary.

At the end of a long section of Balfour School requests, *Mr. Councillor Ward reported that a number of useful articles had not been removed from the Loder Road premises. The Chairman (Mr. Councillor Lane) and Mr. Councillor Ward were requested to interview the Chairman of the Sites and Works Sub-Committee (Mr. Councillor Teasdale) in regard to this matter.*

June arrived but there was no let-up in activities related to putting finishing touches to the fixtures and fittings of the new school. Such as the next entry:

It was reported that the Committee had decided that the Surveyor should be instructed to arrange for certain work to be carried out under the western classroom in the way of providing a storeroom for the storage of tools, furniture, etc., in lieu of the purchase of a shed.

The Surveyor was definitely in the Managers' sights, as the next instruction appears to heading in the same direction.

Resolved:- That the Surveyor be asked to give the matter of the erection of the Sun Dial prompt attention.

There is still no escape for the Surveyor.

Resolved:- That the Surveyor be requested to complete the removal from the school of any furniture, apparatus, etc., which is of use.

Now in July, and it is back to staffing.
The appointment of an assistant for the Senior Mixed department was considered.
A letter was received from Mr Hughes pressing for the appointment of a teacher who is a good Pianist and requesting that the Mistresses in the service might be invited to become candidates. It was agreed that applications should be invited from Mistresses in the service of the Committee and that Mr Privett, a master, this day recommended for the "Appointment List" should be sent to the school temporarily on September 1st next.

(This was the first time the name of Mr Privett was seen in the records but definitely not the last as he was mentioned many times in the oral histories we received from past pupils who had been at Balfour during the 1930s.)

Still in July, letters from Mr Hughes and Miss Seward in regard to various matters were submitted.
Resolved:- That the following requests from the Head teachers be forwarded to the Sites and Works Sub-Committee for consideration and that the last request, for a maypole fixture in the Junior Mixed Department, the Managers recommend that the request be granted.

That an additional picture rail to run the length of the room in each of the five classrooms in the Senior Mixed Department.

That a Bunsen burner be provided in the Senior Mixed Department

That the window on the Head mistress's landing in the Junior Mixed Department be hinged and made to open both sides.

That the under surface of the glazed roof of the veranda of the Junior Mixed Department be green washed to obscure the glaring light.

That the Maypole fixtures be set in the nursery floor and similar fittings in the asphalt of the Playground.

Resolved:- That the following requests from the Head teachers be forwarded to the Requisition Branch Sub-Committee for consideration.

That another school clock be provided for the Senior wing of the school.
That boxes be supplied for paper in all lavatories.

It was agreed that instructions should be given for all pianos to be tuned.

Resolved:- That the Surveyor be requested to arrange for the following works to be carried out during the forthcoming Summer Holidays.
Provision of storeroom under Junior Wing
Provision of satisfactory protection of the nursery window such as by zinc washing or by the means suggested by the late Clerk of Works
Provision of the Sundial
Provision of Sun Blinds on the nursery windows and on S and SW windows of Hall
Hire of Electric Heaters and Caretaker's Copper
Brass arm fittings to two windows (left incomplete by the Caretaker)
Spring bells on main entrance doors

It was also agreed that the Chairman of the Sites and Works Sub-Committee should be *requested to endeavour to arrange for those of the foregoing works, which have been ordered by the Committee, to be expedited.*

It was also agreed that the Surveyor *should be requested to expedite his report to the Committee on the provision of gateways and steps leading to the playing field and that the attention of Mr Councillor Teasdale should also be drawn to the matter.*

It was agreed that *no action could be taken on the request in regard to the allocation of the Playing Fields for use by the school.*
No surprise there, not even now that the new Balfour Road School was actually built on part of the playing field. However, help was at hand on this situation as we can see in Miss Seward's Log Book

Now into the autumn term, *the question of an appointment of a T.C.A for the Senior Mixed department was considered, together with the observations of Mr Hughes on the candidates. Miss M S Funnell, Mr A W Privett and Mr H Webb were interviewed by the managers.*

Resolved:- That Mr A W Privett, an "appointed List" master, who has been serving temporarily in the School since September 1st, be now appointed permanently as Trained Certificated Teacher for full-time service, at a gross salary at a rate of £207.10s per annum according to the Scale of the Committee. This appointment will date from the 1st September 1924, subject to the normal conditions.

Also in September, a letter was received from Mr Hughes and Miss Seward as to the question of further storage accommodation.

Resolved:- That the letter from the two Head teachers as to the use of the Storeroom which has been provided, be forwarded to the Sites and Works Sub-Committee with a recommendation that, if possible, the wishes of the Head teachers may be complied with.

Another letter from Miss Seward was received with reference to various matters.

Resolved:- That the requests of the Head Mistress of the Junior Mixed Department for pictures and for Readers, to be referred to the Requisition Branch Sub-Committee for consideration.

It was agreed that Miss Seward's remarks as to the Electric Heater being supplied through the same meter as the lighting, should be referred to the Surveyor of the Committee for his information and any action necessary.

It was agreed not to take any action on the request for the removal of the platforms, Junior Mixed Department.

Another September letter was receive from Mr Hughes, submitting various requests.

Resolved:- That the following requests from the Head teacher of the Senior Mixed Department be referred to the Sites and Works Sub-Committee for consideration.

    (a)   For the re-painting and re-varnishing of an old but useable cupboard.

    (b)   For the provision in each of four classrooms of an additional wooded rail for the exhibition of drawings, maps and plans, etc.

Resolved:- That the following requests from Mr Hughes be referred to the Requisition Branch Sub-Committee for consideration and that the Committee be informed that it is understood that the Bunsen Burner cannot be provided as gas is not installed at the school.

    For the provision of:

    (a)   A cupboard for the accommodation of teachers' reference library and reference books

    (b)   A cupboard for Science apparatus

    (c)   100 Bibles

    (d)   Certain Science apparatus

    (e)   A small collapsible table for Science Demonstrations

    (f)   Two pairs of curtains for Staff Rooms

    (g)   Two footballs and small flag posts

    (h)   Hooks for accommodation of gardening tools

    (i)   About 2 dozen small utility hooks for maps, etc

    (j)   Pictures, Class books, Teachers' Reference books

It was reported that the Committee had decided to take no action in regard to the following recommendations sent forward at the last meeting:-

    Provision of Bunsen burner, (Senior Mixed Department)

    Hinging of window on Head mistress' landing (Junior Mixed Department)

    Green washing of the glass rook of the verandah (Junior Mixed Department)

It was further reported that the Committee had deferred for six months the decision on the matter of the Maypole fixtures (Junior Mixed Department)

It was reported that-:

    (a)   The committee had decided that a special grant for pictures and readers for the Junior Mixed Department could not be entertained, but that they should be provided out of the amount per head allowed for books, apparatus and stationery.

    (b)   The provision for each of the four classrooms of the Senior Mixed Department of an additional wooden rail for drawings, maps and plans, etc., as requested at the last meeting, had already been ordered by the Committee.

In December it was resolved that:-

The Committee be informed that, despite the provision of a rail, the window of the Nursery Room is still unsafe and that Managers recommend that it be made safe as soon as possible.

New Year and the question of the picture rail in the Senior Department was still exercising the Managers' attention.

It was resolved that:-

The Surveyor be informed that it was the intention of the managers that an extra rail should be provided in each of the rooms, and that the Managers will be glad if he will put the work in hand.

In April, the Head teacher of the Senior Department, Mr Hughes was granted a salary increase *from £492.10s to £494 per annum (gross) according to the Scale of the Committee, to date from 1st March 1925.* (Approximately one half of one percentage point and not exactly inflationary by any means)

Also at the April meeting, the managers considered the HMI Report that had been produced following the Inspector's visits in February.

Reports of the H. M. Inspector on the Senior and Junior Mixed Departments were submitted, together with the observations of the Head teachers therein.

Resolved:- That the Reports be received:

(Copies of the Reports are attached)

BALFOUR ROAD SCHOOL

Copy of Report by H.M.I. Mr. E. F. Davidson, after visits on 16th and 20th February 1925

GENERAL

The School was transferred nearly a year ago from the temporary premises in Loder Road to an excellent new building.

At present, some children in both Departments are doing Standard III work; it would be well to decide definitely which Department Standard III children are to work. If children are to be retained in the Junior Department until they are 10, they should, as a rule, be able to proceed to Standard IV on entering the Senior Department.

SENIOR MIXED

A new Head Master has been in charge for about nine months, and since his coming there has been an earnest effort to raise the School from the unsatisfactory condition to which reference was made in the Report of June 1922 and which continued for nearly two years after receipt of that Report.

Much of the work, notably the Arithmetic, is still very weak, but the tone and discipline have improved, and there is a new spirit among both children and teachers.

Classification has also been improved. The worst part of the School is the lowest class, where the teaching is unsatisfactory.

The Head Master has made useful schemes with full suggestions for the guidance of the Assistants, and has reported on the work of each class. A successful attempt has been made to cultivate fluency in Composition, and to encourage enjoyment of good literature. The importance of accuracy both in understanding and in expression will doubtless not be overlooked and development of the English work in this direction will be helped by the careful study of passages of literature and by thorough correction of Composition.

Some modifications of History, Science and Drawing Schemes were discussed with the Head Master, as was also was the need of more advanced work for children spending a second year in the First Class. In Needlework, as there are only three groups, and girls spend a considerable time in each, provision should be made for progressive work within each group; more careful training should be given in the use of thimble and needle; more complete records of each child's work should be kept; and some better arrangement should be substituted for that by which the two Women teachers take alternate lessons with the middle group.

JUNIOR MIXED AND INFANTS
The work of the Junior Department is decidedly good. The Head Mistress and her team are keen. The children are well advanced in the elementary subjects. They are evidently happy and talk readily.

In the last sentence of the Report of 1922 reference was made to the desirability of giving more time to Observation Lessons and language-training generally, and the time allocated to these is still somewhat scanty. Certainly in the lowest class, where the children are under 5, the programme should contain far more conversation and story lessons, in which the children are trained to talk freely and distinctly.

In response to the Report, the Managers concluded thus:
Resolved:- That the observations of the Head teachers of the Junior and Senior Mixed Departments on the recent H.M.I Reports be forwarded to the Elementary Schools Sub-Committee and that the Committee be informed that the Managers regard the Reports as satisfactory. In respect of the remark by the Inspector, the Managers consider that Standard III should be taught in the Junior Mixed Department.

The Chairman brought forward the question of the allocation of the Hall between the Junior and Senior Departments.
It was agreed that a deputation of the managers consisting of the Chairman, Mr. Councillor Ward, Mrs Reid, Miss Turner, Mr Gibbins and Mr Long should visit the school at 11am on Friday next, the 1st May, to consider the matter and report to the next meeting of Managers.

A question of the provision of screens for the School was considered'

Resolved:-

That the Managers recommend the provision of a portable screen for each of the Departments in order to give more privacy to the medical inspections when these are conducted in the classrooms.

The Chairman reported the decision of the Sub-Committee appointed at the last meeting in regard to the allocation of the Hall in that the south portion of the Hall should be assigned to the Senior Mixed Department.

The action of the Sub-Committee was approved.

Two more Resolutions:

(a) *That the Managers recommend that the land adjoining the School be now used for organised games by the scholars attending the School as much time is wasted visiting Preston Park.*

(b) *That the letter from Miss Seward requesting the removal of the grass from the plot at the rear of the Junior Mixed Department and also the removal of the rubbish in the Playing Field be forwarded to the Sites and Works Sub-Committee with the Managers' recommendation that the matters may receive favourable consideration.*

Later, more on the Playing Field story:

Resolved:- That the Higher Schools Sub-Committee be requested to arrange for facilities to be afforded at the earliest opportunity for the scholars to have the use for organised games at such times as it is not occupied by scholars of the Secondary Boys School of the ground that has been allocated to Balfour School.

Back to the screens;

Resolved:- That the Committee be informed that the Managers protest strongly against the decision of the Requisition Sub-Committee that portable screens for each department in order to give more privacy to medical inspections when they are conducted in classrooms, cannot be supplied as they are unnecessary. The managers consider it to be most undesirable and strongly to be deprecated that children should be medically inspected in the presence of other children who are either being taught or being prepared for medical inspection.

In July, Miss Seward sent a letter with assortment of requests:

The letter opened with an expression of thanks to the Managers for their consideration of recent requests and then gave them another list of requests:

(a) *The provision of wire to the bottom of the gates at the entrance to keep out the dogs*

(b) *The provision of a load of sandstone for the construction of rockeries at the edge of the Nature Study Pond.*

(c) *The planting of one or two trees in the autumn to provide shade for the open air classes*

(d) *And, the creation of a notice board to keep the big lads off the field at the weekends.*

The Managers response was quite straight forward – fix the wire to the gate, deliver a load of sandstone, deliver two or three trees (one more than requested) and provide a warning board at the south-west corner of the field to stop trespassing at weekends.

Oh dear, the next meeting didn't satisfy any of the expectations

It was reported that the Elementary Schools Sub-Committee had decided that the Managers should be informed that the Committee are still strongly of the opinion that screens to give privacy during medical inspections at this school are unnecessary.
AND
That the Sites and Works Sub-Committee decided that the requests agreed upon by the Managers at the last meeting in regard to various matters cannot be granted as it is considered inadvisable to do so at present.

However, like Robert the Bruce's indefatigable spider, the Managers are not beaten yet on the question of screens and, at their next meeting, resolved as follows:
That the managers respectfully renew their request for the provision of simple portable screens similar to those used on hospitals and that failing approval to purchase ready-made articles, the Managers recommend that the necessary material be supplied with a view to the framework of these screens being made by the boys at the Handicraft Centre and the covering fabric by the girls in their needlework lessons

More requests were made in October, this time by Mr Hughes.

Resolved:- That the attention of the Sites and Works Sub-Committee be drawn to the report (made in the Caretaker's Report Book), that "the water lies on the floor of the verandah very badly on wet days and some provision for draining seems very necessary.

Resolved:- That the attention of the Sites and Works Sub-Committee be called to the fact (reported in the Caretaker's Report Book), that the Caretaker at this School has no means of heating water for the necessary cleaning of the School, although in April of last year, the Committee decided that a portable copper should be provided for this purpose.
Also resolved, that the notice Board bearing the names of the Head teachers, which now stands in the road against the school gate, be placed just inside the grounds to prevent it from being damaged.

The next item on the same agenda was another letter from Miss Seward listing the familiar "various matters", a format that must have become very familiar to the Managers. This time, their resolutions were:

Resolved:- That the remarks of the Head Mistress of the Junior Mixed Department requesting permission for afternoon school in this department to begin and close half-an-hour earlier in the during period November to January or February inclusive be forwarded to the Committee with a strong recommendation that the request be granted.

Resolved:- That Miss Seward's request for an additional mistress be forwarded to the School Staff Sub-Committee with a strong recommendation that the Committee will consider favourably their decision in this matter.

Into December 1925, and the question of the adjustment of wages of the Caretakers on completion of the house was considered:

Resolved:- That, as from the date of their entering into occupation of the Caretakers' house, which is nearing completion, the wages of Mr. and Mrs. Weller be reduced by 10/- per week, which amount has been allowed them in lieu of a house.

In the same meeting, the Managers received a report from the Sub-Committee listing the decisions it had made on all the items that the Managers had previously referred to them. In Balfour Road School, these were, in brief:

(a)   No, the junior department cannot alter the beginning and closing times during the November to January period.

(b)   No, the Notice Board at the entrance to the school cannot be moved

(c)   No, the request for an additional teacher cannot be accepted

(d)   Yes, you can have two screens, which it appears were already in store at the school all along!!!

> **In 1926** – In Balfour's third year, there were many fewer requests for materials but Miss Seward was in a battle to get an additional teacher and the Caretaker was battling to get a few bricks removed from the Veranda to assist in the draining of rain water. Miss Boxall's name appears for the first time, another teacher who would still be at Balfour until her retirement.

In January, undaunted, Miss Seward decided to continue a policy of 'if when at first you don't succeed – try again', in a letter *requesting the provision of five collapsible tables and ten chairs. Resolved: That the Managers recommend that the request of the Head Mistress for the tables and chairs be granted.*

In March, an interesting note in the Minutes appeared which looked a bit like a secondment policy but it isn't and it would not be workable today.

It was reported that, in order to save expenditure on 'supply' teachers, the committee had decided that the following schools should be placed on a list of the more favourably staffed schools, which might in emergency, lend a teacher to fill an accidental vacancy, viz:-

Balfour Mixed Seniors
Preston Road Boys

A second note also caught the eye:
A question of the powers and duties of Managers representing Parents' Associations was considered.
The Chairman reported that the representatives have the same powers and duties as an ordinary Manager, subject only to the qualification necessary for Managership.

More letters were sent by Miss Seward in March including one about the state of the playing field after the winter weather.
Miss Seward requested:

(a)   That the playing field, which is in a very bad condition, may receive attention.

(b)   That the pond may be raked clear of the rubbish which has been deposited therein by trespassers during the week-ends.

The Chairman was requested to make enquiries into the condition of the playing field and to bring the matter before the Sites and Works Sub-Committee if he should consider it to be necessary.

It was agreed that the Caretaker should be instructed to rake the pond and, on entering the occupation of the Caretaker's House, to endeavour to prevent the trespassing on the ground and buildings.

The question was raised as to the inability of the Committee to grant permission for certain trees to be planted at the request of Miss Seward. It was agreed that Miss Seward should be informed that the Committee were unable to grant the permission requested, in view of the undesirability of planting further trees, having regard to the fact that objection was taken by the residents in Loder Road to the trees already planted as being likely to overshadow the rears of their houses. In May, the Chairman, who, at an earlier meeting undertook to investigate the issue of the screens that Miss Seward requested for use at medical inspections, reported that he had arranged for the screens to be adapted for the purpose.

In June, Miss Seward requested the appointment of an additional teacher, again.

Motion made: That the Manager recommend that the request be granted.
Amendment made: That the request be referred to the School Staff Branch Sub-Committee with a recommendation that consideration be given to the question of the desirability of transferring a class from the Junior to the Senior Department.
The amendment, on being put, was carried, and on being put as a substantive motion, it was:
Resolved: That the request from the Head Mistress of the Junior Department for an extra Mistress be referred to the Sub-Committee with a recommendation that consideration be given to the question of the desirability of transferring a class from the Junior to the Senior Department.

Before the above request for an extra member of staff (or the transfer of a class to the Senior Mixed Department) was answered, Miss Seward wrote another letter to the Managers for their next meeting in July, again asking for an additional teacher. [It has to be remembered that the Minutes of the meetings do not provide a continuous narrative of activities – presumably decisions on referred items from the Managers, may get answered directly without further reference to the full committee at their next meeting. Responses to recommendations made by Managers do get recorded at subsequent meetings, either positive, negative or no decision yet, but there is evidence that some requests simply drop of the agenda.]

So, we don't know why Miss Seward has repeated her request *as to an additional teacher and as to the absence owing to the illness of Miss English.* These comments *were noted by the Managers.*

It did look as though Miss Seward was now seeking two additional teachers.

At the next meeting it *was reported that Miss English, who had recently been appointed to the Junior Mixed Department had desired that she might be re-appointed to Finsbury Road Infants' School and that, on medical advice and on the authority of the Committee, this had been done.*

This left *the question of the appointment of a successor to Miss English, which was considered. It was agreed that applications for the post should be invited from teachers in the Committee's* service and the appointment should be considered at the next meeting.

At the same meeting, it was noted from the Caretaker's Report Book that the latches in the lavatories and the drinking fountain in the Boys' playground required repair and it was agreed that the Surveyor to the Committee should be asked to give early attention to the matter.

Still in the meeting, *another letter from Miss Seward was received about the need for the appointment of an additional mistress.*
It was agreed that the letter should be forwarded to the School Staff Sub-Committee for consideration.
This would appear to be a repeat prescription for the earlier request for the same teacher.

The repetition worked this time because the next meeting in October focussed on Miss Seward's staffing needs. It turned out that Miss Seward was going to succeed to getting two teachers – one additional one and a replacement one for Miss English

It was reported that the Committee had decided that an additional mistress should be allowed for the Junior Mixed Department and applications for the vacancy this created and for a mistress in place of Miss English, were submitted.
Letters (23.9.26) and (14.10.26) from Miss Seward were received, giving her observations and the following candidates were interviewed by the Managers, viz:-

> Miss D A Boxall
> "   G M Kimber
> "   M H Wilson

On a vote being taken, there appeared

	For	Miss Boxall	4
		Miss Wilson	4
		Miss Kimber	1

Resolved:- That the following mistresses be appointed as T.C.A's in the junior Mixed Department for full-time service and exclusively in the capacity of teachers at salaries set out below according to the Scale of the Committee and subject to the normal conditions.

Name	Salary	Appointment to date from:-
Miss M. H. Wilson	£162 p.a.	30th August 1926
Miss D. A. Boxall	£288 p.a.	25th October 1926

At the end of the year, it was reported that the Sites and Works Sub-Committee would not entertain sowing grass seed on the banks at the back of the school. If they waited long enough the banks would probably be covered with self-grown grass.

Once more, the Caretaker's Record Book has been noticed in relation to repairs needed. This time it was the lawn in the Senior Department's playground that was in a bad condition and there was still a need to provide a way of creating a self-draining verandah.
Resolved: That the managers recommend the removal of the grass, which is in a bad state and replacing it with asphalt.

Resolved: That Managers recommend that some means be provided such as the removal of a brick at suitable points to enable the verandah in the Junior Department to be self-drained of water, which collects in wet weather.

These recommendations got a speedy response from the Committee – effectively, no
They said that the idea for draining the verandah *could not be entertained; the Caretaker should persist in the use the squeegee* for the purpose.
They also said no to an asphalt playground; again, no alternative solution offered.

By 1927 – the last three years of meetings, which have been packed with requests for all kinds of materials, have now been replaced by a few common place issues to deal with and the overall volume was beginning to decline. Several important items were discussed; the suggestion about developing a school's catchment area much as would be used today; Mr Hughes requested a testimonial and. temporary accommodation for additional children in the Junior School was also considered

---

In May, it was the Managers' turn to repeat a recommendation that had already been refused when they renewed their request to *have bricks removed at suitable points on the verandah in order that this may be self-draining.*

This was followed by a second straightforward item by which they *agreed that arrangements should be made for labels to be attached to shrubs in the school garden.*

If a decision to approve the use of garden labels seemed rather trivial, the third item was anything but. The question of school admissions' policy and the catchment areas, on which they are generally based on, can be a politically sensitive issue today. The next item is an early example of that very issue.
A letter (14.3.27) was submitted from Mr Hughes, suggestion the formation of a zone for admissions to the school.
Resolved: That the letter from the Headmaster as to the formation of zones be forwarded to the Elementary Schools Sub-Committee for consideration.

In another May meeting, *it was reported that the Committee had agreed that they were unable to approve the provision of labels for the shrubs at the school. However, Miss Ansell undertook to see Mr Hughes as to the possibility of the boys of the school making wooden labels at the Handicraft Centre.*

Mr Hughes was the subject of the next item on the Agenda; initiated by a letter he sent raising the issue *of the reduction of the Grade of his Department and consequent loss of salary.*
Resolved:- That the letter from Mr Hughes be forwarded to the Committee with a request that the reduction may be suspended pending the putting into effect of the Committee's reorganisation proposals.

A letter in June *was submitted by Miss Seward stating that a teacher had been certified as mentally ill and had been admitted to Haywards Heath Mental Hospital and requesting that a 'Supply' Teacher be sent to the school in her place and that the 'Supply' sent in place of Miss Boxall may be replaced by another who would be more suitable.*

It was agreed that every possible effort is made to comply with these requests.

Six days after Miss Seward's letter had been received, the Managers were informed that the teacher, who had been committed to the mental hospital, had died.
It was agreed that an appropriate letter conveying the Managers' sense of loss and of their sympathy should be sent to the brother of the deceased.

The question of the appointment of a successor was considered, and a letter was submitted from Miss Seward in regard to the matter.
It was agreed that a circular should at once be issued inviting mistresses in the Committee's service and the appointment should be considered at the next meeting.

In July, a letter was received from Mr Hughes requesting that Managers would give him a testimonial in connection with his application for acting Headship of Elm Grove School.
It was agreed that the following testimonial should be sent to Mr Hughes:-

---

The Managers of Balfour Road School have much pleasure in speaking in the highest terms of Mr Owen Hughes, who is a candidate for the post of Acting Head Master at Elm Grove School, with a view to restoring his status and financial position as Head Master of a Grade III School, Balfour Road Senior Mixed School having recently been downgraded owing to a decline in the average attendance.

Mr Hughes came to the service of this Committee as Head Master of Balfour Road School in May 1924 with excellent credentials, and the high promise given in his appointment has been amply fulfilled in the service he has rendered at the School.

Mr Hughes is a progressive Head Master and has exerted a beneficial influence upon the School, in which improvement in the tone and discipline is noticeable

The Managers feel that Mr Hughes' departure would be a real loss to Balfour Road School, but they regard his desire for transfer as a natural one and therefore unhesitatingly support his candidature in the assurance that his appointment to any Headship under the Committee would be fully justified.

At the first meeting of the autumn term, action, as the Managers had agreed should be taken quickly to fill the vacant post following the loss of the teacher who died, was effected by the selection of Miss Muriel Purchase from a group of seven candidates. One of the unsuccessful candidates here in 1927 was Miss E. M. Cowton, who went on to join the staff and was still at Balfour when I left her class and the school in 1952.

An item of Health and Safety is next, and this particular issue has surfaced before – and has continued to do so through the ages, although nowadays it is more likely to involve the potential danger of parked cars at the same site, which is identified in the item below.

The question of the provision of a "stop" at the bottom of the steps between Osborne Road and Balfour Road to check children dashing from the steps to the road was considered.
The Chairman undertook to arrange for the matter to be dealt with in the most expeditious manner possible.

Also at this October meeting *the question, as to the temporary accommodation to meet the increases in numbers of Junior Mixed scholars next September, was considered.*
The Chairman was requested to look into the matter of the necessity of the provision forthwith of temporary accommodation.
Resolved:- That subject to the enquiries to be made by the Chairman of the Managers rendering such action necessary, the Committee be requested to arrange for the provision of temporary accommodation at the Balfour Road Junior Mixed School at the earliest possible moment.

In 1928 – There were several important discussions at the Managers' meetings that helped to shape Balfour's organisation and structure, which would be confirmed by the 1944 Education Act (the Butler Act). We learn from the notes below, that a shortage of accommodation for both primary and secondary children led to a rapid decision to build a two-classroom extension at the west end of the school (as seen in the 1930s aerial view of the campus) and the transfer of some senior girls to Varndean School. Mr Hughes, who had asked earlier to be given a testimonial, was in fact successful in the ensuing interview and had resigned. The senior girls were given permission to take gardening lessons by the Government's Board of Education, following a re-organisation of the education in Brighton, which created a Senior Girls School at Balfour in place of the Mixed Department. Finally, another named new teacher, Miss Bishopp appears on the list in 1928 and was still at Balfour when I left in 1952. (And yes, she did spell her name with two p's – I have her autograph to prove it)

The issue of additional accommodation has moved on. It was reported *that temporary accommodation for 33 scholars from the Senior Girls' Department had been provided at the Secondary Girls' School during the erection of two additional classrooms at Balfour Road School, which was noted.*
Resolved:- That the Elementary Schools Sub-Committee be requested to take into consideration the question of sufficiency of accommodation at this school, after taking into account the extra classrooms that are being provided; the managers being of the opinion that the numbers showed a tendency to increase, and to portend the very undesirable continuance of the class use of the Hall on return of the girls now in the Secondary Girls' School premises.

The next Minute below links in with several of the earlier issues. One is the resignation of Mr Hughes, Head of the Senior Mixed Department in July 1927. No replacement Head was reported in the Minutes after his departure. The above Minute was concerned about finding additional accommodation in the north of Brighton and, in particular, the need for more places for Senior Girls at Balfour.
The letter below indicates that, although no previous reference had been made to it, the Mixed Senior Department at the School was about to be re-organised into one of a Senior Girls' Department.
The good news in the letter from the government education department was that it appears that it will be in order for girls to receive Gardening instruction if they are "the type of scholars" deemed appropriate to receive it. (I hope this is a clumsy way of saying the "type of scholars" are girls not boys. When Mr Weeks applied for permission, he specified "boys of below average ability".)

1 Brighton   26th July 1928
2 Balfour Road Council School, No. 35

Sir,

Up to the present time, instruction in Gardening has been given to the scholars attending the Senior Mixed Department of this School, which is at present organised in Junior Mixed and Senior Mixed Departments. As from September next the School will be organised in Junior Mixed and Senior Girls' Departments, the latter of which desires to give this instruction in future.

I should be glad to receive a copy of any form which it may be necessary to submit to the Board in connexion with this change in the type of scholars receiving this instruction.

I have the honour to be,
Sir,
Your obedient Servant

JHS
Secretary

The Secretary,
Board of Education,
Whitehall, SW.

GARDENING - SENIORS
Fig 44

The above picture was copied from the 1939 Education Week Brochure and, although no school was mentioned, there is no doubt that it was taken at Balfour Road and relates to the letter from the Board of Education's letter

Now, turning to a very different issue.

The Chairman was requested to see the Borough Surveyor with a view to the Chairman communicating with the appropriate committee of the Council with regard to the provision of a stop at the bottom of the steps between Osborne Road and Balfour Road to check children from dashing into the road. It was:

Resolved:- That the Sites and Works Sub-Committee be requested to make representation to the same effect.

Still in October 1928, *Miss Seward requested the appointment of a mistress in place of Miss Puttock.*

Resolved:- That the Elementary Schools Sub-Committee be requested to declare a vacancy in the Junior Mixed Department in view of Miss Puttock's protracted absence and to authorize the Managers to circularize the vacancy as soon as possible.

Also, Miss Seward requested a supplementary requisition allowance for the Class IV that had been added to her Department. A similar request came from the Head Mistress of the Senior Girls' Department and both were referred to the Requisition Branch Sub-Committee.

(At this point in the record of Minutes, no reference had been made of a new Head Mistress for the Senior Girls Department.)

The Chairman (Councillor Ward) reported as to the need for further accommodation at both Balfour Road and Ditchling Road Schools.

Resolved:- That the attention of the Elementary Schools Sub-Committee be drawn to the urgent need in the Balfour Road district area of accommodation for senior girls, and also for the fact that children are being refused admission to the Infants' Department of the Ditchling Road School, owing to the crowded condition of the Junior Mixed Department.

Finally, for this meeting, the Managers renew their request that a brick may be removed from the verandah at suitable points, in order that the verandah may be self-drained.

At the last meeting of the year, the Managers accepted the resignation of Miss Puttock, C.A. at the Junior Mixed Department who had been granted a breakdown allowance by the Board of Education. They then turned their attention to a series of interviews of candidates seeking to fill a number of vacancies existing across the group of north Brighton schools.

For Balfour Road School

Three candidates were interviewed: Miss E. A. Tidy, Miss E.V. Belasco and Miss H. M. Bishopp. There were two vacancies at Balfour and they were filled by Miss Tidy and Miss Bishopp, who was to remain at the School for the rest of her career.

In 1929 – The big issue in this year was again the need for more accommodation in north Brighton and the managers learned that there had been a decision to open new school in Hertford Road to relieve the over-crowding at Ditching Road School. The new school would add another school to the Managers' group and did attract over 60 children presently at Balfour to transfer, probably on grounds of location.

The first Balfour issue to be tackled was an old issue, the one about the allocation of the use of the Hall between the Mixed and Senior Girls' Departments.

The question of the use of the Hall by the Junior Mixed Department, was considered, and a letter (2.1.29) from Miss Seward in regard to the matter.
Miss Smith was interviewed by the Managers in regard to this matter, and it was understood that satisfactory arrangements in the circumstances had now been agreed upon between the two Head Mistresses, the Junior Mixed class being accommodated in the North part of the Hall and the Senior Girls in the South part, the whole of the Hall being made available for assembling by the Senior Girls' Department.

An application was submitted from the Caretaker (Mr. E Weller) for an increase of wages in view of the enlargement of the Junior Mixed Department.
A letter was submitted from Miss Seward, supporting the application.
It was agreed that the application could not be entertained.

One more example of the developing problem of finding sufficient accommodation for children from Brighton's growing population.

The question of the necessity for the provision of further accommodation for senior scholars at this school was further considered.
Resolved:- That Managers renew their reference as to the necessity for the provision of further accommodation for senior girls in this district, and will be glad to receive an assurance that provision is being made to meet the need.
(It was agreed that the foregoing resolution should be accompanied by information as to the number of scholars who may expected to become due for transfer to Balfour Senior Girls' School during the next three years.)

The response to this resolution came quickly; the Managers were informed at the next meeting thus:
It was reported that the need for further provision for Senior Girls has already been noted.

The next item at the meeting wasn't about Balfour but was about a school that would shortly be joining this group of Managers, adding to their work load.

Public Notice of intention of Local Education Authority to provide a new School for 270 junior mixed and infant scholars in Hertford Road was submitted and noted.
(This is the first time that the now familiar acronym, LEA, was mentioned in any of the Minute Books.)

Also recorded at this time was the list of teachers at Balfour Road Junior Mixed Department detailing their salaries for the coming academic year. They were:
Misses Horsley, Sharman, Young, Bishopp, Knight, Wilson and Mr Privett. Apart from MissWilson, all the other teachers were still at Balfour at the time of the Second World War.

At this time, a note was sent by the LEA to the Board of Education, which specified that the maximum roll for Balfour School, as of July 1929, was 230 Senior Girls and 380 Mixed Juniors.

Later in 1929, the Managers were told *that the Committee had decided, as a result of the recent survey of all staff in the town, that the Senior Girls' Department should be reduced by one teacher.*

Following this statement, two Balfour teachers resigned their posts, Miss Sharman from the Senior Mixed and Miss Wilson from the Junior Mixed. These were accepted by the Managers who then received a letter from *Miss Seward requesting that the question of a successor to Miss Wilson be considered.*

(It would seem, from what we now know about the teachers who were in post during the period of the 1930s to the 1950s that Miss Sharman may have left in order to await an opportunity to teach in Junior Mixed Department. She did, in fact, return to Balfour Road later.)

The Managers responded to Miss Seward's request that a successor to Miss Wilson by agreeing to employ a temporary "Supply" teacher.

In 1930 – Nothing very much happened and what was reported were a few comings and goings of teaching staff including the resignation of Miss E. Horsley from the Senior Girls School. Miss Leigh-Pirie, who had taken Mr Hughes' place as Head teacher of the Senior School would, herself, be replaced by Miss Horsley.

In May 1930, the vacancy *left by Miss Wilson's resignation was considered, and it was resolved that Miss B. R. Quigley, an "Appointment List" Mistress be appointed as a TCA in the Junior Mixed and Infants' Department, to take effect from 1st September 1930, subject to the normal conditions.*

(This is the first reference noticed where the Infants are indicated separately from the Junior Mixed section.)

Shortly after this, another resignation from Balfour was encountered, this time *Miss E. M. Horsley from the Senior Girls' Department to take effect from 1st August 1930.*

The appointment of a successor was considered and it was reported that Miss D. Bowe, an "Appointment List" Mistress had been sent to the school as from 1st September 1930. It was agreed that the consideration of the permanent of Miss Bowe should be deferred to the next meeting.

So it was, and at that meeting, Miss Bowe was confirmed as a permanent member of staff.

Now a break from the comings and goings of Balfour staff, *it was resolved that the letter from Miss Seward and Miss Leigh-Pirie as to the darkness of the school drive and pathways, be referred to the Sites and Works Sub-Committee.*
(Miss Leigh-Pirie was the new Head teacher at the Senior Girls School but not mentioned as such before in these Minutes.)

At this point in the record of the Minutes of Managers' meetings were damaged by what seems to have been the effect water infiltration making the sets of Minutes unreadable.

However, further research elsewhere has revealed that in 1931, the Local Education Authority received formal permission from the Board of Education to appropriate land being used presently by the secondary school, for use by the elementary school. It was six years ago, when the Higher Schools Sub-Committee were asked (not for the first time) to allow children from Balfour School to have use of the playing fields that surround the school. The issue didn't reappear in the Minutes but commonsense did eventually emerge and Miss Seward did record in her Log Book the many occasions when she was using the playing fields from 1925. The Government Department's formal confirmation below was merely a rubber stamp on legislation that had been in operation since 1921. But, what a palaver!

Sealed 9 December 1931   County Borough - BRIGHTON

No. 31/694 E.   Appropriation of land for the
                                             purposes of Elementary Education
                                             Education Act, 1921, Section 113 (1) (ii)

BOARD OF EDUCATION

WHEREAS the Local Education Authority for the County Borough of Brighton proposes to appropriate for the purposes of elementary education, until such time as the Authority with the consent of the Board of Education otherwise determine, the land specified in the Schedule hereto, being land acquired by the Authority for the purpose of higher education '

NOW THE BOARD OF EDUCATION, in exercise of the power conferred on them by Section 113 (1) (ii) of the Education Act 1921, hereby CONSENT to the appropriation.

SCHEDULE

Land containing 15 acres or thereabouts, situate off Loder Road and between Surrenden Road and Balfour Road, at Varndean, in the County Borough of Brighton

---

A new year started with a very modest request from the Junior Mixed Department, which the Managers *resolved to recommend that the Committee provide boot racks at the School.*

The next meeting was in June and some good reports to reveal.
The Chairman submitted, for the information of the Managers, a letter that Miss Seward had received from Mr Arthur Deane, informing her that his son, who was formerly a pupil at the School, had recently gained a scholarship tenable at Eltham College, and thanking Miss Seward for all her past kindnesses and help towards enabling his son to accomplish this.

The Managers were gratified to learn of the scholarship successes, which were reported thus:

Balfour Road	*7*
Ditchling Road	*11*
Hertford Road	*2*
Preston Road	*4*
Stanford Road Junior Mixed	*14*
Stanford Road Boys	*2*

(Five other scholars passed the examination but were ineligible owing to parents' income being in excess of that allowed by the regulations.)
The next entry was back on very familiar territory for the Managers whose time was increasingly devoted to the comings and goings of staff.

The resignation of Miss M. Knight of the Junior Mixed Department was noted and accepted as from 28th August 1932

Inter-school sports events were somewhat limited by comparison with the present level of competitions. Here is one that was held in 1932.

Miss Seward reported that the Juniors had won the Shield for Swimming in Division II having scored 28 points.
It was agreed that Miss Seward should be congratulated on the achievement.

More unusual, were the letters from the Caretakers of Balfour Road and Ditchling Road Schools asking *for certain redecoration at their houses, which were referred to the Sites and Works Sub-Committee for consideration.*

In September, it was reported that the Committee had appointed Miss E. L. Chaffer in place of Miss Knight who resigned recently. Miss Chaffer was another of the teachers who had been appointed over the last few years who was still teaching at Balfour up to, and beyond the Second World War.
At the last meeting in 1932, there was an interesting HMI Report on the newest School in the North Brighton group, Hertford Road.

HERTFORD ROAD SCHOOL

Copy of Report of H. M. Inspector, Mr. C. F. Markham after visits on 15th and 19th September 1932

The site of this School is well chosen, away from the noise of busy traffic; and the premises are modestly and suitably placed on the site, no attempt being made to secure the advertisement of a prominent frontage.

The School, which is of Juniors and Infants, and boys and girls, opened in 1931, and, owing to a transfer of children from Ditchling Road Schools, has rapidly filled. There are six classes, one for each age-group, the number of children in the age-groups below that of the ten-year-olds (which presents a "bulge")   is fairly even, suggesting that the number on the books is likely to be fairly stable.

The work has been carefully planned, and smooth running has been established. The influences that have been brought to bear on the children, are, it is felt, wholesome. The children, for their part, appear to be well cared for and happy; in general they are making useful progress; the older ones in particular display both willingness and intelligence.

The present report will not go into detail; but it may be worth while saying that Reading aloud, declamation, and (in some classes) oral answering, all merit perhaps a little more attention, if the standard which should be attainable by these children is to be reached. The teaching of Needlework is in an experimental stage, the work showing some good aspects and some which need further consideration. The scheme, methods of teaching, and the possible level of attainment were talked over.

The school is fortunate in having a Caretaker who takes a real interest of the working and cost of the electric heating system, and who, in addition to keeping the premises in tidy condition, is a good friend to the children when they need "first aid".

It was agreed that a letter should be sent to the Caretaker (Mr Austin) congratulating him upon the Inspector's recognition of his work and in connexion of his services when first aid is required.

On the same agenda, was a letter from the two Balfour Head teachers with a list of requests: they were applying for:
   (a)   The appointment of a gardener exclusively for the School
   (b)   The removal of the broken down fence
   (c)   The provision of lighting for the approach and the lavatory
It was agreed that the question of the removal of the fence and the provision of lighting should be referred to the Sites and Works Sub-Committee.
Councillor Hone kindly undertook to confer with Mr. MacLaren on the matter of the untidy condition of the garden.

In December, the Managers received an answer to some of the above requests.
It was reported that the Committee had decided that they were unable to accede to the managers' request for the removal of the broken down fence and for the provision of lighting to the approach and lavatory.

In 1933 – There was a large amount of business to get through, which was probably caused by the inclusion of the fifth school, Hertford Road. The Balfour items included staffing issues and a letter sent jointly from the Head teachers requesting the appointment of a gardener, the removal of a broken fence and more outside lighting. The reply to the three requests came in December. Three negative responses and no reasons given.

Salary increases for Miss Smale and the Caretaker

Then, a letter was received from Miss Seward with two points to make.

(a) *As to the bad condition of the playing field and the infrequent marking of the pitches*

(b) *The acceptance of a gift of a bird bath from a parent.*

It was agreed that the reference by the Head Mistress to the bad condition of the playing fields should be referred to the Sites and Works Sub-Committee for their information.

Also, it resolved that Mr A Over of 7 Dover Road, a parent of one of the scholars, be thanked for his kind gift to the Junior Mixed Department of an octagonal pedestal bird bath.

The resignation of Miss Creagh from the Junior Mixed Department was accepted as from 31st August 1933.

The question of a successor to Miss Creagh was considered, and it was reported that the application forms of the "Appointment List" teachers who had not yet been appointed to any schools, had been submitted to Miss Seward for her consideration

It was agreed that the teacher chosen by Miss Seward should be sent to the School after the Summer Holidays and that the question of the appointment of such teacher should be considered at a later date.

In July, the Head teachers wrote *to request a separate telephone exchange for the school.*

Resolved: That the request be forwarded to the Finance Sub-Committee with a strong recommendation that the request be granted,

Returning to the question of a successor to Miss Creagh in September, it was reported *that in accordance with the decision of the Managers, an "Appointment List" (Miss Whewell) had been sent to the School pending consideration by them of the question of a permanent appointment of a successor to Miss Creagh.*

It was further reported that Miss Whewell had since applied for a post in another school in the town, and in view of the possibility of her appointment thereat, it was agreed that the vacancy should be circularized.

Finally in 1933, the last meeting resolved the problem of finding a successor to Miss Creagh. Four candidates were interviewed and, taking Miss Seward advice into account, the Managers' *ballot resulted in votes for only two of the candidates:*

For	Miss J. M. Bone	5
	Miss J. E. Watterson	1

So, Miss Bone, who had been teaching at Elm Grove School, was appointed as a TCA in the Junior Mixed Department subject to the usual conditions.

In 1934 – There was one overriding issue on an HMI report from 1933, to which Miss Seward made a full response and took the opportunity to raise the issue of the use of the Hall that had been the subject of much argument between the two Head teachers. The more mundane issues amounted to a report on an offensive smell from the urinals and a request from the Caretaker for hot water but he was also in a bit of hot water himself with the Managers who felt his work was not exactly satisfactory.

There was one report from the end of 1933 that didn't reach the Managers until the first meeting of 1934 (March), which was another HMI Report. This one was focussed on the Junior Mixed Department.

Copy of the Report of the H. M. Inspector, Mr. C. F. Markham, after visit of 19th and 20th July 1933

JUNIOR AND INFANTS' DEPARTMENT: (Head Mistress, Miss H. F. Seward)

This School of 395 children comprises 8 classes, 5 of which have over 50 children on roll. There are seven good classrooms but it is a matter of regret that one class has to work in a partitioned-off portion of the Hall and the use of the remaining portion of the Hall is shared between this and the adjourning department.

The Head Mistress and the staff work well. The scheme is satisfactorily planned, work is duly tested, records are systematically kept and terminal reports are critical and useful.

Work throughout the school progresses steadily. Particularly thorough work is done in the top two classes. The Needlework lessons are interesting and in this subject a very good foundation is laid for the work of the senior schools. The handwork is well graded and in the various classes much commendable work is to be seen.

8.11.33

Resolved: That the Report be received and it was agreed that a letter of congratulation should be sent to the Head Mistress.

The Managers were content to congratulate Miss Seward but I found a document in the school, written by Miss Seward that demonstrated her discontentment

Miss Seward responds to the 1933 HMI Report

Below, is an interesting reply made by Miss Seward in response to the HMI's report in November 1933. In a nutshell, she wanted more HMI reports made about her school and she agreed with the inspectors that the Hall was too small and not fit for purpose (and it was to remain so). Something that didn't remain unresolved was her suggestion that use could be made "by opening up the commodious space under the New Wing, which was built in 1928". Well, it was eventually developed just as she wanted – but the wait for the decision to call in the builders lasted nearly 80 years. That is, not until Balfour Junior School was extended in 2009 ahead of the decision to merge with the Infants' School.

Observations on HMI's report issued on 8th November after visits of 19th & 20th July 1933

Headmistress – H. F. Seward

This is the first report issued since February 1925. There has been a succession of inspections by HM Inspectors, of two days length each time, in; 1928, 1930, 1931, 1932 and 1933.

Reports have been promised after each visit, but have not arrived until this issue of 8th November 1933. Thus the school has worked, without recognition, for eight long years.

The one regret of the HM Inspector is the regret also of the Headmistress, and it has existed ever since the opening of the school in 1924.The Hall has never been known to be a Hall and the only conclusion to draw is that the building is not large enough.

The school which stands in spacious, delightful grounds and on a site which has never, and never will be paralleled in Brighton, is small for the district. I would like to suggest again, that the Junior quarters be extended by opening up the commodious space under the New Wing, which was built in 1928. The iron girders are there to give support. At the same time, the lavatories (which are now a "blot on the landscape" and stand out pre-eminently on the main front), could be moved and built on the East and West extremities of the school.
The occupation of the Hall means much curtailing of the Junior curriculum
1. There is no musical programme other than singing
2. No drill except in fine weather
3. No space for medical inspection
4. The class is turned out when the Hall is required for lectures, etc, and house in a senior classroom or packed in a junior classroom where there are already 50 children making 90 – 100 scholars in one room
5. Last, but not least, the class is subjected to all noises, striving to work against, (1) Singing and Folk Dancing, the latter with gramophone accompaniment from the Senior Department and (2) Singing of the Junior classes

There are very few periods of peace for this class.

With regard to the actual report of the work, I am more than delighted that the Inspectors have noted the steady progress throughout, which leads up to the particularly good work of the Upper Juniors. Good steady progress is essential and produces a foundation for good accumulative results.
Remove the great handicap of the Hall Question, and we can go ahead furthering the curriculum and ideals of work.

H. F. Seward Headmistress   14.11.1933

And now back to the Managers who try again to get more light on the subject:

That the Managers again desire to draw the attention of the Sites and Works Sub-Committee to the danger of the absence of any sort of lighting in the approach to the School and recommend that the Sub-Committee take steps to deal with the matter.

Later, *a report by the Head teachers in the Caretaker's Book with reference to the work of the Caretaker, was read out.*
It was agreed that a letter should be sent to the Caretaker informing him that it has been brought to their notice that there is a very offensive smell from the urinals and hope he will take steps to effect an immediate improvement.

Later still, *Councillor Hone undertook to confer with the Surveyor in regard to the matter of the offensive smell from the boys' lavatory.*

And yet again, the Managers try to press their requirement for more light by *resolving to recommend the favourable consideration of the Committee for the provision of an extra light in the approach to the School as, in their opinion the present one is insufficient.*

At the same meeting, a letter from the Caretaker concerning the *means for obtaining hot water for cleaning purposes in the school, and applying for the installation of a power meter and two electric points and an electric fire, in his house.*

The Caretaker is in the spotlight again

The Chairman kindly undertook, when she was visiting the school, to see Mr. Weller, the Caretaker, in regard to his work, which it was considered by the Managers to be not altogether satisfactory.

In 1935 – It was time for something different. The question of removing the platforms in each classroom to make more space (as asked for 10 years ago) was raised again. Lavatories and the smell returned but the Caretaker seemed to have got back into good books. Managers said they would look into using a gas ring for hot water. Unfortunately, gas wasn't supplied to the school. A modern idea was advanced about co-ordinating occasional school holidays, which would help parents with children at different schools

---

Mr Becket raised the question of the necessity for the removal of the platforms in each of the classrooms which are never used and which would make available more space.
Councillor Hone undertook to look into the matter, and it was agreed that he should be empowered to refer the matter to the Sites and Works Sub-Committee if he feels that the work could be done satisfactorily.

In May, *the Chairman reported that she had visited the school and was of the opinion that there was an improvement in the cleaning of the premises by the Caretaker.*

Later in the meeting, Councillor Hone supplied two reports about previously raised questions.
- (a) That the offensive smell from the boys lavatories is attributable to their improper use, and he was proposing to confer with the Headmistress on the matter
- (b) That the Surveyor had promised to inspect the walls of the classrooms as to the practicality of removing the platforms

The next item on the agenda was the same as the previous one – lavatories

- (a) That the Committee be informed that the seats in the lavatories become very wet in inclement weather, and the Managers recommend the provision of a movable glass screen (or louvre) to prevent this.
- (b) It was reported that Miss Seward was anxious to use part of the Hall to form a class, and it was agreed that the formal consent of H. M. Inspector should be obtained when the Committee had made a decision on the application, which Miss Seward had made to them on the matter.
- (c) A letter was received from Miss Seward to the effect that the electrical installation for heating water had been supplied, but that she had been informed that owing to

the provision of a copper boiler, it was not possible to draw water for drinking purposes, except her own risk.

Mr Box kindly undertook to make inquiries as to whether it is possible to provide an extra gas ring in the Head Teachers' private room, and that the matter should be further considered at the next meeting.

It was agreed that Miss Seward should be informed that the Managers sympathise with her in this matter, and that her letter is receiving their consideration.

(d)   A letter was received from the Caretaker (Mr. Weller) thanking the Managers for recommending his request for a hot water heater for the School and the electric fire in his house.

Next meeting in July, Managers returned to consider again the question of a gas ring for Miss Seward to use for heating drinking water. Unfortunately, gas is not laid on at the school. It was agreed that the matter should be deferred sine die.

It was also reported that the Committee had decided to give permission for the formation of a second class in the Hall up to the August holiday, and for an extra temporary teacher to be allowed, and the whole matter should be further considered by the School Accommodation Committee.

Finally in the July meeting, an interesting point was discussed which even today, causes parents of children at different schools to raise an eye-brow or two.

Resolved:- That the Elementary Schools Sub-Committee be informed that in the opinion of this Board of Managers there appears at times to be a want of co-ordination amongst Head Teachers in choosing days for closing their departments for occasional holidays, and suggest that a circular might with advantage be sent to all Head teachers in the town recommending that if Head teachers propose to close their departments within a day or two of each other that they should endeavour to arrange for the holiday to be taken on the same day as it is felt that otherwise the attendance of the department remaining open is adversely affected as is also the domestic arrangements of parents.

In 1936 - Managers had just three relatively minor items for Balfour Road to deal with in three meetings. Surely by now, they must have been aware that the current management system's days were numbered

---

(February) *The provision of wire mats or scrapers at the bottom of the verandah steps, referred to in the Caretaker's Book, will be looked into by the Chairman.*

(May) *Letter from the Head Mistress requesting the provision of curtains and fittings for the West windows of the two south-west rooms, which was referred to the Sites and Works Sub-Committee with a recommendation that the request should be granted.*

(September) *A letter was received from Miss Seward requesting the provision of a wardrobe for her staff.*
It was agreed that the matter should be referred to the Chairman.

> **And in 1937** - at the meeting on 17th March, the Managers were informed of their collective fate but not before they took one more decision, collectively.

A letter was received from the Head teachers of the Junior and Senior Departments complaining of the excessive pruning of trees and shrubs. The Chairman reported that he had already had his attention drawn to this matter and that he had referred it to the Surveyor to look into.
It was agreed to await the Surveyor's report.

But, as the letter below from the Chairman of the Education Committee, Dorothy Stringer makes clear, the days of the existing Boards of Managers were over. The last four items that were dealt with by the Managers over the past 13 months, wire mats, curtains, a wardrobe and tree pruning rather underline the reason given for re-organising the system of school governance.

However, under the 1902 Education Act, all public elementary schools provided by the Local Education Authority were to have a body of Managers, including up to 4 LEA representatives. It was decided in 1903, that schools in Brighton would grouped together as were those in the north of Brighton. As we see below, the LEA decided to replace the Boards of Managers with individual boards of Managers in each school. At some point, these boards came to be called school governing bodies and their functions, roles and duties have been expanded and developed through successive Education Acts ever since. The earlier bodies were comprised largely of LEA and Church representatives as shown recorded in the Managers' Minutes of 6th October 1906.

THE END OF BUSINESS

54 OLD STEINE BRIGHTON 1

F. Herbert Toyne BA
Education Officer
To whom all communications should be addressed   Telephone: Brighton 4104

26th February, 1937

SCHOOL MANAGERS

Dear

   The Education Committee have, as you are probably aware, decided to abolish the bodies of managers of "Provided" Schools from the 31st March next. A primary reason for coming to this decision is that many of the duties of Managers as at present organised are of a routine nature and involve duplication of work both by the administrative staff and by members of the Committee who are also severally members of managing bodies. In the committee procedure some delay is unavoidably caused before a necessary change can be effected, but if the matter has to await the prior consideration by managers this delay is often greater than those anxious to see the improvement made, would wish. Furthermore, the pressure of business on members on the Committee and others interested in public affairs makes it increasingly difficult to find members who can spare the time to bring managing bodies up to the membership required under the Committee's regulations.

   The work connected with the routine administration of the schools, has, however, formed but a section of the duties of Managers. Perhaps the most valuable contribution has lay in the personal connexions they have established with the schools. In their visits to the schools, they have always shown a keen interest in, and contributed much to secure, the contentment of the teachers, the welfare of the children, and the goodwill of the parents. The schools have gained much from these personal contacts and from their other valuable services which Managers have so readily bestowed. The Committee are fully appreciative of their loyalty and public spirit, which they have devoted to their duties, often involving a considerable expenditure of time, and I have been asked to express on behalf of the Committee their full recognition of the interest and devotion they have shown in the cause of education.

   In thus relieving the Managers of routine matters, the ultimate decision on which rests with the Education Committee, the Committee hope that the managers will, in the capacity of Visitors, could continue to render the services which have proved most valuable in the past, namely maintaining the contact with the schools and the teachers, and bringing to the Committee's notice any improvements in the building or in the organisation of the school, which they consider desirable. Many of those who are willing to serve as Visitors will undoubtedly wish to continue their connexion with the schools they served as Managers, and they will be free to decide whether they wish to maintain contact with the whole group or with one particular school. The method of carrying their duties whether by rota or by pre-arranged meetings in the schools will be a matter for experiment.

(Unfortunately, the copy of this letter had been glued to the last page of the Minute Book which now prevents sight of one of the last two sentences of the letter. This was probably a final direction to the Managers about arrangements that would be put in place to involve them in the new process.)

In the meantime, we should be most obliged I you would inform us in due course whether you would be willing to serve as a Visitor and with which school or group you would wish to be associated.

               Signed: D. E. Stringer

Chairman of the Education Committee

Reminiscences of schooldays past written by the pupils from the Loder Road (temporary) School, pre-1924 and from those who went to the 'new' Balfour Road School, 1924 – 1939

Up till now, Balfour's history has been told largely through the records found in the Head teacher's Log Books and the Minutes of the Managers' meetings. The latter source of information has come to an end. Now it is an appropriate opportunity for the many past pupils to have a voice. Over the years, they have sent their reminiscences to the school in writing, photograph collections and other items of memorabilia. This material was then put on display as part of 60th & 75th anniversary celebrations of the opening of the school on the Balfour site. There is one very important text missing here, which is Owen Williams' account of life at the Loder Road School, which was included at the start of Chapter One to help set the scene in 1905. His is the only substantial account we have of what it was like to be a pupil at the Loder Road School in those days. (See Appendix 3)

1. **Memories from the Loder Road School, including yet another name it was given by those who attended there.**

I am 85 years old and was born in Bates Road. I went to the then Loder Road School and it had a corrugated iron roof and when it rained, it was so noisy we had a job to hear the teacher speaking.

Muriel E. Elms (nee Watts)

I am interested in your 75th anniversary, and as I have just reached 75 years of age you can reckon the School had only just moved up from the old Loder Road Tin Hutment. One family member recalled how she attended Loder Road during the First World War and walked home with candles in jam jars!

I was lucky to start at the newly built school and one of the teachers Miss Young was there to make me feel at home. She had been a training teacher with two of my aunts.

Nora Cox

Note: Nora Cox was well informed by her aunts and had a good memory too. Miss Young was indeed employed at Loder Road School for a six-month trial period starting at the beginning of 1922 and was appointed to the permanent staff as a result.

2. **Memories of pupils who went to Balfour Road School between 1924 – 1939**

These two contributions were sent in to Balfour Junior School in as part of the Jubilee celebration (1924 – 1984)

I was at the school from 1925 – 1931, which must have been just after it was opened. I was at that time, an only child with very little previous contact with the outside world. It says much for the atmosphere of the school that I retained such happy memories.

Built in bungalow style, with light, airy classrooms opening on to verandas in the front, flanked by flower borders and bounded by playgrounds on one side and a field at the back, the premises must have been the envy of less fortunate schools situated in older parts of the town.

The Head teacher, Miss Seward and her staff took an immense pride in the school. School caps and hat bands were introduced with constant instructions as to the behaviour when wearing them. Waste paper and vandalism were almost unknown. Monitors were sent round the playgrounds to clear any scraps around. The staff were ably assisted in this by Albert Weller the caretaker, a pillar of the Brighton Labour Club, who not only rose at 5 o'clock in the morning to get the school warm, but who was seen at the other end of the day, keeping order at the gate as we all streamed out down Balfour Road.

The two teachers, who made the most impact on the children at that period, were Miss. E. Young and Mr. A. Privett who were in charge of the two top classes. Miss Young had tremendous enthusiasm and energy. She must have worked all hours to produce the visual aids and work-cards, which we found so stimulating, all hand-written in her large open script (Italic handwriting had not yet arrived in schools).

One of her great interests was teaching us to swim. Every week we were escorted to St Lukes' Baths in Queen's Park where she went into the water with us, holding us up under our chins and willing us to gain confidence. She was determined that we should all leave school with at least a 10 yards Certificate.

Mr Privett was also a great character, ruling the boys with a rod of iron, but with a sense of humour. He kept the bright section of the class on their toes and the school had a good record of passes in the eleven-plus scholarship exam. The class was large – over forty. I am not sure how the less able fared.

The creative arts were much encouraged by the women. We did painting, modelling in clay, embroidery and drawing with pastels. Miss Knight, the nursery class teacher had artistic talent – her brother Charles who lectured at the College of Art, exhibited at the Royal Academy and became well known in Sussex. She was allowed to take Art with the higher classes from time to time.

Memories of a few events remain with me. The school took part in the Greater Brighton ceremonies when we were taken out (wearing our school colours, of course), to beat the new boundaries with sticks, a process that left us with blisters on our hands. At this time, the Pylons were erected between Patcham and Pyecombe.

Then there was the introduction of school milk, when Miss Seward and the staff all stood drinking bottles of milk to encourage us to pay our two and a half pence per week for added nourishment. I can still see Mr Privett winking at us and scandalising Miss Seward by saying, "I'd rather have a beer."

Then there were the journeys to other schools to "sit for the Scholarship" in three parts, a knock out contest which left few at the end.

The previous year, the school had produced "Top Boy of Brighton", a certain Howard Smith who was in later years to have a distinguished diplomatic career.
*[**Note:** It certainly was a distinguished career; Sir Howard Smith, who was born in Brighton on 15 October 1919, went on to study Mathematics at Cambridge University. After just one*

year, he was drafted into the Bletchley Park team of brilliant mathematicians who helped to break the German codes during the Second World War. After the war, he didn't return to Cambridge but joined the Foreign Office instead. There, he rose to become the Head of Chancery in Moscow in 1961, at the height of the Cold War and supported the Ambassador during the Cuban Crisis. Following that, he became the Ambassador to Czechoslovakia in Prague. Finally, he became the Director General of MI5 for three years before retiring in 1981. A fuller picture of his life's work can be seen in several obituaries that are available on Wikipedia.]

The year I entered for the examination, a number of us gained entry to Varndean, another girl and myself being lucky in obtaining a Hodgecock Scholarship with a small money grant, for which we received much glory. I was also made School Captain with a blue and gold enamel badge, a boy called Eric Bone being Vice-Captain.

After Balfour Road, school was never so enjoyable again although I was very happy at Brighton School of Art as it was then called, but the end part of the training was over-shadowed by the disruption of the war years.

My husband was an ex-pupil of Varndean although not of Balfour Road. We have both now retired from long and, in my case, varied, teaching careers, and have four children.

Margaret Johnson (née Fry)

A second letter was found alongside the one above, but there was no signature or covering letter.

Memories of Balfour Road School, Brighton
(In the 20's and before)

The Babies' class was tucked away in the west alcove, full of toys and interesting frames with coloured counting beads which slid along the rods, wall pictures and mats. In the afternoon the little ones had to rest on the floor part of the time.

Most of the children in the school had time to go home for lunch.

In the second classroom we started to learn reading, writing and arithmetic. Maths tables were chanted over and over again, and then there were reading lessons by taking turns round the class, followed by some writing with pencils.

Milk was distributed at 11am in small bottles (1/2 or 1/3 pint each) from crates, and straws were given to drink it from the bottles.

All classes were taken out on to the tarmac during school hours for physical exercises, games, and when fine, everyone spent their time out there when not in their classes.

About May-day, we were shown how to dance round the Maypole. As we progressed through the school we arrived at Miss Gladys Young's class. She called herself "Irene Mee" (after Arthur Mee), and compiled an interesting magazine every so often. She was an enthusiastic teacher who took us out for nature study walks, and produced many items of interest in the classroom such as jars of tadpoles, and pots of beans to grow. Then we went up to the Hollingbury Camp and we were shown how it was built centuries ago with a ditch around and where the positions of the post holes and entrances were. We visualised the people who occupied the land in ancient times and included even the Ditchling Beacon in our excursions – all on foot.

Mr Privett was the only male teacher and had about 40 in his top class and what a noise they made. He concentrated on coaching the children to enter exams to obtain Scholarships to Secondary Schools and the entrance exams. Mostly it composed of general knowledge quizzes, and it is possible he found it almost too much for him to contend with all those lively, and sometimes naughty children. Boys were usually sent off to Head Mistress, Miss Seward for a few strokes of the leather-thronged tawse, or cane for punishment. The girls probably had to write lines.

Miss Seward lived in Surrenden Road and most of the children were fairly local too. Punctuality had to be kept, but children always found time to play on the way to and from school. The boys played marbles in the gutters. The girls had skipping ropes or joined in a long skipping rope right across the road (not much traffic then). When frost was about in winter time, everyone spent their time making slides on roads and pavements to the hazard of elderly people. Then, in the spring, out came spinning tops, yo-yos, bat and ball on elastic, hoops (wooden and iron), and in the little shops many interesting items could be brought, including favours for the "Boat Race" in navy and pale blue. Even politics had its turn ("The Gunpowder Plot"). Fireworks were bought and hoarded up ready for Nov. 5th with little back garden parties. Then, the popular mechanise were roller skates, scooters, small bicycles, boxes on wheels, sledges and dolls prams.

Familiar faces on the streets would be the Muffin man with a tray on his head and ringing a bell, the scissor-sharpening man, the cane repairer sitting on the pavement and the photographers who waited for the children coming out of school to take their photographs and then came back a few weeks later to sell what they could!

Before the 20's

There are a few people about who went to Balfour Road School when it was just an old building with a tin roof. During the First World War it had to be shared and there were shared session with Ditchling Road pupils who only went part-time. They went home in the dark and carried jam jars with lighted candles to see their way.

(Anon)

All the following contributions were sent in to be displayed at the 75th Anniversary

Pond attracts attention, as do the outside toilets

I joined the school in the autumn 1927, when I was nearly six years old. I left at the end of the summer in 1932 having won a Scholarship to Varndean. Teachers I remember were Miss Knight who looked after the first year, Miss Boxall, Miss Young and Mr Privett. Miss Seward was the headmistress.

Memories are of morning assemblies in the Hall with the hymns chalked up on a blackboard; visits to the pond in the field behind the school to see the wild life; skipping in the playground with a long rope; reciting 'times tables' and 'Daddy Longlegs' in the toilet block in the middle of the playground.

W Mary Jackson (nee Wakely)

Fig 45

This photograph shows the pond in an early stage of development; a later one will show it fully developed as a focus for nature studies.

Early sighting of Brighton and Hove Albion footballers

I can remember many good and enjoyable things about my days spent at Balfour Road between September 1928 and 1934. I am in touch with Hazel Adams (nee Turner) who is also in touch with George Braysher of our years. I can remember Denis Chubb, Mary Scott, Elizabeth Hillier, Bernie Moore, Jackie Ball (both of football fame) and many more.

Trips to the old barn by Varndean Holt to see the owls, to swimming at St Lukes' baths and exercises in the playground on boards 3ft x 2ft because it was dirty on the ground!
All teachers were really great especially Mr. Privett. I had a duty of dusting Miss Seward's office which made me feel special.

Jean W. Gardner (nee Pettit)

An incentive to be really good

I was a pupil at the school from 1928 to 1934/5 in the juniors. I was 5 years old and started in Miss Knight's class, which was at the end of the school building in those days. The other two classrooms were added afterwards.

Miss Seward, the headmistress used to bring a most beautiful doll to the classroom if we had been really good! My father made a dolls house for that class, which lasted for many years – I don't know if it is still in existence.

Mrs Vivian P Winter (nee Maddox)

So much remembered, and the toilets

I remember:

(a) The steps from Osborne Road to Balfour Road forming the boundaries of the County Borough of Brighton and Steyning before the town extended northwards in 1928.

(b) Balfour Road was unmade and not developed until 1905 when the houses were built, although there was a farm track and farm building and two hoses for the farm on the way to where Varndean School is now.

(c) I watched a steam-roller construct Balfour Road with chalk hardcore, sprayed with tar and with a surface of grit.

(d) I played in the roads – Herbert, Gordon, Bates and Loder Road – football, cricket, marbles in the street; spinning tops, and long skipping ropes for Easter. There was a Maypole erected on the lawn opposite the school for St Georges Day when cubs, etc., wore their uniforms We also played in Preston Park, where we climbed on the Great War I tank, much to the annoyance of the park attendant! Sometimes, we watched polo matches by the cavalry in the park who held a tattoo annually.

(e) One of my aunts went to the old school when it was a corrugated iron structure in Loder Place where the caretakers lived in a new house.

(f) I started school in September 1929 and the uniform was yellow and black for cap and tie, and grey shorts and yellow and black socks. The outfitters were Potters in York Place, which has since moved to George Street, Hove.

(g) The staff were Miss Bishopp, Miss Boxall, Miss Young, Miss Purchase, Miss Seward the headmistress, Miss Quigley and a man, Mr Privett.

(h) The outside toilets were uncovered and very cold in winter.

(i) The number 8 bus with solid tyres and a spiral staircase to the top. The terminus was the corner of Loder and Balfour Road. The bus had a conductor. There was a water hydrant for the steam-driven lorry but most trade was delivered by horse and cart.

(j) The school was brick built with an open veranda and a boiler/chair store in the basement. The steps went down to the fields where there was a pond for nature study. During the war there was a 'Dig for Victory' and so my father had an allotment in the field.

(k) As a class, we used to go over to the Barn to watch the Barn Owl

(l) In the infants' class, we wrote on slate pads and the education was the '3Rs'.

(m) In the morning break, all children were issued with 1/3 of a pint of milk with perforated cardboard top and straw. In the winter, the milk was warmed by standing by an open stove and it tasted revolting!

(n) The asphalt playground was often frosted over and we used to slide the length of the playground just when the assembly bells sounded and we ended up in a pile – boys and girls.

(o) I remember going to St Luke's and North Road baths by tram; to Preston Circus for a change to St Luke's or staying on for North Road, travelling, of course, upstairs on the top open deck. Hungry after swimming, we used to purchase a stale roll of bread at the shop on the corner of Marlborough Place for ½d.

Malcolm Hampton (Sept 1929 to Dec.1935)

3.   Memories from the 1930s

Penny concerts and Mr Privett - again

I was a pupil at Balfour Road School from 1931 or 32 until 1936/37. My name was Beryl Moppett. I remember Miss Bone who taught us my first poem – 'Abu Ben Adam – may his tribe increase' was the first line. Then there was Miss Boxall. In her class I learnt knitting and the boys did too! Children I remember were Beryl Roberts, Winnifred Edwards, John Reid and the Mitthias sisters. Also Mr Privett was there and Miss Young. Friday afternoons in the former's class were spent on drama and we acted plays we'd made up ourselves.

The adjoining school was for senior girls and they put on 'Penny Concerts', which must have been outside school hours and I really enjoyed them.
I remember Olive Adams (my age) had the tawse – Goodness knows what for as she was quite a mild girl. This took place during assembly in front of the whole school.
Mr Privett used to read a book to us on alternate Friday afternoons. It was 'The Invisible Man'. He sneezed and pushed the book right off his desk pretending it was the force of his sneeze.

Beryl Fenton (nee Moppett)

A serious punishment episode

When my family moved to Brighton in1933, I was just 5 years old; I started Infants School in that year. I was placed in a corner classroom to the left of the Hall. We sat at small tables with single chairs. Each of us had a plywood box to keep our books, papers and pencils. These were collected each evening and passed around each morning. We had a rest time every afternoon when heads were allowed to rest on our arms at the tables.

I moved through the three infant classes, and as I recall, my first schooling was happy and I do not remember any time of difficulty. The three teachers were pleasant and committed. Their names were, as I remember were Miss Bishopp, Miss Bone and Miss Chaffer.

On arrival at school, we were met at the gate by the caretaker, Mr Weller, and we played in the playground until the head mistress, Miss Seward, walked to the balcony and rang a large hand bell. We lined up in class order and marched into the school classrooms.

At this time, I went to school with my sister Molly who was 12 years old, and we parted at the drive way, as in those days, half of the school was Balfour Road Senior Girls. There was an iron fence across the playground. I often met my sister at the fence at mid-morning break for a chat or a swap of sweets.

I moved on through the junior school and my memories were always pleasant ones of the three teachers, Miss Boxall, Miss Quigley and one other (but cannot recall her name). When I moved into the fourth class 4A, I found the going harder. I think this was my growing up and the fact that I had lost interest in the 3 R's. My only love became sport and Balfour lacked any facilities and did not have a sports teacher.

We played our own games in the fields and swimming was taken once a week at North Road Baths. We turned up at school with our costume and towel rolled up under our arms and, after walking down Balfour Road, we took the tram to North Road. The water was always freezing cold and we were glad to get out of it. The teacher would walk alongside the pool with a pole held a couple of feet ahead of you. I do not remember a teacher ever getting into the pool with us.

Discipline at the school was, or so it seemed to be, upheld by the teachers and the children themselves. I never saw a cane but the leather strap resided in the Head's room. I only ever saw the strap used once, but did experience a rap in the knuckles with a wooden ruler. I did see chalk and a blackboard rubber thrown.

The one time the strap was used, the whole school was assembled in the Hall. Miss Seward set out a long lesson as to why the two girls standing on the platform were to receive the strap, which was to be rendered by Mr Privett, the only male teacher. It appeared that some days before, workmen were called to repair the boys' toilet block. Part of the work consisted involved re-rendering the inside walls. The workmen reported that when returning the next morning, the rendering was covered in hands and feet marks. It was believed that some boys had done this, but they were not forth coming in admission despite the threat that the whole school would be kept in at playtimes, other nice things would be stopped including a school outing to the Isle of Wight. This brought forward the unbelievable admission that two girls had done the damage. The two were marched, with teacher escort, to the toilets and hands and feet were inserted to make a match.

And so, the strap was used four times and I can say, not a tear was seen in the eyes of the girls. Miss Seward never quite understood that girls are as tough as boys.

These are the 4A class members that I can remember:

Edna Andrews	John Nunn	Evelyn Miles	Bobby Burgen
Jean Presbit	Joan Presbit	Colin Curtis	Colin Page
Michael Potts	Roy Pretlove	Pat Young	Jeffery Burtenshaw
Grahame Edwards	Sylvia Guy	Iris Hughes	Yvonne Donaldson
John Walford	June King	Ronnie Stevens	Enid Hutchinson
George Mackensie	Monica Son		

John Booker (1933- 1939)

What follows towards the end of this section is a brief round-up to include two school documents found at school, also from this period.

The documents are:

1. A Day in the Country

The first piece was found in an old exercise book containing a Scheme of Work in which the teacher had left a copy of a notice of the coming of the annual school outing, about which I have been able to date from information in Miss Seward's Log Book. It took place on Saturday, 29th June 1929. Anyone who is familiar with this territory will see that this outing incorporated four or five potential visitor attractions, Arundel, Chichester, Midhurst, Petworth and Bramber, all in one go. The journey's end might have seen a large number of very tired children at about 7pm.

As in her Log Book entries, this notice, which is an exact copy of the original found, has Miss Seward's hallmark of underlining important information.

THE ANNUAL OUTING OF THE CHILDREN AND STAFF OF BALFOUR ROAD JUNIOR SCHOOL WILL TAKE PLACE ON SATURDAY, JUNE 29TH. THE START WILL BE MADE FROM THE SCHOOLS AT 9.30 A.M. AND THE PARTY WILL PROCEED VIA SHOREHAM, SOMPTING AND WEPHAM WOOD TO ARUNDEL. (HERE LUNCH WILL BE TAKEN). AFTER A REST THE PARTY WILL PROCEED VIA FONTWELL, WESTHAMPNETT, CHICHESTER, MID LAVANT, WEST DEAN, SINGLETON AND COCKING TO MIDHURST. HERE TEA WILL BE TAKEN AT SOME TEA GARDEN. A VISIT WILL BE PAID TO THE RUINS OF COWDRAY CASTLE. THE RETURN JOURNEY WILL BE MADE VIA COWDRAY PARK TO PETWORTH, PULBOROUGH, STORRINGTON, WASHINGTON, STEYNING, BRAMBER AND OLD SHOREHAM TO BRIGHTON ARRIVING ABOUT 7 PM.

2. A School Harvest Festival

A newspaper article found tucked in the Visitors Book, records another annual event, this time the School's Harvest Festival. The assumption that can be made is that this event took place in 1932. The "happy tradition of eight years" in the article's first line, would suggest that the new school, opening in the February of 1924 went on to hold a harvest festival in the autumn. The date is rather less interesting than the reporter's description of the festival, and especially so in the detail in which the harvest's copious bounty was recorded in the second paragraph.

In accordance of a happy tradition of eight years, the Balfour Road Junior Mixed School celebrated on Monday, its harvest festival. "Celebrated" is just the right word, for the school was thrown open to the parents for the afternoon and some 380 fathers, mothers and friends enjoyed the experience of watching lessons in the beautiful open-air classrooms which are a feature of this school. That the children for their part, enjoyed being watched, goes without saying.

The little people were extremely proud of the School Hall, where there was a great collection of foodstuffs and groceries of all kind, numbering in all more than 700 separate gifts, brought by the children to be distributed by the Queen's Nurses. Among the gifts were 208 lbs of sugar, 13 lbs of cocoa, 15 lbs of cereals, 133 packets of custard powder, blancmange and jellies, 47 lbs of jam, 9 marrows and various other offerings ranging a crate of silver paper collected during the year to a packet of salt. There was a 3 lb jar of honey.

When lessons were over, the children gathered in the playground, and in the brilliant sunshine of a perfect autumn afternoon, sang a sweet and simple service of thanksgiving, which included the Te Deum, the Lord's Prayer and several bright hymns. They were very proud of the fact that they were accompanied not only by the school piano, but by a nine-years-old boy violinist from among their number.

The Headmistress (Miss H. F. Seward) told them of the good work done by the Queen's Nurses, and Miss Turner one of the school managers, thanked Miss Seward and the staff for all the organisation that had gone into the making of the delightful festival. The three shrill cheers which the kiddies gave for the Queen's Nurses (after three for their own headmistress) must have gladdened the heart of Mrs Galbraith, the Lady Superintendent for Brighton, who was an interested spectator.

Before the service, there was an exciting basket-ball match in which the boys beat the girls – but it was a near thing.

Finally in 1939, with the Second World War approaching, the Education Committee organised an Education Week involving all schools and colleges; starting with a Service at St Peter's Church on 19th February and ending on the following Saturday with Concerts and an art and craft exhibition at the Dome

Events and exhibitions were held in every school with Balfour School's contribution being held on the Wednesday afternoon. The brochure that was published for the occasion contained many photographs showing the range and diversity of provision of education in the town, some of which have been included in this book. The one below is an interesting flow-chart of the provision that was in place in 1939. One or two of the fee levels shown would be mouth-watering were it not for the date!

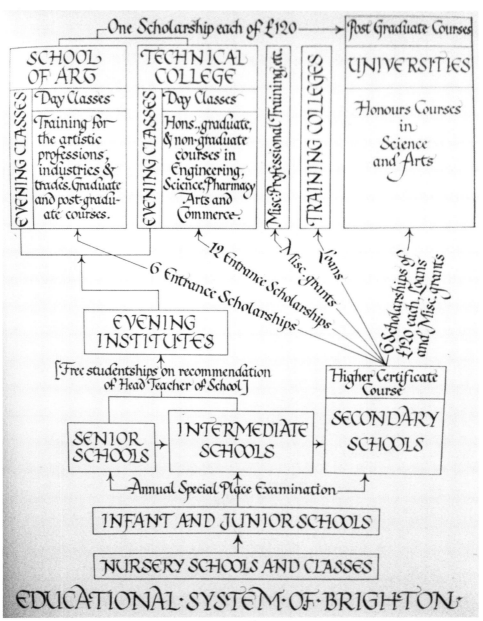

Fig 46

This flow chart of Brighton' system of education was copied from the 1939
Education Week Brochure

Section II

Documents relating to the Second World War (1939 – 1944) including references to local schools linked to Balfour

More memories from past pupils who were at the School during that period

Log Book entries describing the events, trials and tribulations in coping with the situation.

World War Two started on 1st September 1939 when Germany invaded Poland and ended in Europe on 8th May 1945. On 25th June 1945, the Armistice between France and Nazi Germany was signed also at Le Francfort nr. Compiègne.

It is now the turn of former pupils who were children at Balfour Road School during the Second World War to describe rather different experiences to those that befell the pupils at the Loder Road School during WW1. Not this time, a war fought mainly in a foreign field but one that was also brought to the doorsteps of towns and cities in this country as well as those world-wide.

The day the German bomber flew over and more, much more

Right from the first day, I loved school, which was nowhere near the size that it is now, of course. There were seven classes as far as I can remember (one for each year), and the whole of the school was housed below the old Hall. The building above the Hall was Balfour Senior Girls School, under the Head mistress, Miss Horsley; to us a terrifying being. I was later to learn that she *was* human, and a very kind one. The toilets were in the middle of the playground, about a dozen for the whole school, junior and seniors. There were railings across the playground separating us from the seniors.

The three infant classes were at the west end of the building with the 'baby class' in the large room in the corner. I can vaguely remember beds coming out in the afternoon, when we all had to have rest. If it was really fine, the beds were on the veranda. Imagine this happening now! Two of the infant teachers, names were Miss Bishopp and Miss Chaffer.

The awful day came when we lost our building and it became a soldiers' hospital, where all the patients wore blue suits. I hadn't a clue what was going on, but I heard the word 'war' bandied about in adult conversations. For a long time, (I am not sure how long) we had to share school buildings with Ditchling Road Junior School (now Downs School). It was a fair walk for us, (no cars then, they were all demobilised), and times were dangerous.

One week we went to school in the morning, and the next in the afternoon, alternating with the Ditchling Road pupils. For the other half of the day, we would go to different halls to play games. I remember two of the halls; one at Stanford Road Methodist Church and the other at a church in Cumberland Road. We seemed to manage to learn something in spite of our disrupted teaching.

The mothers in our area used to take turns to take us to school. About three mothers for fifteen children, all with our gas masks in cardboard boxes hanging round our necks. On one occasion

I remember getting to Havelock Road, and suddenly an aeroplane was coming very low towards us. Someone shouted 'German' and we all laid down in the gutter. Why we thought this could be safe, I have no idea. However, we were machine gunned and bullets ricocheted all over the place. It was miracle that we all lived. The drama was over, but one of the mothers shouted, "in here quickly" and we charged through someone's front door. Even to this day, I have a vivid picture of a woman standing at the top of the stairs, with her hair in curlers, and her mouth wide open when she saw about 15 frantic children come charging through her door. On investigating the damage, one child had a bullet through the wrist and another through the lapel of the coat. As I said – a miracle. We then continued on our journey to school, and just carried on (without counselling); I expect we had forgotten the incident by the time we arrived at school; this was one drama among so many.

Another time, on my way home, without warning (the planes used to fly very low to avoid detection) we heard the whistle of bombs, and looked up just in time to see several roofs fly up in the air. I think that was when Dover Road was hit.

Eventually, our time at Ditchling Road School came to an end and we moved up to a corridor in Varndean Grammar School for girls. At least the girls did, the boys went to the Boys' School. So we were split. The classes were then only half size, so every two years were grouped together. So, there was a wide range of ages in each class. I can even remember being given the task of teaching Arithmetic to some in my class who were really a year below. I knew then that I wanted to teach when I was older, and I did. I don't know which teachers went with the boys, I can only remember one male teacher, a Mr Privett, who had to 'go away to fight the Germans', which was the way we put it.

So began a new era, with girls only. The head teacher was Miss Seward, and her room was a box room under the main stairs of the school. She was not at all well, and often the school was run by Miss Young.

I can remember running errands to Miss Seward's house in Surrenden Road, or across to the Boys School and it was wonderful to be able to go across the fields or down the lane where normally we were not allowed to go. I have just thought that a bomb could have dropped at this time, but never did. I seem to remember that most of our lessons were done in the air raid shelters at the back of the school.

Another of the teachers was Miss Boxall. She was very strict and nobody dared put a foot wrong. She was a very good teacher, and we really learnt what she taught us. Two things in connection with her particularly stand out in my mind; drawing and playtime. She was marvellous at drawing and at Christmas time while we watched she would cover the whole blackboard from one side of the classroom to the other with Christmas drawings. All filled in with coloured chalks.

I can remember Santa coming out at the top of the chimney and a dog curled up with the presents at the bottom of the Christmas tree covered in lights and decorations, which were hard to come by then. These drawings would stay there for the last few days of term.

Also, I can remember the playground, which was the first half of Varndean Terrace. Miss Boxall would join us, and we loved the games she played with us. Two in particular, 2s and 3s and the long skipping rope, which she would turn for what seemed hours.

One day, a new girl arrived, and she was German. I can remember our reactions and wondering why on earth '*a German*' was in our classroom. We only thought about Germans as our enemies, people who dropped bombs and tried to kill us. She was introduced to us as a German Jew, and it was only years later that I thought what horrors that girl must have gone through in her own country and then to be stared at by a load of hostile English children. We had no idea then about the Jewish problem. She did not stay long with us.

I never went back to Balfour. In 1944, I moved on to Varndean Grammar School

Rita Shipp (nee Hollands) (1937 – 1944)

I went to Yorkshire

I was a pupil from the age of 4 years (1938), until I went on to Brighton Intermediate School, York Place, and later named Margaret Hardy

In 1940, I was evacuated to Yorkshire for 4 years. We returned during the time Balfour was being used as a hospital. During this time, we went to various schools, mornings one week and afternoons the next. We went to Clermont Road Church Hall, the Downs School and Varndean Girls School. We spent many lessons in the air raid shelters.

I can still remember Miss Young, Miss Chaffer and Miss Bishopp, who were our teachers. Miss Seward was the Headmistress. Miss Horsley was Head of the Senior School, where my sisters were pupils.

Patricia Long

Yet more wartime memories

I was a pupil from 1938 to 1944 and my two brothers attended from 1947 to 1953 for one and 1953 to 1959 for the other.

I attended the present building for just one year when the year started in 1939. I remember my first few months aged 5, in Miss Chaffer's class, when part of each afternoon was spent resting on little camp beds, covered by blankets each with a different animal embroidered on them. I also recall the toilets' situation in the centre of the playground, very exposed to the wind and the rain.

At the outbreak of war, the school was used as a military hospital, with a large white cross painted on the roof to indicate to the German bombers that it was a hospital. I remember then, having classes in various golf and tennis huts in the vicinity, then being allocated some classrooms in Ditchling Road School.

Towards the end of the war, we were allocated half the ground floor at the eastern end of the Varndean Girls' School.

Many children were evacuated, of course.

I remember having to carry our gas-masks, in brown cardboard boxes, to school every day and the frequent practices being called to put the masks on and do our school work in them, very suffocating.

While at Varndean Girls' School, as Balfour children, many hours were spent in the rabbit warren of air-raid shelters underneath the field at the back of the school. These shelters had wooden-slatted chairs along both sides of the tunnels and voices echoed through them as hundreds tried to continue lessons but we usually ended up singing until the all-clear siren sounded.

I remember too, the great paper shortage for exercise books. All new exercise books were cut in half, each child given one half-book to use, and only being given another half when the first book was completely used up. Pencils were also cut in half before being distributed.

I can remember seeing a German plane break up in the sky and then the pilot parachuting out as I looked from the high vantage point of the Varndean School windows.

I have very fond memories of the teachers at the time, the Headmistress, Miss Seward, the two teachers of the 'baby' classes, Miss Chaffer and Miss Bishopp; also Miss Young, Mr Privett, Miss Boxall, Miss Purchase and Miss Bone.

I also remember Mr Weller, the caretaker, who used to help the children quite a lot.

Margaret Rich (nee Pavey)

And more again

My sister (Mrs Elizabeth Ridgley, nee Samson) and I both attended Balfour between the years 1944 and 1950. I commenced my primary schooling aged 5 at Varndean Girls School at the top of Balfour Road as Balfour school was used as a recovery hospital for wounded soldiers. I believe that the headmistress was Miss Seward. I see from my school reports that in 1946 Miss Pickett was headmistress and in 1947, Mr E D Slater was headmaster and remained so for many years, I believe.

During the years of shortages after the war, we used to be asked to bring in all used envelopes to the school and they would be opened flat and we practised our writing exercises, etc., using very thick pencils.

Richard Samson

Now the wartime Log Book, which provides a diary of events written as they happened, by Miss Seward and Miss Young, who covered for her at times of ill-health.

Second World War at Balfour Road School

- *Balfour Road School was commandeered* by HM Government at the beginning of September*
- *School is holding sessions at Ditchling Road - 18th Sept onwards with Juniors in the Senior School and the Infants in the Infant School*
- *Great difficulties have been experienced in removing stock, first to Varndean Boys, and thence to Ditchling Road.*

It can be assumed that the close proximity of Varndean Boys School was the reason that the stock was moved there first in order to comply with the government's request for speed. We know that the WW1 requisition at York Place was ordered to be completed in 24 hours.

A request for speed, which probably led to the stock being loaded into containers without any inventory being taken, was the likely reason for the disappearance of the school's Punishment Book. A new one was started in 1941when staff were unable to record an outstanding entry in the missing Book.

*In 1939, as Headmistress of the Balfour Senior Girls' School, Eleanor Horsley experienced an incredible co-incidence when she was again involved in the evacuation of a school that had been commandeered, this time by the Ministry of Defence. She had been a sixth- former at York Place in 1914 where she helped the younger children to move their belongings when the school was evacuated.

- No Halls are available until November and then only one for use of the school and that to be shared with Colbury London School, amounting to two afternoons a week. Wet weather prohibited attendance on many afternoons.

(Presumably the walking distance was a limiting factor.)

- *December 11th*
  Two Halls – St Saviours' Crypt and Clermont Hall given as under:

Crypt	*Clermont*
Monday	*Monday*
IV a & IV (If wet)	*Infants*
Tuesday	*Tuesday*
Junior IV a & IV	*Junior: I and II*
Wednesday	
Staff – Billeting	

The reference to 'Billeting' indicated that provision was being made for teachers who were attending to the children who had been evacuated to Brighton. Brighton had been designated a 'safe area for London children to be housed. Brighton children were offered the sanctuary of Yorkshire when Brighton seemed less safe.

Thursday	*Thursday*
III & IV a	*Infants*
Friday	*Friday*
Class III	*I & II*

In January 1940

- *The children remained in the same Halls and Buildings but in September, the Junior School was transferred to the Junior Department at Ditchling Road and the Infants' School was transferred to the Varndean Girls' School, starting on 5th November 1940.*

Two days later, the Log records that there can be:

- *No games or singing in classrooms as this will disturb the Varndean girls. A section of the dining room was allocated for singing and drill lessons were restricted to being held in the field. This ruled them out of being held during the winter months.*

At this time also, the Head was engaged yet again in transferring the cupboards and stock, this time from Ditchling Road School up the hill to Varndean Girls.

The year ended on a calmer note as there had been:

- *No alerts so the school has gone on happily this week and closed for the Xmas vacation on Friday 20th December.*

1941

- *Started with a problem with milk being delivered in quart bottles leaving the Head and teachers doing the sterilising of the measures, jugs and then packing everything away.*

186

Presumably this change in practice was connected with the exigencies of wartime – shortages of resources and staff.

In March, lessons were interrupted by sessions of registration involving the children whose parents had opted for them to be evacuated. By the end of March, the school of 250 carried on with two teachers short owing to the evacuation. Miss Young (Deputy Head) and Miss Bone have accompanied a party of 46 to the Yorkshire West Riding villages around the Holme Valley and Holmforth.

Back at Balfour, it was a week of alerts.

At the end of April

- *The Junior School transferred to Varndean Girls School. Balfour Road Junior and Infants were now working as a compact whole.*

This might have been a well-timed move as, two weeks later, two teachers were removed for service in Yorkshire with the evacuated children and none sent to the school to take their place. With the two groups of staff together, it would have been a bit easier to cover for the missing teachers

The year continued in this disjointed fashion with much evidence of staff illness and injury caused by accidents, mainly in severe winter conditions. With echoes of the conditions so prevalent at the temporary Balfour School, the classrooms were often very cold in temperatures in the region of 40°F.

Then in September, another school re-organisation this time, reversed part of the April re-organisation with the Junior Boys transferring to Varndean Boys and the Junior Girls and Infants remaining at Varndean Girls.

Perhaps the Log entries for the month of November are a good example of the recurring variables.

- *Miss Bone has resigned from Yorkshire to take up a post at Horsham. There are now only twelve of junior children in Yorkshire, scattered over several villages. Only three are in the district in which Miss Bone teaches.*
- *A request from Mr Toyne to send another teacher to Yorkshire to replace Miss Bone has been received. Objection to such a request made by Miss Seward to the Education Committee, without avail.*
- *The school has had unceasing interruptions since 1939.*

Quite so, as Miss Seward said, and before the month ended, she recorded the following:

- *Change in the school sessions took place Nov. 9th – 27th as follows:-*
  9.30 – 12.30p.m. and 2.00 – 4.30p.m.
- *Miss Chaffer leaves today, 27th November for Yorkshire for a stay of six months.*

1943
The Log Book records that Miss Bishopp replaced Miss Chaffer in Yorkshire on 4th May 1943 and Miss Chaffer returned to her class in Brighton.

Another event brought the War right into the staff room.

Mr Privett, the only male teaching at Balfour at this time, had been given several 'leaves of absence' during 1942 to attend camps run by the Air Training Corps (ATC). The ATC had been established in 1941, growing out of the Air Defence Cadet Corps which was formed in 1938, and was focussed on training young men for service in the Royal Air Force.

School summer holidays began on 29th July with Mr. Privett expecting to be 'called up' for service in the RAF but had not heard anything official. By 3rd September, when the school returned for the autumn term, Mr Privett had left. Miss Urquhart had been appointed to take his classes IV(a) and IV Boys at Varndean Boys.

The good news was that he did survive the War.

1944
In the summer there were Air Raid warnings of Flying Bombs, which caused some disruption to lessons that involved transport to them, especially ones like swimming.

By the 1st December 1944, any reference to Air Raids and other wartime consequences appeared to have disappeared from entries in the Log Book and the next entry sums up perfectly the sudden change of emphasis:
- *Week ending 8th December 1944*
- *Invoices for Balfour School canteen have arrived and are now handed over to Mr. Weller (Caretaker) to check in goods. Decorators have arrived at Balfour Road, but apparently only two men and a boy are at work, consequently the prospect of moving before Xmas seems impossible.*

This was undoubtedly frustrating but any concern expressed would, equally undoubtedly, have been answered along the lines that there has been a War on.
- *The Roll stands at 334 this week and classrooms are full*

With the Roll at 334, the average class size would have been almost 56.

As we saw earlier in the section on WW1, other schools in the area had wartime experiences that overlapped with those at the Balfour Road School.

1. Varndean Girls School, (1884 – 1984)

In preparing for the 'anticipated' possibility of War, Brighton had been designated as a 'safe-area' (from aerial attack), and VGS prepared to take 50 evacuated girls from the Grey Coat Hospital School, but by 1940, the picture dramatically changed. The girls were found a safer refuge.

Varndean had to find 100 places for 100 infants displaced by the military hospital at Balfour. Brighton was now declared a "dangerous-area" subject to evacuation, and all girls were given the opportunity to move to Yorkshire if they and their parents, wished.

On 18th March 1941, the first group of Varndean girls set off for an unknown destination in Yorkshire. Altogether, some 220 girls were evacuated, together with several members of staff, whilst a slightly greater number stayed in Brighton. For the next 1½ years,

Varndean was split in two parts under two second mistresses, Miss Everden in Yorkshire and Miss Price in Brighton, with Miss Warmington providing the unifying element by her constant journeys between the two.

The evacuated group found themselves sharing the buildings of Holme Valley GS and were billeted in the villages of the Pennine Valley of Holmfirth.

The School back in Brighton continued as best that it could. One "novel" experience was fire watching duty for the staff and members of the Sixth Form, who each spent one night a week guarding the school. It was no idle duty – on one raid, fire bombs were spread spectacularly across the vegetable patch that had once been the "sloping hockey field".

By the autumn of 1942, Hitler's threat to the South Coast seemed to have receded and most of the evacuees returned, creating a considerable accommodation problem, since Varndean was still providing rooms for the Balfour Road children.

2. Ditchling Road School, (1890 – 1954)

A whole book could be devoted to the efforts which all schools made to serve both education and public needs in the Second World War. But the events are sufficiently fresh in most minds to require only the slightest reminders and space will permit no more.

Ironically enough, March 1939 saw the successful Education Week in which this school took its full share, and which was to be, for more than seven years, the sole possible demonstration of complete whole-time education.

Gas Mask drill; initiated in July, was a vague omen of rigours to come. In September, it was decreed that Balfour Road Junior and Infant Departments, together with two evacuated Croydon Schools, should share these premises, and "double sessions" became normal hours. "Out-of-hours" activities followed in the local Church Halls and crypts; teachers took the extra duties of Billeting Officers and Fire Watchers; Air Raid Wardens became as frequent visitors as members of the Committee had been.

This period of interruption and indecision coincided with a time of widespread epidemics and severe weather. Mid-1940 found the trenches in constant use and it was indeed a good day when visits to the "subterranean classrooms" did not total more than two and a half hours. Morning sessions were held on Saturdays in an endeavour to make up for lost teaching time.

A voluntary evacuation to the West Riding of Yorkshire was arranged in March 1941but a large majority of children and parents preferred to stay and endure the worst. It is difficult, unless one endured these vicissitudes, to appreciate the relief which "VE" and "VJ" days brought or the heartfelt thankfulness when normal routine was restored.

Section III

Reminiscences of pupils who went to Balfour between 1944 and 1955

Log Book entries as the School recovered from the effects of the War and moved into a more settled period.

With the Second World War coming to an end, the school was being prepared to receive pupils again after it was decommissioned by the Ministry of Defence. Before we pick up on the Log Book again, which was left at the end of December 1944, we should hear from the pupils who were at Balfour at this time.

A little bit more of the War and much more besides

I was at Balfour Road from 1944 until 1950 so started before the Second World War had ended' For a while we had to go to Varndean Girls School because Balfour had no bomb shelter.
Infant teachers included Miss Bishopp and Miss Chaffer – one never mentioned one without the other. Miss Chaffer added to the trauma of that first day of school by accusing me of kicking someone under the table. Oh, the injustice!

Then there was Miss Boxall who tried with great patience to teach me to do proper joined-up writing. She had regular spelling tests for which the whole class stood at their desks. When you got a word wrong you sat down, until only the winner was left standing to receive the grand prize of a threepenny bit. I often won and remember being devastated – and puzzled – when Miss Boxall said on one occasion that she wished my manners were as good as my spelling. What could she have meant?
Mr Comer was my hero. He had been in the RAF during the War and though I now realise that he might have been just a humble clerk in an air force office, to me the RAF meant that he must have flown Spitfires and Hurricanes. He was Rockfist Rogan and Biggles rolled into one and he had a moustache like Clark Gable's. He used to tell us stories from Shakespeare – I vividly remember being mesmerised by Julian Caesar, especially the cunning cleverness of Mark Anthony's "Friends, Romans, countrymen" speech. The love of Shakespeare that man inspired survived all the boring grind of reading around the class, which was the norm at Varndean.

One shameful incident remains in my mind: for the class Christmas party my big sister had made a special cake with elaborate and loving care. I took it proudly to Mr Cromar who duly admired it, making me feel even grander. He said that I should put it away in the cupboard and he would bring it out as the climax of the feast. But I grew impatient and fetched it myself before his signal. As I carried it I stumbled – was I tripped? (If so, and the culprit is reading this, will he please own up?)
Of course the cake fell, icing down and my pride fell with it. It was almost 30 years after the event that I was able to tell my sister about it.

In the "top" class we had Miss Bottomley whose unfortunate name was the subject of many smutty schoolboy jokes. But I enjoyed that year and recall a BBC Schools broadcast about the world's great cities. Miss Bottomley divided us into groups to prepare our own studies and my group chose Mecca for a reason that escapes me now. Amongst other activities we made a clay model of the Kaaba.

We read that this holiest of holies reeked with all the perfume of the East so we assembled our own version from various household items. Taking it to school in a screw top jar, we duly announced our Kaaba. The diabolical smell lingered in the classroom for days.

Also in this year we had a brilliant student teacher who involved us in a study of medieval Preston by giving us all the names and trades from the Doomsday Book. We had to write stories about our characters and this really brought history alive in a very special way.

Balfour Road was excellent at sport in those days with an especially successful football team. I was hopeless at the game but loved to stand on the touchline and cheer. The star player was my friend Brian Blacker who lived just up Gordon Road from me. Our street gang also included Balfourites Alan Watling, Frank Saunders and John Wingate. But the divisive 11+ exam caused the parting of the ways as Brian, Alan and Frank "failed" and went to secondary modern schools. When Mr Slater signed my autograph book on the day I left to go to Varndean he wrote in it the school motto: "The days that make us happy make us wise". Balfour Road certainly gave me happiness but I am still waiting for the wisdom.

John Funnell, Melbourne, Australia (1944-1951)

Some eclectic memories

My first day at school has long since faded from memory, so I can't tell you that I bawled my eyes out or clung desperately to my grandmother's leg. My earliest memory is of Miss Bishopp's infants class in the room at the bottom corner of the school, and a board on which she had hung little plywood cut-outs representing the day's weather. I didn't understand the need for this as it was only necessary to look out of the window to see what the weather was doing. Anyway, hadn't we already trudged through the prevailing atmospheric conditions to get to school? All lying down on little camp stretchers and having an afternoon nap is another recollection that has lingered also.

Note: The photograph below was not taken at Balfour Road School. It appeared in the Brighton Education Week Brochure in 1939. From my memory, the three beds at the left corner were the ones used at Balfour.

REST—THE NURSERY SCHOOL

Fig 47

191

Moving up year by year towards the Hall there were other teachers, Miss Marshall who got married and became Mrs Mayes perhaps. Miss Lindop who breezed in from Kenya or Tanganyka or somewhere, and who wore fancy leather boots, the first I had ever seen, and who I thought was very exotic.

The percussion band: I was always in tambourine, triangle or castanets…..girls' instruments. Never did I get to play the drums. There was status in playing the drums, but it never came my way. Still, that little band gave me some modest start in my appreciation of music that has remained with me 'til the present day. One of the teachers had a series of books on the lives of the great composers, which I found very interesting.

At about this time there was an accident in the Hall during PT in which a boy from another class lost his life. We were kept in our classrooms in silence while the teachers ran about. We didn't know what had happened until later but we had some idea that something very serious had occurred.

School dinners. We used to have little green wooden tokens to show that we had paid. Just why that should come to mind I have no idea. I don't remember the food, but then again there have been many restaurants in which I have eaten since those days where the meals were forgettable also. The canteen, if that is what it was called, was in a separate building down a set of steps at the end of the building.

Mr Slater. What can I say? We didn't like each other. I remember him pulling my hair once just after I had scored a goal in a football match out at the back, the one and only time I have scored in any organised football in my entire life. I have no idea why he did it. Perhaps it was an "own goal". Then there were the daily processions up the stairs to his office at morning playtime to get our work stamped. An oval green "Good", a purple "Very Good" or a rectangular red "Excellent".

I am pleased to say that I earned one or two of the greens and purples. But never the latter.

Isn't it odd how your mind works? I'm now up to the Hall and the offices. Mr Slater used to refer to the toilets as "the offices", as in "Have you all been to the offices"? It's a wonder that ex-Balfour Road pupils of the era didn't engage in anti-social behaviour in their later business life.

On the other side of the Hall, my memories are rather dim. I remember Mr Divall, although he was never my teacher, as he was the only male member of staff save the aforementioned Mr Slater. I would sometimes see him walking home as he lived up in Hollingbury somewhere near us. I also remember the 11-plus from this time, and Balfour Road served me very well in that regard as I was successful in gaining a place at Varndean.

Oh! Country Dancing on the lawn. Hated it.

The Coronation. There were, as you can imagine, great celebrations. I still have the blue commemoratory glass that we were all given to mark the occasion, it has pride of place behind the bar. And there was a pageant of some kind down in Preston Park and we all sang "Land of Hope and Glory". Something I can still do with gusto (and a tear in my eye) when the last Night of the Proms is on TV (to the great embarrassment of my family). Preston Park reminds me of the school games. I was never in them nor was anyone I knew, all I remember is the march past to "Sussex by the Sea".

Peter Clark (1947 – 1954)

Lunchtimes were memorable too, and lots more

My first recollection of Balfour Road Primary School was when I joined Reception Class in 1947/48. I have a vague recollection of the layout of the room but distinctly remember having to lie down on a camp-style bed in the afternoon to 'rest'. I could never understand this as I was never tired!

I moved through Miss Chaffer's class and into Miss Sharman's class where I remember being very upset by the death of 'Captain', a ship's cat on which we had done a project.

Lunchtimes live vividly in the memory. Playing in the playground, going down a long flight of steps to the field, playing marbles and being marched down the path to the School Canteen, a flimsy looking hut close to the Loder Road entry to what is now Dorothy Stringer School. Obviously as children, we did not appreciate the post war shortages of food, but two things stick in my memory. Friday was stew day – it was repulsive – I can still taste it now. Mr Slater, the Headmaster, was a rotund fellow who liked his food. He was ably assisted by the Canteen Staff who without exception piled his plate high everyday totally disregarding the shortage of basic food. We weren't allowed to leave anything – not even the repulsive stew.

Class sizes in those days were large as evidenced by the photograph of Miss Marshall's class of 1951. For some reason, unknown to me, this is the only class photograph I have in all those years at Balfour.

Miss Marshall, soon to be Mrs Mayes, took us for two years after which we went to Mrs Moore and begun in earnest our preparations for the Eleven Plus which culminated in Miss Cowtan's class the following year. I believe that when I went into Miss Cowtan's class we had all been streamed into those likely to and those not. This was pretty horrible for those being labelled before they had a chance to prove themselves.

Mr Divall, who I believe was the only other male teacher in the School apart from Mr Slater, took the other class. There was much excitement amongst the boys when he announced that he was going to take a party to see Sussex play the Australians at Hove. It was a case of who got there earliest got the places.

Good pieces of work were rewarded with a green stamp for 'good', a blue one for 'very good', a mauve stamp for better than that (it was a blue and green stamp combined) and a red for excellent. The red stamp was square in shape while the others were oval. The excellent stamp was a rare event resulting in much rejoicing.

When the 'great' day dawned when we were given our Eleven Plus results we were allowed to go home to tell our parents the good (or bad) news or we were told to telephone from the phone box close to the entrance to the school. This was great if you passed but pretty awful if you hadn't.

During our stay at Balfour, King George VI died. Mr Slater came round and told all classes the bad news. We spent much of the day imagining sitting on his throne with his crown on and dying there! By the time we went home that evening, the trolley buses that ran up and down Surrenden Road had black triangular flags draped over their conductor poles. I had a piano lesson that night (I didn't like playing piano) but the piano teacher hadn't heard the news!

Nick Armstrong

A very successful career built on a Balfour education

I want to write to tell you that I spent one happy year at Balfour Road, from September 1948 to July 1949. I was in the 11+ class and my teacher was Miss Boxall. I have always thought that my Balfour experience was very important and informative. I was happy at school, became an enthusiastic learner (my academic results improved dramatically during the year) and I played on the rounders team and the netball team.

I trained as a primary school teacher in Birmingham, emigrated to Canada at the age of 22, married and had two sons. Over the years I have taken undergraduate and graduate work at the University of British Columbia and taught in schools and community colleges. Also, both my husband and I taught in Nigeria for 4 years. Much later, after 30 years in education, I had a career change and moved into the field of International Development and later became the Executive Director of Save the Children Fund of British Columbia. I now work as a consultant in the areas of education, youth and international development.

The high standards of excellence in academic achievement by the teachers of Balfour Road School set me on a path in the right direction. I will always be grateful for the excellent teaching I received.

Elizabeth Bannister (nee Rider)

Mr Privett continues to feature in dispatches

I still remember with affection and respect my teachers at the school; particularly Miss Boxall in my early days and Mr Privett when in class IV, and, of course, Miss Young and Miss Seward. My reports show that class sizes were then in the 50s – surely a tribute to the teachers who gave us all such a good grounding for the educational ladder still to be climbed. I can remember Mr Privett, in one of the last classes before I left, giving us an introductory talk on algebra, but warning very sternly at the end that we were not to imagine that we now knew all there was to know on the subject!

Peter G Swan

An Eclipse of the Sun

The most noteworthy happening that I experienced during my time at Balfour occurred on 30 June 1954, when I was 10 years old. This was the date of the Eclipse of the Sun.

As this was due to happen later in the day, the teacher, knowing that I had an interest in Astronomy, asked me to explain to the class what was going to happen later in the day. I quickly referred to the book I had with me, Descriptive Astronomy, and set about drawing a diagram on the blackboard.

Later, the moon began to pass across the Sun – and we followed this, during the dinner break, using some kind of eye protection (probably smoked glass) and I made a series of drawings. The only paper I had to hand was some embossed wallpaper, which made this rather difficult. Unfortunately, I lost the drawings almost immediately. If only I had them now, what a marvellous memento they would be.

This was the very first time I was asked to give an astronomy talk – since then, as part of my job as Interpretative Officer at the Foredown Tower, I give them all the time.

It is interesting also to note that this eclipse was the last one visible as Total somewhere in the British Isles (The Shetlands) and your anniversary occurs when there will be another visible as Total, from Cornwall.

I hope this is of some interest.

Mike Feist

This one rings a bell

I vividly remember my first day, running home, crying all the way at lunchtime I only lived in Loder Road, opposite to the entrance to Stringer.

My first teacher was Miss Snook, down the steps in the sort of basement classroom and of course, there was Mr Slater, an awesome figure.

Having afternoon naps when I first started

The large round pond down the steps, made of concrete – great for newts, frogspawn, etc

Maypole dancing in front of the school

The outside toilets in front of the hall – unheated, obviously

Most of the older children got a chance to ring the hand-bell to signal the end of classes. When my turn came I must have been too nervous because I rang it straight away, several minutes early and earned a severe reprimand from Mr Slater.

The badge system: Every Friday, Mr Slater would come round with a tray of badges, awarded for different levels of achievement, marks, etc. – green was good, blue was very good, but red was the one to aim for.

Trips out were few and far between – I remember one to a bakery and two cinema visits (Oliver Twist and Henry V) to the Continentale in Kemptown.

I can remember very little parental involvement (neither can my parents)

I've just realised how big the classes were by looking at the old photos – two of 47 and one of 38.

David Hughes 1954 – 1960

More memories in a Personal Footnote

The marvellous mixture of reminiscences a number of times and been impressed by the variations of, and reflections on the events that were remembered, I feel that I too, should reveal my memories of the period 1945 – 1952. I have had the distinct benefit, of course, of having access to so many reminders of past school life, characters and events.

I will not repeat the stories that have already been told save to say that, had I started with a blank sheet of paper and with no prompts available, I would probably have written down just two examples and then made tracks for another coffee break.

Unsurprisingly the two examples that immediately sprang to mind are ones that have already been mentioned more than once. Yes, the afternoon naps in the first infants' class was an easy one but the second one, the very sad outcome of the accident during a PT session, is one that I will expand on here.

This event has been etched on my memory for the last 64 years. As the Log Book entry that was made at the time reported, John Crossthwaite slipped and hit his chin on a bench. The injury proved fatal.

We were running around in a circle at the end of the PT lesson when I caught the sight of John tripping and falling against what I now know is called a Swedish bench, which was very near to the east door of the Hall. I can still see this image in my mind's eye just as I can also see a teacher on her knees bending over John trying to resuscitate him as we were led slowly in a line, out of the door and up the steps to Mrs Moore's classroom.

It was a pure accident, which ironically occurred after a lesson full of wall bar climbing and jumping over the other items of gym apparatus.

Mr Divall organised a radio in the Hall, which allowed us to listen during our lunchtimes, to the early days of the BBC Test cricket commentaries, the forerunner of Test Match Special,. I can recall hearing the exploits of Len Hutton, Cyril Washbrook and Denis Compton as described by John Arlott and Rex Alston.

There were other kinds sporting connections with Balfour, as Jean Gardner recalled by identifying the names of some of her class mates that she remembered, including Bernie Moore and Jack Ball (both, as she said, of football fame). In fact they both went on to play for Brighton and Hove Albion. Bernard Moore played during the Second World War and his last season was 1947/48 while Jack Ball who played in goal, remained with the Club until 1952/53.

I watched Jack Ball play in my last 3 Balfour years and managed to get his autograph along with most of the 1951 team, including Brighton's other goalkeeper, Harry Baldwin. And, in doing so, I learnt a salutary lesson by asking Harry for his signature. "MR Baldwin to you, young man". "Thanks Mr Baldwin", I said quickly moving on to safer ground.

It may have been through Jack Ball's influence that Jack Mansell, Brighton's very successful full back, came to Balfour in 1951 to take some coaching lessons in much the same way as Albion players have been doing in recent years. In fact, like the old boys, Jack Ball and Bernie Moore, Balfour still provides the Albion with local talent – recently, Lewis Dunk and Tommy Fraser played for the Division One team and Dunk still does in the Championship.

Fig 48

By the fifties, Balfour had developed a strong commitment to competitive sport, with teams representing the school in swimming, netball, cricket, football and athletics. My particular memory concerns Balfour's football team's presence in the 1952 final of the FitzGerald Cup, which was against Elm Grove Primary School. Cllr. Fitzgerald, who chaired the Education Committee and was a regular visitor to Balfour, handed the cup to the winning side, Elm Grove, who beat us 2 – 1. This cup competition continues to be held to his day and Balfour teams have enjoyed the success in the recent past that eluded us in 1952.

Another lunch time break activity, when there were no radio broadcasts, was to walk over to the barn on the edge of the woods at Varndean Holt and watch the blacksmith at work shoeing the working horses that were still being used by various trades in Brighton. Deliveries of coal, collections of 'rag and bones' and keeping public houses well supplied with the brewery products, all kept the blacksmith busy. One assumes that the smithy was operating at the time the Loder Road School was opened as the first Scheme of Work set out in the Log Book in 1905, includes the topic "the stable (blacksmith)" amongst the items listed for Nature Study.

A very personal recollection, which may well not have applied to many children, came back to my memory early in 2013 as a result of watching the first episode of the BBC series, "The Village". Set in the period 1914 – 1920, the main character, Bert as a young boy at school, was made to hold out his left hand, which was repeatedly caned while he said that "the left hand is not the right hand". That is, not the hand that can be used for writing. Only the right hand would do. This sentence was more or less repeated by my teacher during a meeting with my mother, who had been summoned to the school to hear it. I wasn't in any danger of getting the cane like Bert, but my mother was told that she should insist that I used my right hand for writing.

This was a bit confusing for my mother as she was left-handed, a natural trait she used unhindered at school – the Downs School!

Several past pupils have mentioned that their parents did not get many invitations to come into the school. As I remember, the one day when the call did come was in July - Open Day - when displays and events like some of those that are shown in the Postscripts under the heading 'Sports and PE', are pictured.

However, parents would normally wait at the school gates for the bell to ring. My mother said that she often approached the gates hoping that Mr Slater's booming voice would never carry my name on its sound waves when he, as he often did, bellowed the name of a miscreant to return to him for a 'little advice' before continuing on the journey home.

Mr Slater was always a slightly Larger than Life character but the booming voice was reserved for the playground and the football touchline. I remember a softer voice in the classroom when he turned his attention to reading to us from a book that, in retrospect, seems to have been a particular favourite of his. One piece has stayed with me entitled, "A Dissertation Upon Roast Pig" by Charles Lamb, an 18th century poet and writer. No, I didn't remember the full title but I did remember roast pig and Charles Lamb, which was enough to trace the origins of the text using 21st century technology. In fact the book wasn't called a dissertation on anything. It was the "Essays of Elia" published in 1823 and the 'dissertation' was one in the collection of essays.

Remembering snippets of linked text from the past like "pig" and "lamb" has lead me to explain (to myself), the context an event that happened over 65 years ago and involved 'Box' and 'Hassocks'. I can remember being taken on a school outing to Hassocks where we played on a lawn and had lemonade and cakes. The house and lawn belonged to Mr Box.

The School Log Book however, records an annual Nature Study trip to Hassocks taking place for the Lower Infants (the two classes of 5 year olds). Elsewhere, there is a record of visits made by Mr Box (sometimes he signed in as George Box) to check registers or to attend special events like Harvest Festival and to act as Father Christmas. In fact, he had been a manager on the committee of north Brighton Schools' Managers before it was abolished in 1937 after which the managers were invited to become 'Visitors', which he clearly did as one who had taken a particular interest in Balfour School. That I have always remember his name perhaps stems from the instructions we might have received before we went to his house, in remembering to say "thank you, Mr Box" as we boarded the coach home. I do remember the food and drink; I don't remember learning anything concerned with the Study of Nature, though

I hope we did thank Mr. and Mrs. Box and I have plenty to thank Balfour Primary School for, but I cannot better what Elizabeth Bannister has already said:

The high standards of excellence in academic achievement by the teachers of Balfour Road School set me on a path in the right direction. I will always be grateful for the excellent teaching I received.

They did the same for me and their example continues to remind me of the vital importance of a good primary education.

Balfour Road County Primary School Log Book (1945 -1955)

Having heard from the past pupils' about their memories from the10 years that followed the end of the War, we can now move to see different perspective this period through the eyes of the Head teachers who recorded the changing times on the pages of the School Log Book.

We left that narrative at the end of December 1944 when the decorators had just started work to prepare the school for the children to return from their temporary residence at the Varndean schools. At that time the average class size had risen to nearly 56.

1945

In the event, the school opened again in February and the average class size was almost at its maximum of 60. Between February and July, the entries being made by Miss Seward were weekly and limited to recording which teachers were available, or ill, or helping out at another school. Miss Seward was herself, one of the absentees at times. Her health had been poor during the War, something which could not have been helped by the great burden she carried throughout.

And so to 13th September 1945, when the school opened again after the summer holiday and by which time, Japan had surrendered (15th August). The only significant reminder of the war that could now be seen on the campus, was the row of 'pre-fabs'; temporary houses that had been constructed between the Balfour and Varndean Schools.

The first Log Book entry describes a situation that was to become an ever recurring theme at Balfour when parents submitted their school preferences for the coming year.

- *A good number of under fives were refused owing to the lack of accommodation*

Just one week later, Miss Young took over responsibility for making weekly entries (as she had done on occasions during the war) and the circumstances were going to be no less depressing for Miss Seward's friends and colleagues.

- *22/9: Miss Seward absent with acute rheumatism; Miss Young deputising*
- *29/9: Miss Seward reported to be "desperately ill"*
- *5/10: Miss Seward died on 2nd Oct; school closed on 4th Oct in the afternoon as a mark of respect and to allow teachers to attend a Memorial Service held at St. John's Church, Preston*
- *12/10: Cllr. Leak, Chairman of the Sites and Works Committee visited and approved the position of the Bird Bath, which it is proposed to erect in memory of Miss H. F. Seward*
- *The picture, "All Things Bright and Beautiful", the property of Miss Seward, has been left to stay in place (in the Head's room) amongst us by the kindness of Miss A Seward.*

Miss Seward had led the school from the last couple of years at Loder Road to the start of the post-war period 23 years later. She was 61 and like so many working people 70 years ago, the length of retirements were often very short indeed when compared with the situation nowadays. And this will not be the last time that I will draw attention to this subject before the last page is reached.

Miss Young, now the acting Head, continued to complete the Log Book in her own, very different style. It was sparse on mundane facts and figures, which were replaced by more whimsical and observational thoughts.

- *2/11: The gardens are being tidied; the beds are being dug and wallflowers planted; the shrubs have been given what they most needed – a severe prune. While the school was in military occupation, the shrubs had much rampant growth and it is a joy to stand on the veranda and see the school assembled in the playground without our having to crane our necks and strain our voices through the foliage!*
- *30/11: In the Junior School terminal examinations have begun this week. The teachers are conducting their own exams and I am helping with some of the marking and reading and releasing the teachers from their classes for marking while I take the junior classes in turn.*
- *7/12: Teachers are busy writing the reports of individual children.*
- *14/12: The windows are being cleaned this week; it is wonderful to see the bright sparkling panes once more. The "black out" had all been removed by the caretaker before we had returned to our building.*
- *21/12: We are decorating a large Christmas tree and having a "whole school" concert on Wednesday afternoon. Mrs Field, mother of John and Richard, (two former pupils of the school, the latter being Brighton's Top Boy in the Scholarship list of his year) has brought two toys to the Babies Room – a lovely almost-new push wagon and a farmyard. Most classes have made Christmas gifts, cards and calendars to take home to their parents this week.*

The autumn term had started with a familiar problem of too many children applying for places and it now ends with another familiar problem – dogs.

- *Dogs are great nuisance while children are in the playground – it would be a great advantage to have some kind of protection from them if this can be arranged.*

So, with this comment, Miss Young completed her year-long temporary role as Acting Head.

- *21/12: Miss E A Young signed off*
- *Miss A C Pickett commenced duty as Head teacher.*

1946

Oh dear, a new Head teacher and dogs to report on again. Miss Pickett had the Constabulary to deal with as well

- *11/3: A police constable came over to enquire about a dog that had torn Miss Plummer's coat (one of the college lecturers)*

It must be assumed that the tree mentioned below was ordered a few months earlier in 1945, when it would have been 21 years since the new school building was opened.

- *13/3: The tree given by Varndean Girls as a 21st Birthday present and as a token of the friendship existing during the time that the School was evacuated to Varndean School – was planted at 2.15pm*
- *26/3: We had the editor of the Argus and a Fireman to talk to Classes III and IV respectively about Newspapers and Transport*

As was recorded in the wartime section of the Log Book, Mr Privett had been released by the school for a number of periods in order to train as a pilot with the ATC and was eventually called-up by the RAF

- *25/4: School re-opened to-day. Mr Noonan commenced duties here as a permanent member of staff until such time as news is received as to whether Mr Privett is wishing to return.*
- *10/7: Open Day will be held for the parents this afternoon. It was a marvellously sunny afternoon and the school was crowded with parents who were most interested in the work being done and especially thankful for the healthy conditions under which we work. I spoke to a crowded Hall at 3.30pm*
- *17/7: Junior Swimming Sports at North Rd Baths. We came 2nd in Division 2 with 4 points less than the top school. The children gained 5 firsts, 1 second and 1 third*
- *2/10: This afternoon (1st anniversary of Miss Seward's death) we had a meeting on the lawn to see the Bird Bath erected as a tribute to Miss Seward's work here)*

Pupils were reminded of the War in 1946 when they received a letter (below) from the King celebrating the ending of the War and thanking everyone for their efforts in helping the Allied Nations to bring about the victory.

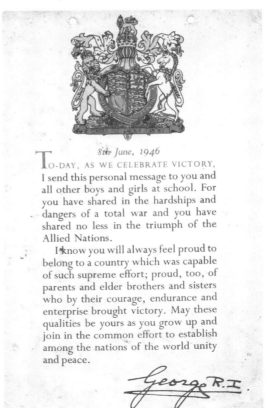

8th June, 1946

TO-DAY, AS WE CELEBRATE VICTORY, I send this personal message to you and all other boys and girls at school. For you have shared in the hardships and dangers of a total war and you have shared no less in the triumph of the Allied Nations.

I know you will always feel proud to belong to a country which was capable of such supreme effort; proud, too, of parents and elder brothers and sisters who by their courage, endurance and enterprise brought victory. May these qualities be yours as you grow up and join in the common effort to establish among the nations of the world unity and peace.

George R.I.

Fig 49

1947

The year starts with a cold reminder of the days at Loder Road School

- *27/1: School closed owing to the weather conditions and wasn't opened again until 3/2*
- *3/2: By the efforts of the caretaker, sufficient lavatory accommodation was available for the remainder of the severe weather. Physical work outside has been impossible and children have had to be in the classrooms for playtime and after Canteen during the entire term so far.*

Followed by another déjà vu moment, I am afraid.

- *29/4: Miss E A Young is in charge of the School*
- *12/5: Miss A C Pickett sent her resignation as Head teacher owing to ill-health*

The Hollingbury Sports' Pavilion, that is mentioned below was in Ditchling Road opposite the top of Balfour Road and was constructed very much like the Loder Road School building had been. It was demolished only a few years ago.

- *19/5: Preparing Sports Pavilion in the adjoining field for the class now occupying the Hollingbury Sports' Pavilion.*

As Miss Young resumes her duties as Head she continues to record school life in her own style

- *22/5: The gardens are looking very beautiful now that the shrubs and trees are in blossom. The Sports' Pavilion (belonging to Fawcett School) is now ready for our occupation on 4 June*
- *4/6: No under fives were admitted as there is no room in the Reception class. Sports' Practices are being taken in the field whenever space is available and the weather permits.*
- *9/6: The gardeners are busy making the flower beds look gay with bright geraniums, lobelia and alyssum: it is a joy to see them.*
- *10/6: A General assembly of the whole school took place in the Hall is morning. The Acting Head spoke to the children and showed them the gift bought with the money the children and staff had collected for Miss A C Pickett. The purse with notecase attached, is being sent to Miss Pickett who was not well enough to be present with us.*
- *In the dinner hour Mr Cromar started to take Boxing Exercise with six of Class V boys in the space under the west wing.*
- *11/6: The children are installed in the Sports' Pavilion: they have polished the desks and are making it look much brighter. Several of the staff have been busy altering the School Sports' frocks – so that the girls may run in blouses and shorts. The children have stencilled the School number 1 on to calico.*
- *13/6: The School was shut this afternoon for the Inter-School Sports held in Preston Park.*
- *17/6: In General Assembly, the runners in Fridays sports were congratulated. Last week in General Assembly, while the Acting Headmistress spoke to the children, the staff went to visit the Loder Road canteen. The children of Class V are going to visit the kitchen and canteen tomorrow morning and the morning afterwards, the class being divided into groups of approximately 20 so the children can get some intimate* acquaintance with the machinery, etc.

- *19/6: We are putting stones (rolling larger ones) into the pond. On our visit to it we noticed dragonflies, water boatmen, whirligig beetles, newts and water snails were already at home in its water.*
- *24/6: Class V (with Class teacher and Acting Headmistress) are going to Shoreham marshes on a school outing tomorrow afternoon. The class is studying plant and animal life likely to be met, and working out sums from bus time-tables.*
- *Several children have been allowed to take part in the Brighton Music Festival and those who took part in the pianoforte classes played to the school in General Assembly this morning. Class IVp in two relays are visiting the Loder Rd canteen. Mr Burgess is very kind in taking these classes round and the children are writing him letters of thanks.*
- *27/6: Several classes have visited the pond to see the fine dragonfly display there.*
- *The class occupying the Pavilion are finding that the water now laid on to the lavatory and water basin on its south side, is a great facility: paint boxes can be washed there and fresh water is available in case of emergency.*
- *The Infant classes are making the most of this lovely weather and are having lessons on the lawn, in the field, and are taking walks around the school.*
- *It would be of educational value to our school to have some protection around it. The pond and school premises would be safer.*
- *30/6: I learn that several of the Class V children planned an expedition to Shoreham Marshes for last Saturday and had a very enjoyable time.*

And now another situation that will familiar to present-day Headteachers; children, which were absent from school as a result of family holidays, to add to the previous two 'to-be-expected' happenings, more children applying than can be enrolled and dogs!

- *Several children are absent due to Father's holiday; this is making the attendance low*

Clearly, Miss Young was very keen on making school trips locally and also liked to make maximum use of the school pond. I have absolutely no recollection of the pond although I must have seen it. With hindsight, it is likely that infants like me were kept well away from it. No health and safety legislation at the time, just commonsense.

- *3/7: Class IV (40 children) with Acting Headmistress and Class Teacher, went to Lewes Levels: we started from school at 12.30pm and had a bus to Lewes Prison, and the children arrived home shortly after 4pm. It was a very enjoyable outing though plants for the pond were not so easy to procure; but the children saw arrow heads and flowering rush growing beautifully in their natural habitat.*

Fig 50

By now, this was a well-developed pond that was used for nature studies; here by senior girls and it was clearly a subject for photographers

Miss Horsley, the Head teacher of the Senior Girls School, which occupied the half of the building closest to Balfour Road, did offer support to the Primary School when necessary and did so again a few months later

- *4/7: Miss Horsley kindly allowed one of her secondary girls to help us out with the young children yesterday*

Big changes are on the way. A new canteen was built away from the school, directly below the west end classrooms and alongside the path that leads from Loder Road to the site now occupied by the Dorothy Stringer School.

- *Stock and furniture belonging to the canteen is to be removed to the new dining hall this afternoon as we are starting dinners there on Monday*
- *7/7: Nearly 200 children (193) are dining in the new canteen dining hall in one sitting.*
- *10/7: Examinations in all the junior classes are proceeding this week. The subjects tested are English and Arithmetic and in the 3 top classes, Intelligence Tests. Individual reports on each child will be sent home to parents*
- *During Miss Bottomley's absence, the Acting Headmistress tested Class A in Reading, Number and Written English. She has heard the children in Class III and Class B read as well.*
- *The dinner numbers have reached a record to-day –221*
- *21/7: Acting Headteacher is continuing organisation of school for next September*
- *Several children absent owing to Father's holiday.*

Those away on family holidays may have missed the round of educational musical chairs played in the Headteacher's study with announcements of a new Head, Mr Slater, a new Headship for Miss Young and yet another Acting Head to replace the current Acting Head. The latter appointment was not a surprise, as Miss Horsley was already on site at the Girls School

- *30/7: School closed until Sept 4th 1947*
- *Miss E A Young appointed Head Teacher of Hertford Road School*
- *Mr Slater appointed Head Teacher of Balfour County Primary School*
- *4/9: I (Miss E M Horsley) have been appointed as Acting Head until Oct 31st when Mr Slater will commence duty.*

The interviews and appointments must have been made very late in the summer term but Miss Young did manage to get back and say goodbye as she would have wanted. As the records show, she was with Miss Seward as a trainee teacher at Loder Road and transferred with her to the new building in 1924, 23 years ago

- *29/9: The school assembled in the Hall to bid 'Farewell' to Miss Young as this had not been possible at the end of last term.*

In a repeat of the event that Miss Mills reported in1920 at the Loder Road School when children were given the opportunity of going to see Earl Haig in his visit to Brighton, some children were given the chance to another famous wartime leader, Mr Churchill.

- *3/10: Miss Boxall and I took 33 children from Class V to see Mr Churchill as he drove along the sea front*

And finally, Miss Horsley's last six entries; a rather mixed bag including my least favourite 'treat', which was drinking milk. Not sure that it didn't always taste the same.

- *8/10: L Adrienne Scanes (V) was taken to the Municipal Hospital as her arm was injured while in the field after dinner. We later learned that she had a green-stick fracture three inches from the wrist.*
- *19/10: The heating was put on for the first time this winter.*
- *21/10: I left school at 3pm to attend a meeting of Secondary Head teachers concerning the employment of a film projectionist in the town, for the schools*
- *24/10: Mr Slater visited the schools*
- *28/10: A number of children complained of their milk this morning. It had an unpleasant taste of oil. On reporting this to the dairy I am told it is due to the change over in the feeding of the cows and is quite harmless.*
- *30/10: The name plate for Varndean's presentation reached me to-day, Mr Bachelor (in charge of grounds) is seeing to fixing it safely.*
- *I finished duty at this school.*   *Miss E M Horsley signed off*

Mr Eric Slater was now in charge and would remain so for the next 25 years. He retired in July 1972 having held the post of Head teacher in three schools for a total of 40 years. Sadly, he died suddenly 5 month later,

- *4/11: Mr. E D Slater commenced duties as Headmaster of Balfour Primary School, Junior and Infants Dept*
- *20/11: All school closed today on account of Princess Elizabeth's Wedding to Philip, Duke of Edinburgh*
- *29/11: The School Football Team, under Mr. Cromar, played its first Junior Football Match and won 6 – 0*
- *3/12: Approximately 300 children taken to the Savoy Cinema this morning to see the films of the Royal Wedding (The Savoy cinema was at the corner of East St and Kings Rd)*

1948

Mr Slater provided speedy evidence that writing lengthy records in the Log Book was not one of his priorities. 'One-liners' have a different meaning nowadays on the comedy circuit, his definition was, I think, to be concise and to the point and not too often, either. Here are some of the events and happenings that fell outside the normal recording of teachers absent, teachers returning and supply teachers coming and going.

- *12/ 1: School opened today. Miss Ruby H Prew commenced duties as a qualified teacher from Canada*
- *19/2: 404 children on the books and the percentage attendance was 91.2%*
- *5/3: Film show given in School Hall to Infants on account of the wedding of Princess Elizabeth*

I said, at the start of 1947 above, "Another Déjà vu moment, I am afraid" when describing another Acting Head role for Miss Young in stepping in to cover for Miss Pickett just as she had often done for Miss Seward. The reason I said, "I am afraid" was because I knew that, like Miss Seward, Miss Pickett would soon die. In fact, she died 10 months later.

- *9/3: Miss A C Pickett, a former Headmistress, passed away today after a long illness.*
- *26/4: The Silver Wedding Day of the King and Queen - all schools granted a holiday in the afternoon*
- *27, 28 and 29/4: Dr Harris joined by Miss G M Eyres Mr W L Roberts to complete the HMI inspection*
- *7/6: Headmaster attended Primary Schools Sub-Committee to hear a Report by HMIs*
- *9/7 : Miss Prew absent for the day owing to Royal Garden Party*
- *15/7: School played the first cricket match in the evening*
- *16/7: Classes IVB, III, II, taken on a Nature Trip to Hassocks during the afternoon*
- *28/7: School closed today for the Summer Holidays. Miss R Prew, the teacher on an Interchange Scheme from Canada finished her year in English schools today*
- *14/9: A very satisfactory HMI Report was received today for the full inspection carried out on April 28th and April 29th (Copy in Appendix 2)*

1949

Mr Slater made a point of maintaining a record of the sporting events in which the school took part.

The examination for entrance to a technical school as one outcome from the 11+ examinations was a development of a provision that was specified in the 1944 Education Act. The secondary phase was sub-divided into grammar schools, secondary modern schools and technical schools. In the event, technical education did not take root at this time although a few local education authorities did make a start. Grammar and secondary modern schools became established as the two routes that were available for 11 year olds, dependent on their performance in the 11+ examinations. Comprehensive schools were introduced in 1965 in a significant change of policy.

- *16/2: Junior School played their first netball game and beat Hertford Road 5 – 0*
- *1/6: Twenty-one boys took the examination for the Technical School, the first time that it was held in Brighton instead of the 11+.*
- *13/7: School took part in the Primary School Swimming Sports and wan the Division III Championship Shield*
- *21/12: School closed today for Christmas. Mr Cromar left the Staff to take up position as Education Officer in the RAF.*

1950

A newspaper cutting was found in the school archives which carried the notice that Miss Boxall passed away in a Brighton nursing home, aged 59 years. She was yet another Balfour teacher at this time who died before reaching the normal retirement age. She began teaching at Balfour when the new school opened in 1924 after spells of teaching at Circus Street School and Richmond Street School.

- *9/1: Mr F D Divall came on the permanent staff of the school in place of Mr Cromar.*
- *17/3: School took part in the non-competitive Music Festival during the week.*
- *5/6: Miss Boxall did not return as she is ill and has sent in her resignation to take effect from 31st August*
- *16/6: School closed during the afternoon as we took part in the Primary School Sports in Preston Park. Balfour won the Championship for Division 2 in the Athletic Sports.*
- *21/7: Dr A N Harris HMI visited the School*
- *24/ 7: Miss Gilbert HMI visited the School*
- *17/11: Miss Trost HMI and Instructor-Commander visited*

1951

I have already mentioned this terrible event in my personal reminiscences and the record below is a direct quote from the Log Book. It is impossible to comprehend how Mr Divall must have felt as a result of what was a pure accident.

- *14/2: Dr A N Harris brought Mr A N Holton to hear the singing and percussion bands*
- *9/3: Mrs Golden HMI came to see the students in PT*
- *31/5: Dr A N Harris visited the School*
- *26/6: The school received a severe shock this afternoon when John Graham Crosthwaite was running in the School Hall in a PT lesson. Apparently, he stumbled and hit his head on a Swedish Bench. He never recovered consciousness and died soon after the ambulance and doctor was called. Mr Divall, the teacher in charge of the PT lesson was very distressed.*
- *27/6: School closed today as the upper classes visited the Festival of Britain in London.*
- *28/6: Mr Divall absent on doctor's advice*

Also on Thursday, 28th June 1951, a report of John's death was carried in the Sussex Daily News under the heading:

Gymnasium Death of Schoolboy

"The Brighton Coroner, Mr Charles Webb, has ordered an inquest on a nine-years-old Brighton schoolboy who died in a school gymnasium. Ambulance men and police were called to Balfour Road School where they found John Graham Crosthwaite of Ditchling Road, dead. It is believed that John, taking part in a PT class, slipped and fell striking his chin on a form and breaking his throat". [This report refers to John striking the bench with his chin, which is what I remember seeing, but it is understandable that the information that Mr Slater was given mentioned for the Log Book varied slightly.]

- *2/7: Mr Divall resumed duties today*
- *10/12: Dr A N Harris visited the School and saw all classes*

1952

This year's selection of entries is something of a miscellany.
The visit of the Mayor and Chair of the Education Committee was recorded in the Log but no explanation was given about what occasion prompted the visit. The Alderman (inappropriate terminology as usual) Miss Dorothy Stringer was soon to have a well-known school on the Balfour campus, named after her. Councillor Fitzgerald's name was given to the cup awarded to the winners of the primary schools football competition – a match between the top teams of the two Divisions. The competition for the Fitzgerald Cup is still held each year.

- *6/2: H.M. King George VI died suddenly, the news received at school at 11.20 am*
- *8/2: Queen Elizabeth II proclaimed Queen today*
- *15/2: Funeral of the late King George VI today, there was no school holiday, but the time table was modified to allow children to take part in Memorial Service.*
- *2/5: Miss Gilbert, HMI, visited the school and made some enquiries into the use of the school broadcasting throughout the school*
- *13/5: Mr Fedurb HMI came with Mr Horton to see the students Art work*
- *26/6: Miss Tann, the Chief Inspector for Primary Schools in All England, and Dr Harris inspected the school from 9.30am to 4.30pm today. At the end of the day, Miss Tann expressed great satisfaction in all that she saw.*
- *10/10: The Mayor of Brighton, Alderman Miss Dorothy Stringer and the Chairman of the Education Committee, Councillor Fitzgerald, accompanied by Mr P Sawbridge visited the school this afternoon.*
- *16/10: The Headmaster absent today attending an official enquiry at the Town Hall. Miss Bishopp left in charge.*

1953

Events this year were dominated by the Queen's Coronation. However, the first entry recorded the second extension of the school when the two new classrooms were ready for use at the east end. No extension though, to the Hall; something that Miss Seward was arguing for 20 years earlier, and which the HMI inspectors agreed was necessary

- *7/1: The School re-opened today after the Christmas Holidays. The top two Junior Classes were transferred to the two new classrooms which were now ready for use. An additional reception class was started under Miss Beatrice Helen Snook who came on the permanent staff.*
- *30/4: Dr Harris visited and saw most classes*
- *1/5: Miss Ellis HMI came the see PE in all infants' classes*
- *19/5: The Mayor of Brighton, Alderman Miss Dorothy Stringer, accompanied by the Director of Education, kindly distributed the Coronation Beakers.*
- *20/5: All the Balfour School children enjoyed their Coronation Entertainment this afternoon. The Juniors went to the Sports Stadium to see the Ice Show while the Infants were entertained by a Magician etc. in the School Hall.*
- *29/5: The school broke up tonight for the Coronation of Queen Elizabeth the Second*
- *2/6: The Coronation*

1954

The appearance of a welfare assistant was a new role in the school. Things had improved and advanced from the days of Loder Road School where some aspects of the children's welfare at school were in the hands of young girls of 14/15 years of age who were appointed as monitoresses.

- *3/2: Miss Gilbert HMI and Miss Falconer HMI visited*
- *12/2: Miss Gilbert and Miss Falconer visited and saw Broadcast lessons*
- *7/4: Centenary of Borough; Open Day for both Juniors and Infants*
- *21/7: Dr Harris visited in the afternoon*
- *30/8: School opened today after the summer holidays. Mrs F.M.Bryant deputised for Mrs Cornford, the new Welfare Assistant*
- *24/9: Mrs Bryant finished today as welfare assistant*
- *27/9: Mrs Margaret W Cornford started today as the School Welfare Assistant this morning*
- *17/11: Top half of the school suddenly decimated by winter vomiting disease*
- *20/12: Dr Harris and Miss Trost called*

1955

This year the HM Inspectors called; the gap of eight years would raise eyebrows now and might beg the question about whether standards were higher or lower when the visits were less frequent. In this context, it is worth pointing out that between 1950 and 1954, 17 visits to the school were made by one or more HMIs. There was a totally different relationship between HMI and schools in the 1950s and 60s in that inspectors offered advice as well as making full inspections.

- *6/6; Dr A N Harris called to make tentative arrangements about a full inspection this term*
- *17/6: Dr Harris and Mr Sidebottom spent the day at the school inspecting classes B and 9 and seeing some of the PE.*
- *5/7: Dr Harris, Miss Trost and Mr Keeney HMI carried out a three day full inspection of the School. Miss McKie HMI inspected the School Meals Section at the same time*
- *6/7 : School won the Division 1 Swimming Shield*
- *13/7: An excellent HMI Report was received today for the full inspection carried out on July 5, July 6 and July 7. (Copy in Appendix 2)*

This seems a good moment to end the history of the first 50 years of Balfour Road School with the publication of "an excellent HMI Report". Reading the collective reminiscences of past pupils, I think we knew that already.

Postscripts

1. A Final Miscellany

Teachers and Classes, School Discipline, School Resorts, Sports and PE and Obituaries

Here is a last round-up of items that were not recorded systematically in the Log Books, or not at all; but they do cover a number of important aspects of Balfour's history.

1. Teachers and Classes

This is an ad hoc collection of photographs, which show that classes with their teacher over a span of 25 years didn't change very much. The oldest one, dated 1925, has the slightly smaller class size reflecting the move from Loder Road before the rapid increase in numbers, which soon followed. Thereafter, size 40 became the norm. I have added two photographs of teachers that were taken half way through this period, which carried the date and names that were not always available on other images (although these have several question marks added).

Fig 51
Mrs Moore's class of 1951 with 40 children on the day

Fig 52
Miss Brogate's class with 39 children on the day

This photograph was dated 1925 and this maybe Miss Young's class with Miss Seward standing behind. There were 34 children on the day but, as the records show, the admissions grew quickly after the new school opened and would soon see much larger classes

Fig 53

Fig 54

This is a pre-WW2 photograph with names of the teachers written on the back, which were:
Back row left to right; Boxall, (?), Privett, Bishopp
Front row left to right; Wilson, Young, Seward, Purchase, Knight

Fig 55

And a second one, which was dated as 1938
Back row: L to R; Bishopp, Quigley, Privett, Chaffer, Purchase
Front row: L to R; Bone, Boxall, Seward, Young

2. School Discipline

This is another aspect of school life that was gradually altered in 'actions taken' on the matter of discipline. Specifically, the amount and type of corporal punishment used, which over the 50 years went from commonplace to a much more limited use, which at Balfour, ceased to be used by 1970, 16years before Parliament made the same decision.

Earlier, it was mentioned that the1890 Code of Regulation gave encouragement to teachers to develop and broaden the curriculum in more enlightened ways. The greater freedom was not constrained by any rules to limit the extent or nature of disciplinary methods used. By 1905, Headteachers were seen as the ultimate arbiter of disciplinary sanctions. 'Being sent to the Head' was a familiar journey, either to get some equipment for the administration of punishment or to be given the punishment.

No Punishment Book has been discovered, which might have been used at the Loder Road School and the one that was in use at the Balfour Road School thereafter, was lost sometime in 1940. Nevertheless, it is still possible to describe the various disciplinary measures that were in force from 1905 onwards.

A key record exists in an autobiography written by Albert Paul describing life in central Brighton at the beginning of the 20th century.

Albert Paul's memories of his own school experience from 1907 onwards will have been the common experiences of pupils in other schools in the town and there is little reason to suggest that children coming to Loder Road in 1907 would have witnessed significantly different practises. Save one caveat, which is that he was in a class of boys whereas the Loder Road Infants' School was mixed.

Would that have made a difference?

Probably, and such evidence as there is suggests that, while girls were subject to the most extreme form of punishment, corporal punishment, the instances of their receiving it were very limited. From the pages of Balfour School Punishment Book, between 1941 and 1955, there were 163 entries of which three entries in 1942 involved two girls and one entry involving a girl in 1948. The other 159 entries involved boys.

On closer inspection of these statistics, the 159 names in the Book can be sub-divided by the number of times each boy received the cane or tawse

87 boys were so punished on one occasion

18	"	"	"	"	" two occasions
4	"	"	"	"	" three	"
2	"	"	"	"	" four	"
1	"	"	"	"	" six	"
2	"	"	"	"	" seven	"

There is, of course, no way to assess the fairness or otherwise of the various punishments on a scale of 1 to 7 but a selection of the stated "offences" include; disobedience, misbehaviour, stealing, lying, hitting girls, bullying, slack work, fire-raising, truancy, swearing and climbing over to the next lavatory (twice!).

Or, put it another way with the benefit of hindsight, "Flicking paper in class" earned one boy 3 strokes of the cane while another miscreant received just one stoke for "punching smaller children".

However, whichever misdemeanour was committed, 87 boys didn't transgress again while 18 had second thoughts after the second punishment, before deciding that was enough. A harder core of 9 boys made it a bit more of a habit to climb the stairs to the Head's room alongside the Hall. They did so on at least three occasions and there were two serial offenders who challenged the Head's patience seven times.

As the next two paragraphs indicate, the local authority eventually moved to limit Head's freedom to go beyond a maximum of three strikes per offence.

At the end of the 1950s, the Education Committee approved new regulations that formally excluded girls and infants from being administered any form of corporal punishment in any circumstance. This amendment to the punishment policy was one of a number that had been made since Albert Paul witnessed the range of punishments being used in his classroom.

These included restricting the number of strikes made by cane or tawse on the hand or buttocks, to a maximum of three by the Head only. Qualified teachers were restricted to one strike, preferably with another teacher present. Such treatment restricted to classroom offences of a serious nature.

Other methods had been ruled out quite early on in the tightening-up processes; so punishments by boxing or cuffing of ears or blows to the head or other parts of the body were forbidden.

Finally, on 1 August 1986, schools were informed that, by narrow majorities in both Houses of Parliament, corporal punishment was abolished in respect of all maintained schools.

It was not so much like Parliament leading the Nation on the issue, but more like following in the wake of decisions that had already made locally. For example, the last instance of corporal punishment being administered at Balfour, after consultation with the boy's mother, was 16 years earlier on 11th May 1970. It was also the case that the last girl to be punished in this way was 36 years earlier on 18th January 1950.

3. The School Reports

A very small selection of school reports, the ones that were sent home to inform parents of progress being made, have been displayed here showing how little changed with the passage of time. From 1935 to 1950, the format was roughly the same. The 1942 version in between, was hand-made because of the wartime shortages.

Another reason for including the reports is to provide a 'compare and contrast' opportunity when looked at in relation to the school report of today. Anyone concerned about large class sizes today had better look away now.

Term ending *Christmas* 1935

Name
Class IVA

No. in Class 51
Position in Class 35

	MARKS			REMARKS
	EXAMINATION		TERM	
	No. Gained	Maximum	General	
Reading	13	20		
Recitation	11	20		
Speech Training	—	—		
Composition	11	20		Denis has had an
Literature	18	20		uphill struggle in
Writing	13	20		his class especially
Dictation	12	20		with spelling. He has
General Knowledge	11	20		done well and is to be
History	—	—	P	commended for his
Geography	—	—	P	continued progress
Paper 1. (Mental)	7/3	10		aw?
Paper 2. (Mechanical)	12	20		
Paper 3. (Reasoning)	10	20		
Drawing	—	—	P+	
Handwork	—	—	P+	
Needlework	—	—		
General Neatness	7	10		
Physical Culture	—	—	P+	

No. of times school open 138
Progress Excellent

" " absent 1
Conduct Excellent

" " late 0

Points won for Team —
Term Marking

Points lost for Team —

Ex. = Excellent
P+ = Good Average
P. = Average
P— = Below Average

Class Mistress or Master.

H. F. Seward . Head Mistress

213

Joy Parry — Upper Four

Easter 1942

Subject	Max	Exam	Remarks
Reading	20	20	
Composition	20	19	An
English Study	20	15	
Writing	20	18	excellent
Dictation	20	16	result.
General Knowledge	20	15	
Mental	10	9	Comment
Tables	10	9	unnecessary,
Arithmetic I	20	19	
Arithmetic II	20	11	Arthur Privett
Totals	180	151	
Number in Class	48		
Order of Merit	4		

★

A. F. Seward.

BALFOUR ROAD JUNIOR SCHOOL

This is wartime school report that had to be hand-made by the teachers because of the absence of any of the officially printed ones. It shows one of the last signatures that Mr Privett would have written before being called up for service in the RAF

EDUCATION COMMITTEE FOR THE COUNTY BOROUGH OF BRIGHTON.
Balfour County Primary School.

REPORT FOR Term ending July 28th 1950

Name
Class 6
No. in Class 48
Position in Class 21

	No. Gained	Maximum	General	REMARKS
Religious Knowledge				
Reading	8	10		Tries very hard
Recitation	9	10		
Composition	7	10		Shows great improvement
Literature				
Writing	9	10		Neat but too small
Spelling	17	20		Works well
Language Study	9	10		Good
General Knowledge				
History	8½	10		Works well
Geography	8½	10		Shows a keen interest
Nature Study	8	10		Tries hard.
Paper 1. (Mental)	9	10		All work has
Paper 2. (Mechanical)	23	30		improved. She has
Paper 3. (Tables)	7½	10		tried very hard
TOTAL	123½	150		
Drawing				Sophisticated but neat
Handwork				Good
Needlework				
General Neatness				Good
Physical Culture				Takes a keen interest

Progress Very satisfactory Conduct Good

General Remarks ... has worked hard. She takes a keen interest in all her lessons. She is a very reliable and courteous little girl E. Marshall Class Teacher.

A satisfactory year's work
E. D. Slater. Headmaster.

214

4. Sports and PE activities at Balfour

Sadly, it was the case that sporting activities were largely the preserve of Balfour Road School when compared with the earlier years at Loder Road. There, Drill was the formal exercise, which was criticised by the HMI as being unimaginative. Physical exercise was often organised 'on the day' as a way of keeping the children warm when temperatures were heading down to 40°F. The main problem, as mentioned many times by the Head, was the lack of space. This was apparent in both the Hall, which had to be used as a classroom when weather stopped outside activities and the playground surface that was useless in most weather conditions for any activity. This was a point that the education committee didn't seem to appreciate when the school was prevented from using part of the spacious playing fields across the road, which would have been an excellent alternative.

In the new school, Balfour was able to use the playing fields to the full and developed a good range of sports and PE, which were mentioned in the Log Book when competitive events were involved. The collection of photographs demonstrates a fair sample of the variety of activities that were on offer. However, there are no photos showing Netball and Rounders but both games were definitely played.

Balfour leads the way at Preston Park at start of the annual Schools Sports meeting

Fig 56

Fig 57
This would appear to be a rehearsal for the Sports Day at Preston Park

215

The programme below listed every race and swimmer

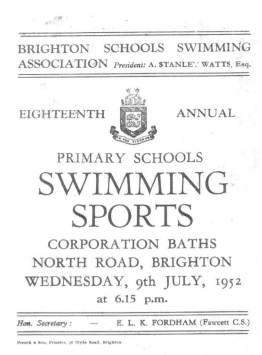

BRIGHTON SCHOOLS SWIMMING
ASSOCIATION President: A. STANLEY WATTS, Esq.

EIGHTEENTH   ANNUAL

PRIMARY SCHOOLS

SWIMMING
SPORTS

CORPORATION BATHS
NORTH ROAD, BRIGHTON
WEDNESDAY, 9th JULY, 1952
at 6.15 p.m.

Hon. Secretary :   —   E. L. K. FORDHAM (Fawcett C.S.)

French & Son, Printers, 38 Clyde Road, Brighton.

Fig 58

The photograph below was displayed in the 1939 Education Week Brochure showing an instance in a folk dancing competition for senior girls that was being held at Balfour Road School

Fig 59

216

Fig 60

Above is Balfour's 1951 football team wearing the school's colours of yellow and black.

Below is a photograph taken an Open Day showing a Gym Display in action on the lawn. The teacher on the left is Mr. Divall. In the background between Varndean Girls School and the heads of two boys in the centre, is the row of wartime pre-fabs that were constructed at the edge of the playing field to provide some temporary housing following loss of homes during WW2 bombing raids.

Fig 61

Fig 62

The 1952 Final of the Fitzgerald Cup between Elm Grove on the left, Balfour on the right, and Cllr Fitzgerald presenting the cup to the winners Elm Grove, by two goals to one.

Fig 63

The 1951 Cricket team with Mr Divall on the left and Mr Slater on the right

5. Obituaries

It is surely fitting at this point, to remember the two Head teachers, Miss Seward and Mr Slater, who played such a dominant role in the successful development of the school. Thoughts of them should be coupled with the memory of Miss Mills who managed to cope, like Miss Seward, with the effects of a World War and, not like Miss Seward, coped with a dilapidated, leaking old building that was often too hot or too cold and was without a playground that could be called one. These were the three stalwarts who led the Balfour Road School for 48 of its first 50 years during what was a defining period in education history that included the 1902 and 1944 Education Acts.

From the days in 1922 when Miss Seward became Head while the school was still in its temporary accommodation in Loder Road through to 1972, 50 years later when Mr Slater retired. Their joint 'reign' was separated only by the brief headship of Miss Pickett and even briefer, acting headships by Miss Young and Miss Horsley. These were the published reports found in newspaper cuttings amongst the stored material

Death of a Beloved Headmistress

The coming-of-age year *(as in 1924 – 1945)* which saw the return of Balfour Road Junior School to its charming home has alas, also seen the passing of the beloved headmistress who dedicated her life to it. Miss Hilda Flanders Seward died in a nursing home on Thursday

She died as she would have wished, almost in harness, for although in ill-health she was at her post for the first few days of the new term. Miss Seward came from an old Huntingdon family. She was a niece of the late Miss Annie Flanders, headmistress of Pelham Street Infants' School, and there she spent many years as an assistant before becoming, in 1922, head of the infants' department of the temporary "tin" school in Loder Road.

Balfour Road quickly made its mark on the young life of Brighton. Everybody who has visited Balfour Road has warmed to its happy, friendly atmosphere. Miss Seward's understanding of little children was a truly precious gift. Balfour Road was her life.

Deep sympathy will go out to the father, Mr George Seward, in the grievous loss that has come to him at the age of 91. He has lived with his daughter at Red Deeps, Surrenden Road for some years past and is amazingly active. Miss Seward also leaves a brother and three sisters.

On Thursday morning the little ones were made aware of the school's loss in a simple memorial service led by Miss Edith Young, her devoted friend and colleague for 21 years

Former Head at Balfour School dies

Only four months after retiring after 25 years as headmaster of Balfour Junior School died suddenly at his home in Nutley Avenue, Saltdean, last week.

Mr Slater, who was 65, had been a headmaster for 40 years. At the age of 25 he was appointed head at Farnham Royal Church of England, Slough and, in1938 was made head of Wexham Road, Slough, County Primary School.

In 1947, when he and his wife Ethel moved to Saltdean, he took up his appointment at Balfour where he remained until July last year. During the early years in the Brighton area he made many friends through his work as chairman of Brighton School Music Festival.

As well as his deep understanding of children he was keenly interested in the encouragement of student teachers and was on the board of managers of Saltdean Middle School.

For many years, Mr Slater and his wife worshipped at St. Anne's Church, Burlington Street, Brighton, but, more recently they attended St. Nicholas' Church, Saltdean, where the funeral took place on Wednesday.

Postscripts

2. A Bit of my Family History

I read somewhere, when researching material for this book that local history is often intertwined with family history. As I had already decided to write about the school I had attended for part of the specified period, this thought seemed, in my case, to be a self-fulfilling prophecy (or a statement of the blithering obvious as was once heard in one of Dennis Potter's TV plays).

This was not so, as I was eventually to find out.

While reading the last few pages of Miss Mills' last Log Book during the May of 2013, I reached the page on which she had recorded the events of April 1920, almost exactly ninety-three years earlier. It is an understatement when I say that I was shocked to read the first paragraph (see page 72), which included the following:

- *Doris Youell, 157 Waldegrave Road, aged 15 years of age (March 29th 1905) has been engaged as the monitoress for this school to commence duties on May 31st next. The present monitoress will be leaving on May 21st next, by reason of age.*

I was seeing, for the very first time, a reference to my mother who was born at the family home a few hundred metres from the Loder Road School and a few weeks before it opened.

I never knew this, despite walking with her on a countless number of times past the corner of Loder Road to reach the Balfour Road School in the 1940s. I do now know that there were subsequent events in her life that she never talked about. These would now not look out of place in an episode of the BBC's, "Who do you think you are"?

I cannot be sure if these events played any part in what now seems to have been a vacuum in my family history and there is little point in speculating about it now. I am sure that one of the reasons was not the one that Miss Mills wrote about in the next sentence in 1920.

She reported that unfortunately, *the monitoress was later hit by part of a window that collapsed.*
No account of any injury was given but my mother did eventually leave before her year was completed.

My mother does make a brief appearance near the beginning of the first chapter where I emphasise the importance of school attendance figures for which children received prizes, much as children would today for good work. The prize of a book she got was for the best attendance at Ditchling Road School in 1914 is shown on page 13.

I wonder now if she was able to use a reference to this prize in her application for the job of monitoress? If not, perhaps another piece of my recently uncovered family history might have played a part. You will see the reference to this later.

My great grandfather and grandmother were members of staff at the Brighton Workhouse at the top of Elm Grove, which is now the Brighton General Hospital. William and Eliza Wright had six children and four of them were listed as staff in 1881. Three of his four girls were teachers at the Warren Farm Industrial Schools. One of them was my Great Aunt Caroline

(Carrie) Wright and, ironically, the only one of his four daughters who wasn't a teacher, was my Grandmother. So I must have taken after her sisters in opting for teaching as a career.

My Great Aunt Carrie sitting in between her sisters in front of a Sussex flint wall

Fig 64

I had always been led to believe that Carrie had taught at Finsbury Road School, but it was only after I discovered in 2014 that schools in Brighton were overseen by groups of Managers, that I started to search the Journals of the group containing Finsbury Road School. Eventually found a reference to Caroline Wright in the minutes of one of their meetings. She started there in 1905 and went on to spend the next seventeen years at the School in the Boys' department. This means that she was one Albert Paul's teachers during his seven years at the School from 1907 to 1914.

Fig 65

221

The Finsbury Road School building is shown above as it is today, no longer used as a school, but still has some original plaques attached to the front that recall its historic past.

Given that Caroline Wright was still teaching at Finsbury Road in 1920 when my mother applied for the post of monitoress, it does seem likely that she gave her aunt's name as a reference.

The family connection to Finsbury Road School doesn't end there. One of my friends, Helen Enticknap, whose son Richard was at Balfour Road School with my son Richard, came to a talk I gave at the School during the Brighton Festival in 2013. During it, she revealed that one of her friends was the grandson of Albert Paul and, through the miracle of new technology, I have been able to introduce him to one of his grandfather's teachers after a span of 108 years. Well, introduced through a photograph of Great Aunt Carrie, that is.

The Brighton Workhouse again figures in my family history through the involvement of my half-Italian Grandfather, Fred Youell, who was one of the Institution's Guardians. He served for many years on the Warren Farm and Relief Committees.

He was a bus driver who hailed from London and turned his hand to steering vehicles variously powered by horses, petrol and electricity.

I know that his route, when his bus was pulled by horses, was from Patcham Village to the Old Steine.

He could have been driving one of the trams mentioned in the school Log Books; perhaps one taking children from the end of Balfour Road to the Preston Circus to get their boots from the Fire Station. Perhaps, but we will never know.

I do know that he was often photographed at the Old Steine, sitting in the driving seat when waiting to take Brighton & Hove Albion supporters to away games at Portsmouth. The picture below is one such image where he is the middle driver of three who would have taken turns at the wheel.

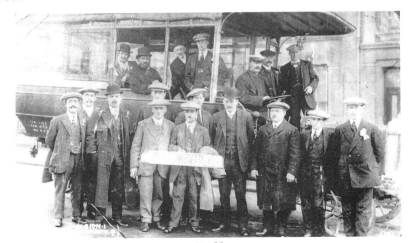

Fig 66

This journey to Portsmouth ended with a victory, Brighton 1, Portsmouth 0

Fred Youell was a member of the Transport and General Workers Union after his small union, the United Vehicle Workers, joined with other unions to create the TGWU in 1922. He was its first Southern Regional Organiser. An article in the local press (14.01.30) reported that he had spent the Christmas "working as hard as anybody waiting on the inmates at the Poor Law Institution and Warren Farm Schools". Sadly, the article goes on to say that his death occurred with tragic suddenness soon after Christmas, when aged 62.

The article names everyone in the different groups of mourners that attended his funeral, which included my mother, Doris Youell, now 24 years old and, at the top of the list of TGWU members present, was Ernest Bevin; the Union's first General Secretary who went on to become the Minister of Labour in the war-time coalition government and Foreign Secretary in the Attlee government after the War. And, in the group of the Brighton Labour Club members, was Mr A Weller. His name now reveals the last bit of local history that has been interwoven with my family history as you will see from this extract from the oral history sent in by Margaret Johnson for Balfour's 60th Anniversary display in 1984.

"The staff were ably assisted in this by Albert Weller the caretaker, a pillar of the Brighton Labour Club, who not only rose at 5 o'clock in the morning to get the school warm, but who was seen at the other end of the day, keeping order at the gate as we all streamed out down Balfour Road".

That my grandfather knew Albert Weller was something else I didn't know about my family history until I found out what I didn't know about the associated local history.

Postscripts

3. And Finally, Thanks

My thanks are due for all the support and help I have received from family and friends and everyone connected to Balfour School over the years; and yes, it was an inordinate length of time in the making! There are a few people I want to thank on the record, starting with the Headteacher, Marcelo Staricoff. I have of course, thanked him for writing what is a very generous Foreword to the book and for sharing his knowledge of publishing. Ben Marle, the Site Manager, has been involved throughout the process as the unofficial voluntary curator of Balfour's history store of documents. Tim Carder, a Balfour graduate, also gave me good advice from his experience of publishing and supplied me with the photograph of Harry Baldwin.

The unfamiliar processes of self-publishing were clarified for me with the help of Philip and Dale Clark at the Brighton Print Centre and Richard Golds at Gemini Printers.

Finally, and definitely not least as I spent many days and weeks variously, at The Keep and Libraries in Brighton and Hove, where the different groups of staff couldn't have been more helpful.

Impossible, but I just wish I could have thanked Owen Williams and Albert Paul for leaving us with their priceless memories of schooldays at start of the 20th century. These ensured that Chapter One contained what would otherwise, have been the missing link – the essential pupil voice that provides due balance alongside those of the teachers and school managers.

Notwithstanding all this assistance, any errors and omissions in this book are down to me.

Appendices

Appendix 1

Footnote on the development of the teaching profession from 1870

The 1870 Education Act established the School Boards, which were directed to fill in the gaps in the local provision of education. In the event, there was an expansion in the first ten years. This was seen in the increased numbers of teachers that were recorded in 1880.

Description	1870	1880
Certificated teachers	12,467	31,422
Uncertificated 'assistant' teachers	1,262	7,652
Pupil-teachers	14.612	32,128
Total	28.341	71,202

This indicator of expansion looked fine on paper but, when the figures are qualified by the situation in the classrooms in 1880, the picture didn't look so good.
- About half of the certificated teachers were not teacher-trained, (they were certified by an HMI who saw them teach), and the training courses had been reduced to one year from the two that had been common practice in 1870. The cost of the expansion had been partly funded by cutting the cost of teacher training
- Of the 7,652 uncertified assistants, 2,352 had no professional qualifications at all
- And the largest section of the teaching force remained the pupil-teachers.

This last point was the most disappointing feature, as it had been hoped that the 1870 Act would act as the catalyst to begin the reduction in the reliance on pupil-teachers.

The author of these statistics, H. C. Dent, in his book, "1870 -1970, Century of Growth in English Education", said it was *a sobering thought that throughout the public elementary schools' first decade as statutory institutions, they were largely run by children between the ages of thirteen and eighteen.*

As we can see from the staff lists in the early years at Balfour Road School, the staffing structure that had existed in elementary schools during the1880s was still largely in place here despite continuing efforts still being made nationally to reduce the numbers of pupil-teachers in schools.

Nevertheless, the first decade of the 20th century was a time of significant change.

The records of schemes of work and educational aims and objectives that Miss Mills wrote into the Log Book at the start of the academic were the manifestation of policy developments following the 1890 Code of Regulation. Among other things, it sought to replace the plain teaching of facts, learning by rote and the cramming for exam passes in the '3 Rs', which together formed the basis of school funding. This was in other words, through 'payment by results'.

Alongside this change, came a new approach whereby teachers would be expected to devise more imaginative curricular and broaden its content. The Code also recognised that it was the duty of the State to care for the physical welfare of the children. Hence, an encouragement for PE, sports and out-of-door teaching.

Evidence of all these changes can be seen in the entries made by Miss Mills as well as her frustration at times when the playground and fields were, for various reasons, unavailable for any use. We can also see that Miss Seward took the same approach in valuing the opportunities for out-of-doors activities that the evergreen Balfour campus provided.

The other significant change that was being attempted, but not publically recognised in the 1870 Act, or the Code of Regulations in 1890 nor even in the 1902 Act giving local authorities control of education, was the desire to end the pupil-teacher system.

The School Boards were set up to fill in the gaps in provision but, as the statistics above showed, the extra provision came with an increase in pupil-teacher numbers. The 1902 Act didn't set out to resolve the problem as it was accepted that there were just too few efficient secondary schools. Instead, restrictions on the employment of pupil-teachers were introduced 1903. They would need to be over 16 years of age, and after 1905, could only serve in an elementary school for up to half the time that the school was open and the other half should be spent at a recognised pupil-teacher centre. One of the centres in Brighton was at the Diocesan Training College on the corner of Ditchling Road and Viaduct Road. In other parts of the country, some pupil-teacher centres were established in secondary schools.

This was a step in the right direction but still only one step. Secondary education was not free. A mixture of scholarships, bursaries and free places meant that there was a patch-work quilt of opportunities in different areas. In affluent areas and in forward-thinking local authorities, the employment of pupil-teachers was gradually being phased out.

In the end, the 1944 Education Act became the milestone in which many incongruities were resolved and through which a coherent system was devised that is still the basis for the current tripartite system of primary, secondary and further education (the latter encompassing different levels of post-16 education up to university level.

Appendix 2

These are copies of the two HMI reports that were published during the period 1945 – 1955. Other HMI reports that have been published since 1905 can be found attached to the appropriate Log Book or Minutes of Managers' meetings.

Report by H. M. Inspectors on Balfour School, Brighton, inspected on 28th and 29th April 1948

This school was opened in 1924, and has a pleasant position with lawns and flower beds in front and playing fields behind. It has passed through a difficult period since the outbreak of war in 1939, and has suffered from a number of disturbances before the present Head Master took up his appointment on 1st November 1947. The children are mainly drawn from the vicinity of the school, and there is an annual intake that varies between 50 and 80, but in the current year 110 have already been admitted. The total roll at the time of the Inspections was 423. In July 1947 four boys and five girls qualified for transfer to Secondary Grammar Schools, and twenty boys and eighteen girls to Secondary Modern Schools. There are frequent changes in the school population as a result of some families moving to a new hosing estate nearby and other families moving out to housing estates in other parts of Brighton.

The premises comprise eight classrooms facing south, with a Hall dividing them, and there is an additional 3-classroom wing built on at the western end. It is a pleasant single-storey building and it provides ready access from the classrooms to the open air. The school possesses two pianos, both of which are in poor condition, and a gramophone. Every room is equipped to receive the relayed radio service.

The Head Master has won the co-operation of his staff and of the pupils, and his quiet, friendly disposition has been instrumental in creating an atmosphere of mutual trust and regard. His sincerity and his encouraging manner have contributed to make his leadership effective. There are 10 qualified assistant female teachers, and one qualified assistant male teacher in charge of classes, and one unqualified teacher who takes lessons in various classes. Together they form a keen and conscientious team with a good balance of experience and vigour, and they meet sufficiently as a staff for effective co-operation to be promoted.

During the Inspection, it was interesting to note the experiment of the teacher trained for work among senior pupils working, at her own request, with Infants. Her special ability in Art has proved an asset in the Department, and her teaching will gain in effectiveness with increasing experience of the special needs of young children.

The school has six Junior classes and five Infant classes, in some of which the age-range is not altogether satisfactory at the moment, but the Head Master has already taken steps towards correcting anomalies of this kind. Special provision has been made to deal with the more retarded pupils (class IVB); they are in the care of a competent and sympathetic practitioner.

The programme of work for both Juniors and Infants is varied and there is a reasonable balance of subjects and activities. Some suggestions were made during the Inspection with a view to improving the daily rhythm in the Infants' classes. Similarly, in the Junior classes the importance of closer co-ordination activity and experience was stressed. However, the children show pleasing qualities of concentration and of keen interest in their work which on the whole reaches a satisfactory level. A high standard of neatness in written work is general throughout the School.

The approach to Reading and Number in the Infants' classes takes into account the varying degrees of ability of these young children. Opportunities are provided for acquiring physical and manipulative skills and the children show a spontaneous and natural zest for what is undertaken. No teachers have spared pains in the preparation of useful teaching apparatus, and the simple projects undertaken by the children give scope for satisfying and instructive occupations. The good work done in the initial stages in acquiring knowledge of Number through appropriate activities could be consolidated in all classes, so that competence will spring from experience rather than from mechanical facility. Purposeful recreative activities are being pursued and both good Art and good group work were observed.

In the Junior Department Religious Instruction is based on a syllabus which comprises suitable portions of the Cambridge and Sunderland Syllabuses. The pupils reveal a real interest in these lessons. The children are acquiring the habit of reading for pleasure and information, but it is suggested that purposeful English might be developed from such reading rather from class manuals in which the exercises are divorced from current work or interest. The encouragement given to some pupils to write poems themselves has already produced interesting results, and similar efforts might be gathered together in the form of a class magazine. History and Geography could be more realistic and related to environment, while retaining the best of the existing features such as the study of interesting people and the daily weather observations. The introduction of simple practical Mathematics for the boys is a good feature that would be equally valuable for the girls, and could profitably include measurements about the school premises and simple graphical representation. There are indications of practical interest in Nature and a pleasant freedom and a sense of colour and pattern in Art. In the Physical Education lessons the team system is working well; effective use is made of simple apparatus, and the good quality of the teaching, particularly with the girls, is reflected of the children about the premises. Dancing makes a special contribution to their poise and enjoyment of school life.

A plot of land has been fenced in and brought into cultivation by the boys of the retarded class. This valuable start in school gardening might include not only the experimental work which is contemplated, but also the cultivation of flowers. Such work could with advantage be planned for every age group in the School.

Promising work is being done in Music although the subject suffers from some past years of unavoidable neglect. The emphasis is on class singing but more use might be made of song books in order to build up a good repertoire of national folk and classical songs in all classes. Some attention to sight reading is necessary and such training could be built upon what has already been achieved in percussion.

Owing to the small size of the Hall, sectional assemblies are held, and services seen were simple and dignified. The mid-day meal is a pleasant feature of the School programme, the tables are made attractive with flowers and the older boys and girls are trained to be helpful.

The School is developing on sound lines. Due regard is given to training on good habits and to the cultivation of standards of taste. The children are natural, polite, talk with ease, and are clearly happy and show the right attitude to their activities in School.

There is much to commend in what is being done, and further developments will probably lie in these directions which were discussed during the Inspection. The prospects here are distinctly good

Ministry's Reference   **F. 62/35/46**

Report by H. M. Inspectors on Balfour County Primary School
Inspected on 5th, 6th, 7th July 1955

The Junior mixed and infants school was last inspected in 1948. Since then the roll has increased by nearly 40% and was 590 at the time of this inspection.

In the three years 1953/55, the number transferring to secondary schools have been 82, 90 and 90 respectively; of these the allocations to Secondary Grammar Schools have been 31, 38 and 40.

The attractiveness of the site has been maintained and two additional classrooms have been added. A small covered playground beneath the west wing has been enclosed to give a third extra room. Despite this, the classes are very large, 10 of the 14 classes having over 45. The enlarged school accentuates the inadequacy and inconvenience of other essential amenities. The tiny assembly hall, for example, is much too small for the large numbers and it is physically impossible for the Head Master to do all that he would wish for the children's musical and physical education. The staff room is also much too small for the present numbers and the toilet facilities both for staff and pupils are inadequate. Some inconveniences must be accepted in schools while age groups containing abnormally high numbers are passing through; the future needs of the school, however, might be approximately assessed and some amelioration of present difficulties provided within the limits of those needs. The premises are well cared for, flowers and pictures add a touch of graciousness, and members of the staff have taken a good deal of trouble to make the classrooms attractive.

It is clear that the Head Master has followed a well thought out plan in providing books for the children. Most of the classes have well chosen books for their use, both of reading and reference. There are gaps, however, and the Head Master does not find it easy to cope with the problem. The movement of the 'bulge' for example, in the next school year results in the number of infants' classes being one less and of juniors' one more; and it faces him with the problem of providing the complete range of requirements for an extra class of juniors. The school could now make good use of more large apparatus for physical education.

The Head Master has an intimate knowledge of his school and a good grasp of its needs so that he has been able to formulate clear aims. He has won the support of his staff and easy relationships prevail despite the wide variation in the teachers' experience. They are thinking about their work, what they are doing is generally apt, and they give generously of their time out of school. An enthusiastic spirit pervades the school.

INFANT CLASSES

Children who come into the reception classes are fortunate in being put in the care of an experienced teacher who knows well how to help them adapt themselves to the strange and new life of the classroom. Consistent training in social behaviour and hygienic habits is given from the very first and this is so effective that it quickly establishes a sensible and considerate relationship between children and adults – an attitude which persists throughout the infant classes.

The children work and play in rooms that are equipped with materials and tools suitable to their needs and every room has a well chosen supply of books always easily accessible. Excellent use is made of corridor space outside the classrooms and occasionally classes are taken on the lawns.

The progress made in each of the infant classes is in every way most satisfactory. The pursuits followed afford interesting opportunities experimenting and exploring, from which ensue conversation of value and a real need to learn and practice the skills of reading and writing, counting and very simple calculations. Some vigorous and colourful painting has been done and some of the pattern making was particularly exciting and satisfying. The variety of constructive handwork is good. The foundations of a broad, sound musical training are given. The children sing sweetly from a well chosen repertoire and are able to attempt quite difficult songs. The percussion band played carefully selected music and also some of their own rhythm compositions with marked control and appreciation. This was a delightful performance.

In Physical Education there is plenty of scope for ingenuity, agility of movement and manipulative skill. The lessons were active, vigorous and well conducted.

JUNIOR CLASSES

Religious Instruction is well taught in the school. In many classes the children keep attractive folders and before they leave they acquire facility in finding their way through the Bible. They are given a rich experience in English language and their writing often springs naturally from studies in other subjects as well as English. In many classes very good standard is reached and all through the school one finds a readiness to write. There is a growing understanding of the value of presenting good literature to the pupils and this has borne fruit for there is evidence of their love of good poetry and prose. The children are encouraged to read widely and there is a strong interest in books. The teaching of History and Geography has led to interesting work some of which has been stimulated either by visits or by broadcasts.

The children have given lively cooperation to their teachers, made extensive use of reference material, produced attractive records and learnt a great deal. There is considerable enthusiasm for Nature Study; the pupils learn to observe both in school and out of school, and many of them are very well informed on Nature topics.

The pupils take great care in working and setting out their Arithmetic. It is suggested that to a great extent the teachers might think of problems and mental work as an integral part of the subject rather than regard the former purely as an application of mechanical work and the latter as only a testing technique. Nevertheless the pupils at the top of the school have a very good understanding of the subject.

Some good, lively, adventurous work in Art is found throughout the school. All the children are given an opportunity of hearing good music; they sing well and have a good repertoire. The older children are well informed about the great musicians. Physical Education also has an important part to play in the life of the school and there is all-round keenness. A variety of work is attempted and in all the activities there is an appreciation of good standards. The lessons are well organised and where allowance has been made for individual differences among the children progress has been most marked.

This school has made thoughtful use of School Broadcasts and a great deal of activity has found its initial impulse in this aid. So far from being content with passive listening, the teachers and pupils have engaged in a number of enterprises of considerable educational value which have been suggested, explicitly or implicitly, by broadcasts.

The school has a pleasant meals service. About 250 children take school meals; they are served in a dining room attached to the central kitchen and there are two sittings. The servers have been at the Canteen for a long time, they know the children well, and they take a pride in their work. Flowers are provided and arranged by the pupils. A good nourishing dinner was served on the day of the inspection.

A number of activities flourish to give the school a full and interesting corporate life and there is justifiable pride in an excellent record of achievements in games and in swimming. The children make steady progress throughout the school; they learn good habits and come to appreciate mutual trust, regard and cooperation as normal attitudes. This is a good school.

The Report was counter-signed by the staff: E.D.Slater, H.M.Bishopp, D.T.Moore, R.Windall, M.J.Bacon, B.M.Jarvis, B.H.Snook, J.M.Cowtan, G.A.Brown, E.Chaffer, M.M.Sharman, J.V.Horne, P.D.Bennett, E.J.Brogate, T.W.Divall.

Note attached to the 1955 HMI Report

This note is based on a statistical analysis that appeared attached to the above 1955 HMI as an Appendix. It details the varying average class sizes in the school's 14 classes during that year from information that would have been supplied by the school before the inspection. I have attached the analysis together with a more general commentary about class sizes.

Nowadays, the issue of class sizes often surfaces as a concern of parents – it has done so at Balfour Junior School. A few years ago, opinion surveys of parents always returned 'class size' as their number one dissatisfaction. Too large, it was said when the class sizes rose to between 33 and 36 compared with the 30 that the Infant School next door was limited to by government policy.

If we look back at Loder Road School's maximum of 60, for which the classrooms were actual designed to hold, we can see that there were, sadly in a way, several good reasons why the class size of 60 didn't appear to have been an issue.

It was a rather theoretical target to maintain. There were many incidences of very low attendance figures because of serious outbreaks of illnesses and episodes of very inclement weather. In addition, there was evidence of a considerable 'churn' of admissions and transfers out. All this meant that the 'normal' class size was probably 50 or less. The real difficulty for the teachers at this time was that it was rarely the same 50 children that would present themselves on a regular basis.

A document was found in archives, which showed an analysis of the class size situation that existed at Balfour Primary School as of 17th June 1955. It was attached to the HMI Report of 1955 and the statistics must have emanated from the school records that were prepared for the Inspectors.

In the '50s, HMIs tended to make individual visits for specific purposes as can be seen from the Log Book records. They were also prepared to offer advice outside the normal full inspection process. An outcome of their earlier visits in 1955, when they may have discussed Balfour's difficulties in coping with larger than normal admissions, seems to be contained in the second and third paragraphs of the Report.

In describing the range of problems that needed additional resources in order to overcome them, the Inspector 'politely' suggested in the second paragraph that the following approach might be taken:

"Some inconveniences must inevitably be accepted in schools while the age groups containing abnormally high numbers are passing through ; the future needs of the school, however, might be approximately assessed and some amelioration the present difficulties provided within the limits of those needs."

Sir Humphrey Appleby couldn't have put it better in the TV series, Yes Minister.

The Inspector was less oblique in the third paragraph when making another 'suggestion' about the additional resources that were needed;

"The school could now make good use of more large apparatus for physical education."

Looking back now, nearly sixty years later, a word that the inspectors used in this Report as shorthand for the *"abnormally high numbers"* of children, was the 'Bulge'. The word didn't need any further explanation then, in describing the significant birth rate rises that occurred following the ending of the Second World War. As the 'Bulge' matured, it became known as the generation of the Baby Boomers who are now reaching retirement age.

Back in 1955, the statistics in the HMI Report, shown below, indicated that the average class size across the 14 classes (a two-form entry school then) was 42 with large variations in individual classes from 23 to 50. Part of the variations might have been caused by the practice of allowing mixed age groups where children could be held back for a year instead of moving forward to the next class at the end of the academic year.

The average class size for the whole school of 42 did hide the divide between the upper and lower school's average class size of 45.3 and 40 respectively. The bulge effect was a temporary one that would be replaced by increases in the numbers of children requiring school places as the town's population continued to increase.

Class and year start	No. of pupils	Average age
E 1955	42	5 y 2m
D 1955	39	5y 10m
C 1954	45	6y 7m
B 1954	40	6y 2m
A 1953	44	7y 6m
9 1953	23	8y 4m
8 1952	39	8y 1m

7 1952	46	8y 3m
6 1951	41	9y 2m
5 1951	50	9y 3m
4 1950	40	10y 4m
3 1950	47	10y 3m
2 1949	47	11y 2m
1 1949	47	11y 3m

The other main statistics in the report were that the total number of children on the Roll was 590, of which 283 were boys and 307 girls

Sixteen former pupils from the 1945 – 1951 sent in their school reports, with class size recorded on each. The average size for this random sample turned out to be 41.9

So, it does seem to show that the school's admissions policy at this time did aim to bring the normal class size down towards 40.

A similar random sample of school reports was sent in from pupils who had been at Balfour between 1931 and 1937, which showed that average class size was 49.

Loder Rd classrooms were built to hold 60; the new Balfour Rd building could hold 50 and the immediate post-war period saw class sizes drop towards 40.

Appendix 3

Extract from "Turn Back the Years", Owen and Doris Williams, published in1991

Owen's Schooldays

I was fourteen years of age, my years of schooling at an end, eagerly awaiting the day when I started work Unaware and uncaring that before me lay seventy years of hard work as I struggled to earn my living. Years that would on the whole prove to be happy, if not always carefree with a few sombre moments woven into the tapestry of life.

But what has a lad of fourteen to do with nostalgic memories and regrets of what might have been when he is about to embark on his working life? An exciting new era was about to begin, his years of acquiring some sort of an education, albeit a pretty basic one behind him.

The task of instilling into a tough bunch of youngsters including myself, some degree of literacy and numeracy was tackled by a dedicated band of teachers, male and female in a Council School in Brighton. Much can be said for their courage and expertise, when against all odds, they succeeded in the task. Especially when the majority of pupils in their charge nurtured ideas and notions far removed from improvement of the mind. The mysteries of what three times three added up to, or the significance of a date, 1066 in our history books, was imparted to classes of ill-clad and undernourished children in a hideously ugly school, with the title Loder Road Council School.

This structure masquerading as a school mainly consisting of solid sheets of corrugated iron, had, as we were told, stood originally on a site elsewhere. Not for education of the young, but to confine the mentally unstable. In short, in the idiom of the 19th century, a lunatic asylum. Presumably used for this purpose for the greater part of the century, the powers that be decided towards the end of it, the grim old building would be quite suitable and adequate for use as a Council school. Accordingly, the former asylum was dismantled and rebuilt in Loder Road to begin life anew as an establishment of education, capable of holding up to three hundred pupils, boys and girls.

And there it remained for the next 19 years or so, despite promises and assurances made from time to time. "Yes the school is shortly to be pulled down and you will be taught in a fine new one." But years went by, so did our school-days, our ugly old school remained, nothing materialised. In 1924, with my school days long passed the old school finally closed and the pupils were transferred to a brand new building. I first crossed the threshold of the Loder Road School in 1908, at the age five years, where improvement of my mind proceeded more or less uneventfully until 1914 when the war with Germany was declared. From that time, our education deteriorated, a factor bothering neither me nor several other of my other contemporaries. Learning was something to be avoided as much as possible. I had grown used to being addressed as, "Williams you blockhead. When will you learn that is not the way to do it?"

I suppose some knowledge did sink into my alleged 'Blockhead', my school reports were average, musical aspiration somewhat lacking perhaps, with two out of ten my usual marks for that subject. I fared better at handicrafts, having a certain talent in that direction, which I developed to good advantage later when I had grown up.

For many of us, boys especially war was exciting, the attendant horrors and tragedies not fully understood.

When troops of soldiers paraded through the town, led by bands playing stirring marches, with crowds of people looking on, cheering and waving flags, we rushed to watch. Army camps were set up on the Downs on the outskirts of Brighton. There were army manoeuvres with mock battles and soldiers firing blank ammunition. My brothers and I with various schoolmates, spent most of our spare time hanging round these camps, eager to see all that was going on. Some folks said, "The war would be over by Christmas." We sincerely hoped not, our ambitions were to be soldiers too and march off to fight for our country.

But gradually, the harsh realities of war became more apparent, the picture changed. Food became scarce; children appeared at school wearing black arm bands or with diamond shaped patches sewn onto sleeves of coats. Mourning fathers and brothers killed fighting in the trenches in France. Most of the able bodied young men disappeared, my older brother among them, swallowed up by the hungry maw of the war machines.

Teachers were now mainly women, lessons, morning only. Another school took over in the afternoons, their premises requisitioned for war purposes. Maps showing the progress of the war were chalked on to blackboards as various battles were fought. Dire consequences awaiting us if Kaiser Bill and Little Willie won the war filled our hearts with dread. We set-to with a will, sewing coarse material into sandbags, one of the tasks we were given in place of some of our lessons. This probably encouraged us to think we were doing our bit, but did little for our education.

However, in the summer of 1918, all this was behind me, my schooling such as it was had come to an end, my years of employment about to commence. A garden boy I was to be, working in the kitchen gardens of the Earl of Chichester on his country estate at Stanmer Park, 4 miles north of Loder Road School.

Postscript

Owen went on to work at Stanmer Park until being signed up in 1942 to do essential wartime work repairing damaged local sea defences and other damaged properties on-land. He was too young to join his brothers fighting in the First World War and too old for the Second.

He stayed with the building company, John Mowlen after the War before finally returning to Stanmer Park in 1961 when his employer was then the University of Sussex, employing him as the Maintenance Foreman.

On his retirement, the University awarded him the degree of Master of Arts in recognition of his service, 1961 – 77.

I think he would have thought that this was a very good achievement for a "Blockhead" from the Tin Hut.

I hope he did.

Appendix 4

Balfour Time-line

1905

Asprin went on sale for the first time

First cornea transplant

Mrs Pankhurst organises the first outdoor 'Votes for Women' protest meeting at Westminster

Foundation of the AA (Automobile Association)

G. B. Shaw's "Man and Superman" and "Major Barbara" both performed at the Royal Court

1906

School meals provided for deprived children

The Government declares that the British Empire covered one-fifth of the Earth, ruling a population of 400,000,000

Parliamentary Labour Party formed by Keir Hardy

First international rugby union match against a foreign country: England beat France in Paris, 35-8

1907

Plans for the first Channel Tunnel were scrapped

School health service established.

1908

First purpose-built cinema in Britain opens at Colne, Lancs

Kenneth Grahame publishes *The Wind in the Willows*

1909

Louis Blerior is the first man to fly the Channel, crossing from Sangette to Dover in 43 minutes

Edward VII opens Victoria and Albert Museum, South Kensington

Girl Guides established to complement the Boy Scout movement

Shackleton returns from Antarctica, after coming within 100 miles of South Pole, he is knighted

1910

Edward VII dies and Prince of Wales accedes as King George V

H. G. Wells publishes **The History of Mr Polly**

Scott sails for Antarctica in *Terra Nova*

First edition of the Times Educational Supplement

Brighton & Hove Albion top the Southern League, Division 1 and beat Aston Villa 1 – 0 in the FA Charity Shield

1911
Lloyd George introduces National Insurance Scheme
Coronation of George V
Official Secrets Act hurried through Parliament in 2 days because of an international crisis
First electric escalators opened at Earls Court underground station
Committee on secondary schools examinations reported that over 80% of 14 – 18 year olds receive no education

1912
White Star liner Titanic strikes iceberg on maiden voyage; over 1,500 drowned
Scottish physicist Charles Rees Wilson devises a cloud chamber to study behaviour of ions
English engineer Charles Belling perfects an electric cooker with fireclay elements

1913
Eric Gill sculpts Stations of the Cross, Westminster Cathedral
Suffragette Emily Davison fatally injured in throwing herself in front of King's horse in the Derby
First stainless steel cutlery
First use of formica

1914 – 1918
There are many local books that have been published about the First World War and its effects on Brighton together with more source material in the Royal Pavilion, Museum and Library.
Fisher Education Act raised the school leaving age to 14yrs in 1918 and ends all fees for elementary education. Conscription caused teacher shortages.

1919
Victory parades in Britain as peace is celebrated
National pay scales introduced for elementary school teachers

1920
Women at Oxford become full members of the University and able to receive degrees
Brighton & Hove Albion join the Football League in the new Division 3 (South)
League of Nations Council first meets at St James Palace, London

1921
Chequers estate becomes a country residence for Prime Ministers
Marie Stopes opens first Mothers' Clinic in Holloway, London, advocating birth control
British Legion founded
Railways Act: amalgamates 123 companies into 4 groups – GWR, LMS, LNER, SR – from Jan 1923

1922
Provisional Irish government takes office in Dublin, headed by Michael Collins
IRA Irregulars ambush and kill Michael Collins
Lloyd George resigns as Prime Minister, ending the coalition, and Bonar Law takes office
New Waterloo Station opens
LCC's County Hall opened
Tomb of Tutankhamen at Luxor discovered by Howard Carter, under the patronage of Lord Carnarvon
Benito Mussolini becomes the Italian Prime Minister
Teachers' salaries cut by 5% and pension contributions introduced at 5%

1923

Liquor Act: bans sale of alcohol to under-18s
Wembley Stadium opens for FA Cup. Bolton beat West Ham 2-1
Sir Arthur Eddington's Mathematical Theory of Relativity helps establish Einstein' theories

1924

Britain gives diplomatic recognition to Soviet Russia
Rise in the cost of petrol (£1 for 10 gallons) fails to curb mounting popularity of motoring
Sunday Express is first British newspaper with a crossword
Death of Lenin; Stalin emerges as Party boss

1925

Churchill's budget speech announces return to the gold standard, based on pre-war parity of sterling to the dollar ($4.86 to £1)
Cyprus is proclaimed as a Crown Colony

1926

Birth of Princess Elizabeth of York, future Queen Elizabeth II
General strike in support of miners
General strike ends after TUC talks with Samuel; miners stay out
Miners call off strike begun on 1st May
A.A. Milne creates *Winnie the Pooh*
First British greyhound track opens at Belle Vue, Manchester
Traffic lights, manually controlled, are introduced in central London
Television demonstrated by John Logie Baird in Soho to scientists from the Royal Institution
Hadow Report on secondary education recommends separate secondary and primary at age 11yrs and Grammar and Modern Schools

1927

The BBC becomes a public corporation
Eric Gill designs the sans-serif alphabet
Rex Whistler paints murals in the Tate Gallery
Henry Williamson publishes *Tarka the Otter*
First radio commentary on a football match (Arsenal v Sheffield Utd) and on the Grand National
Charles Lindbergh flies the Atlantic solo from New York to Paris in 33 hrs 19 min

1928

Equal Franchise Act gives the vote to women between the ages of 21 and 30
Alexander Fleming accidently discovers penicillin at St Mary's Hospital, Paddington
J. L. Baird successfully experiments with coloured television

1929

Sharp fall in share values on Stock Exchange following start of the Wall Street 'crash' on 24 October
GPO introduces the first public telephone boxes: 22 red-painted boxes put into service in London
Virginia Woolf writes A Room of One's Own, essay on feminism

1930

Gandhi begins a peaceful civil disobedience campaign
Arthur Ransome writes *Swallows and Amazons*
Youth Hostel Association (YHA) established
Amy Johnson takes off from Croydon in a Gipsy Moth biplane, seeking to become the first woman

to fly solo to Australia: reaches Darwin, 24th May; receives triumphant welcome when she returns to London, 4th August.

1931
Mrs Wallis Simpson is introduced to the Prince of Wales, Burrough Court, Leicestershire
First Highway Code issued by the Ministry of Transport
House of Lords prevents Bill to raise leaving age to 15 yrs and teachers' salaries cut by 10%

1932
Sir Oswald Mosley founds the British Union of Fascists
George V begins the practice of royal Christmas broadcasts
Stella Gibbons publishes *Cold Comfort Farm*
A Huxley publishes *Brave New World*
First BBC transmission from Broadcasting House; Henry Hall conducts his BBC Dance Orchestra

1933
Trade agreement signed with Germany
Rally in Hyde Park to protest at the treatment of Jews in Germany
Churchill's first speech warning of German rearmament
Designs by Giles Gilbert Scott for Battersea Power Station approved; opens in 1937
George Orwell writes *"Down and Out in Paris and London"*
Hitler becomes German Chancellor

1934
The liner *Queen Elizabeth* is launched at Clydebank
John Christie founds the Glyndebourne Festival of Opera
British wins in both singles at Wimbledon: Dorothy Round and Fred Perry
Stanley Matthews wins first cap for England at football
Jack Hobbs plays his last first-class cricket match

1935
Imperial Airways and QANTAS inaugurate joint London to Australia commercial flights
Road Traffic Act operative: speed limit of 30 mph imposed in built-up areas
London County Council establishes protected "Green Belt" to check ribbon development
Celebrations of George V's Silver Jubilee
Allen Lane founds Penguin Books Ltd to begin a paperback revolution in publishing
LNER trains twice set world speed records on runs to Newcastle; 108 mph 0n 5th March and 112 mph on 21st September
Robert Watson-Watt successfully carries out the first experiment on radar
'Cat's- eyes', self-cleaning and reflecting road studs, first-used
Sir James Chadwick awarded the Nobel Prize for Physics for his work in confirming the existence of the neutron

1936
George V dies at Sandringham; Prince of Wales accedes as King Edward VIII
Jarrow marchers set off for London; their unemployment is backed by their MP, Ellen Wilkinson
Edward VIII tells Baldwin of his intention to marry Mrs Simpson when her divorce becomes absolute
Crystal Palace destroyed by fire
Edward VIII abdicates in favour of Duke of York, who accedes as King George VI. Ex-King created Duke of Windsor
BBC opens regular TV service, reaching only London and the Home Counties from Alexander Palace

William Butlin opens first holiday camp at Skegness, Lincs
German troops occupy the demilitarized Rhineland
Spanish Civil War begins
Nazis seek to exploit the Olympic Games in Berlin

1937

Coronation of King Georg VI
Duke of Windsor weds Wallis Simpson
Duke and Duchess of Windsor visit Nazi Germany and meets Hitler
Constitution of Ireland Act effective: Irish Free State replaced by sovereign state of Eire, within the Commonwealth but having no links with the Crown
G Orwell publishes The Road to Wigan Pier
Frank Whittle shows effectiveness of jet engine, in demonstration on the ground

1938

Warning by Churchill in House of Commons of Hitler's aggressive plans, following German absorption of Austria
Britain warns Germany not to attack Czechoslovakia
Liner *Queen Elizabeth* is launched by the Queen at Clydeside, first ship over 80,000 tons displacement
Munich Conference of Chamberlain, Hitler, Mussolini and Daladier
A. Duff Cooper resigns as First Lord of the Admiralty in protest at Chamberlain's appeasement
Graham Greens publishes *Brighton Rock*
Test Match cricket televised for the first time from Lords
LNER's newly constructed Mallard engine establishes definitive speed record for steam traction reaching 125 mph between Grantham and Peterborough
German troops enter Austria; Anschluss (union of Germany and Austria) proclaimed
German troops enter Sudetenland

1939 – 1945

The same point, as made above about the First World War, can be made here in relation to the Second World War. Different emphasises in this period – mass evacuation of children, school became a hospital this time, temporary house building, shortages of all kinds, an atomic bomb and amid the mayhem, the 1944 Education Act was published. Locally, artist Rex Whistler painted a mural on wallpaper in a house in Preston Park Avenue (5th – 7th June 1945), which was lifted later and is displayed in the Royal Pavilion. It was called the "Awakening of the Spirit of Brighton". Sadly, Whistler was killed on 18th July, five weeks after painting it, while leading his tank corps on the Normandy battlefields

1946

Nationalisation of the Bank of England
Churchill's 'Iron Curtain' speech at Fulton, Missouri; urges joint resistance by the West to the Soviet threat
London Airport opens at Heathrow
Ministry of Town and Country Planning to supervise building of up to 20 new towns
House of Commons approves Bill to nationalise the coal industry
Television service resumes for the first time since 1939; some 11,500 viewers, all in the SE England
Shortage of shipping and of wheat worldwide leads to bread and flour rationing
National Health Service Bill enacted
Royal Commission report in favour of equal pay for women
Sir Barry Jackson Memorial Theatre, Stratford-upon-Avon; Peter Brook produces Love Labour's Lost

with Paul Scofield* as Don Armado. *Paul Schofield went to Varndean Grammar School (1934 – 39)
BBC Third Programme begins, with emphasis on culture
First-class cricket and league football resumes
Supplementary grants for university students announced
Free school milk is introduced but free school meals postponed

1947
National Coal Board takes over running of mines
Coldest weather since 1883 necessitates rationing coal to industry and homes
Princess Elizabeth marries Philip Mountbatten at Westminster Abbey
India and Pakistan become independent
School leaving age finally raised to 15 yrs

1948
Nationalisation of British Railways effective
Britain's first supermarket opens: London Co-operative Society, Manor Park, E. London
National Health Service inaugurated
Gas Industry nationalized
Birth of George V1-I first grandchild, Prince Charles
The austere XII Olympiad opens in London
Ministry of education proposes to introduce, in 1951, the General Certificate of Education, at Ordinary and Advanced levels
Pioneer comprehensives are opened at Potters Bar and Hillingdon, London
Compact Morris Minor and the Rover's 'Landrover' go on sale at the Motor Show
Gandhi assassinated, Dehli

1949
Britain recognises State of Israel
End of clothes rationing
End of Sweet rationing
Iron and Steel nationalisation enacted
Rev Awdry begins a long series of books for younger children with Thomas the Tank Engine

1950
Petrol rationing ends
J Sainsbury opens a purpose-built supermarket at Croydon
Soap rationing ends
Legal Aid becomes freely available to men and women of limited means
George VI opens restored chamber of House of Commons

1951
Ration for carcass meat cut to 18d per week (7p in decimal currency)
George VI opens the Festival of Britain from the steps of St. Paul's Cathedral
State of War with Germany formally declared at an end
Operation on George VI for lung cancer
George VI opens the Royal Festival Hall, designed by Robert Matthew
Opening of the main Festival of Britain site on South Bank after general planning by Sir Gerald Barry in 27 acres west of Waterloo; architectural supervision by Hugh Casson (who also designed Sussex University)
O and A-levels introduced

1952

George VI dies in his sleep at Sandringham; Q Elizabeth II learns of her accession while on a royal tour in Kenya

Identity cards, obligatory since 1939, abolished

Elizabeth II confirms that she wishes her children and grandchildren to bear the name of Windsor

Freak thunderstorms on Exmoor bring flooding and devastation to Lynmouth

Worst railway disaster in England; 112 people killed in triple crash at Harrow

Bill introduced to denationalise iron and steel

Agatha Christie's play *The Mousetrap* opens at the Ambassadors Theatre, London

British atomic bomb exploded in Monte Bello islands off NW Australia

Tea rationing ends

First hydrogen bomb tested by USA, Enimertok atoll, Pacific

1953

Sweet rationing ends

Road transport denationalised

Coronation of Queen Elizabeth

Steel industry denationalised

End of sugar rationing

Everest summit reached by Edmund Hilary and a Sherpa, Tenzing Norgay in expedition led by Sir John Hunt

Rev Chad Varah, at St Stephen's Walbrook, London, founds Samaritans to help people in despair; becomes national movement in early 1960s

The Royal Conservatory leaves Greenwich for Sussex because of increasing pollution in London skies

Cambridge molecular biologists Francis Crick and James Watson postulate the molecular structure of DNA (deoxyribonucleic acid),"the code of life."

Stalin dies; Khrushchev succeeds him as Communist Party secretary

The Hovercraft is invented by Christopher Cockerell

1954

Food rationing ends

Churchill first octogenarian Prime Minister since Gladstone

William Golding publishes *Lord of the Flies*

J.R.R. Tolkien publishes *The Fellowship of the Ring*, being part 1 of *The Lord of the Rings*

Roger Bannister runs first 4-minute mile (3mins, 39.4secs) at Oxford

British Medical Committee's report suggests links between smoking and lung cancer; findings treated cautiously by Ministry of Health

US hydrogen bomb tested at Bikini atoll

The 11+ is said to be wrongly allocating one in three pupils

1955

First ships beginning large influx of Jamaican immigrants reach Plymouth

ITV presents first alternative programmes to BBC television; commercially sponsored

Fashion for tight-fitting jeans for women spreads from America; among young men, there is a reversion to an older style as *"Teddy Boys"*

Floodlit international football comes to Wembley Stadium; England v Spain

Duke of Edinburgh's Award Scheme instituted, to encourage initiative among young people

Martin Luther King begins civil disobedience campaign for black rights in Montgomery, Alabama

The last gas lamps are removed from London schools

The automatic kettle is invented by Peter Hobbs, a founder member of the Russell Hobbs Company.

List of Photographs and Illustrations

No	Image		No	Image	
1	Preston Road School	P	34	Organised outside activities	S
2	Ditchling Road School	P	35	Flagstaff ceremony	S
3	Stanford Road School	P	36	An Outing with Miss Seward	S
4	Balfour Road	P	37	An Outing's comfort break?	S
5	Loder Road	P	38	Gathering for an Outing?	S
6	Diocesan College	O	39	Boarding the char-a-banc	S
7	Stranded Tram at Preston Circus	O	40	Snow scene	S
8	Entrance to York Place schools	C	41	We've just built a snowman	S
9	Art class at York Place	C	42	Snowman with visitors	S
10	Pupil-teacher Centre, York Place	C	43	Snowman with a crowd	S
11	Boots	C	44	Senior Girls' gardening class	S
12	First page of enrolments in 1905	C	45	The new pond	S
13	Advert for Lewes Road School	C	46	Flowchart of education in Brighton	C
14	Prize for good attendance	O	47	Beds for the infants	S
15	Drill lesson	C	48	Harry Baldwin	C
16	Coombe Road School, design example	C	49	The King's letter	C
17	Osborne Road steps to Loder Road	O	50	The now well-established pond	S
18	Brighton Boys football match	C	51	Mrs Moore's class of '51	O
19	New Balfour school building	P	52	Miss Brogate's class	S
20	Teachers leave the Tin School	S	53	Class of 1925	S
21	Another group of 'leaving' teachers	S	54	Teachers' group pre-1940	S
22	Same teachers cross over to Balfour	S	55	Group in 1938	S
23	Miss Seward, Head teacher	S	56	The opening march-pass	S
24	Aerial view of the campus	C	57	Practising the opening march-pass?	S
25	Varndean Girls School	C	58	Swimming gala programme	O
26	Barn at the edge of the woods	O	59	Folk dancing	C
27	Tram rails at the end of Balfour Road	O	60	1951 Football team	S
28	Entrance to new building	S	61	Gymnastics	O
29	Foot of the Osborne Road steps	O	62	1952 Primary schools' Cup Final	O
30	Drive way to the playgrounds	S	63	1951 Cricket team	O
31	Outside activities	S	64	Great Aunts	O
32	More outside activities	S	65	Finsbury Road School	O
33	Playtime	S	66	Albion supporter's bus	O

Index: S = Store of photographs held at school
C = Copied from various sources
P = Purchased from 'Step Back in Time', 36 Queens Road, Brighton BN1 3XB
O = Owned by Derek Betts including items 6 and 7, which were drawn by him